Instructor's Resource Manual

The Writer's Workplace

EIGHTH EDITION

and

The Writer's Workplace with Readings

SIXTH EDITION

Sandra Scarry
Formerly with the Office of Academic Affairs,
City University of New York

John Scarry
Hostos Community College,
City University of New York

Prepared by
Siobhán Scarry
State University of New York at Buffalo

THOMSON
WADSWORTH

Australia • Brazil • Canada • Mexico • Singapore
Spain • United Kingdom • United States

Instructor's Resource Manual

The Writer's Workplace, Eighth Edition
The Writer's Workplace with Readings, Sixth Edition

Sandra Scarry and John Scarry
Prepared by Siobhán Scarry

Publisher: Lyn Uhl
Acquisitions Editor: Annie Todd
Development Editor: Laurie Runion
Editorial Assistant: Dan DeBonis
Associate Content Project Manager: Sarah Sherman
Permissions Editors: Ronald Montgomery and Timothy Sisler

Print Buyer: Mary Beth Hennebury
Art Director: Cate Rickard Barr
Production Service: Newgen–Austin
Printer: West Group
Cover Designer: Dick Hannus
Cover Art: © Steven Chorney 2008

1 2 3 4 5 6 7   09 08 07 06

ISBN-10: 1-4130-3072-6
ISBN-13: 978-1-4130-3072-3

Thomson Higher Education
25 Thomson Place
Boston, MA 02210-1202
USA

For more information about our products, contact us at:
Thomson Learning Academic Resource Center
1-800-423-0563
For permission to use material from this text or product, submit a request online at **http://www.thomsonrights.com**
Any additional questions about permissions can be submitted by e-mail to **thomsonrights@thomson.com**

Preface

This Instructor's Resource Manual supports instructors teaching with *The Writer's Workplace,* Eighth Edition and *The Writer's Workplace with Readings,* Sixth Edition. Teachers using this manual will find a variety of materials geared toward enhancing, reinforcing, and complementing students' experience with the primary text.

This manual has been revised and expanded in order to support the new editions of *The Writer's Workplace,* with an eye toward integrating ancillary material more closely with the objectives, chapter content, and readings in the textbook. Instructors will find comprehensive support for planning and organizing their courses in Part 1, including specific sample syllabi that leverage the exciting new material from the text. This section also includes in-depth discussion on incorporating collaborative learning and the use of journals into the classroom, as well as a section on grading and responding to student writing. Teachers looking for additional assignments to give their students will benefit from the revised chapter guides in Part 2, which offer in-class activities, journal assignments, and responding to reading assignments designed with the goals of each chapter in mind. New instructional essays, drawn from respected colleagues in the field of composition studies, have been added to Part 3 and cover such topics as integrating the teaching of grammar into the composition classroom and using a hybrid model of online and in-classroom learning for composition students. Part 4 now includes a full and revised set of handouts and transparency masters that complement the entire text. Part 5 provides a variety of evaluation handouts that may prove useful for both teachers and students. Two appendices complete the manual, offering sample student writings and a compendium of over 100 additional assignments.

I would like to express my thanks to Steve Dalphin, my former Acquisitions Editor, Annie Todd, Acquisitions Editor, Laurie Runion, Developmental Editor, and Joe Gallagher, Tech Project Manager at Thomson/Wadsworth for their support and intelligent guidance through the writing of this book. I would also like to thank my mentors and colleagues at SUNY Buffalo, who have made teaching composition here a pleasure. A special thanks to Associate Professor of English Tim Dean. My deepest thanks to Sandra and John Scarry, for their wonderful text, their sincere belief in the importance of the written word, and for so much else. Last but not least, an extension of gratitude to my students, who prove every semester that they are teachers as well.

Siobhán Scarry
SUNY Buffalo
September 2006

An Overview of the Instructor's Manual

Part 1 of this manual contains support for instructors planning and organizing their courses using *The Writer's Workplace* as their textbook. The following material can be found in Part 1:

- sample syllabi and course outlines designed specifically for use with the new editions;
- advice on incorporating journals into the classroom;
- a discussion of collaborative learning techniques, including peer evaluation and workshopping;
- suggestions for using student portfolios in the composition classroom;
- information on effective conferencing techniques;
- sample grading rubrics;
- and a discussion on writing proficiency exams.

Part 2 is a chapter-by-chapter guide to the textbook, providing instructors with overviews of chapter goals, tips on effective approaches to teaching each chapter, and additional chapter-specific assignments for students, including:

- in-class activities;
- journal assignments;
- and responding to reading assignments.

Part 3 is a compilation of instructional essays dealing with pedagogical issues relevant to the college composition instructor. The following topics are covered in this section:

- collaboration in the classroom;
- the use of portfolios;
- the role of tutors in college composition;
- ways of meaningfully incorporating grammar into composition courses;
- working with ESL students in the composition environment;
- an argument for a hybrid model of in-class *and* online learning;
- and plagiarism and the Web.

Part 4 contains handouts and transparency masters for the entire textbook.

Part 5 contains evaluation handouts, including instructor and peer evaluation worksheets.

Appendix A contains sample student writings, which cover most of the rhetorical modes, a rough and final draft of a student essay, and a sample writing proficiency exam.

Appendix B is a compilation of over 100 additional assignments contained in this manual. These include in-class activities, journal and writing assignments, and assignments that ask students to respond to readings from the textbook.

Using the Companion Website to *The Writer's Workplace*

The authors of *The Writer's Workplace* have made their textbooks even more dynamic in these new editions by creating a companion website designed specifically for students using the books as their classroom texts:

The Writer's Online Workplace
(http://www.thomsonedu.com/english/scarry/)

This website offers students an opportunity to use the Web as a focused learning tool for writing and composition. Students using the textbook are directed to the website through the Exploring Online feature of each chapter. The Exploring Online segment of the website links students to chapter-specific handouts, quizzes, and other online resources that give students an opportunity to put their new knowledge to use in the interactive environment of the Web.

The Writer's Online Workplace is also a tremendous resource for instructors. Because the site offers students a wealth of information and activities, instructors will want to encourage students to make use of the website as they study each chapter. Or instructors may choose to assign website activities as an integral part of the curriculum, either as homework or as collaborative work. Either way, the companion website will expand students' learning as well as their Web proficiency.

Some of the features of The Writer's Online Workplace include:

- interactive online grammar quizzes;
- links to online resources for writers;
- glossaries and electronic flashcards for each chapter;
- overviews of chapter objectives;
- and online activities that build on chapter material by leveraging the depth and breadth of content available on the Web.

Another way to incorporate new media into the composition classroom is by using *ThomsonNOW for Writing*, available from Thomson/Wadsworth. This online multimedia program covers all aspects of the writing process, from pointers on prewriting techniques to grammar exercises to help with the college essay. Incorporating this new media ancillary as part of the curriculum may prove useful in adding dimensionality and currency to composition courses.

Contents

Planning and Organizing Your Course

Developing a Syllabus and Course Outline

Recognizing the Flexibility of *The Writer's Workplace*

The Writer's Workplace is designed as a flexible resource for both teachers and students, making a variety of course structures possible and allowing for many different approaches in the composition classroom. For those teachers who want to emphasize grammar, Chapters 3–13 provide students with ample opportunities to practice and build their skills. The wealth of readings supplied throughout the book allows for an integration of reading and writing, a focus on the rhetorical modes, and rich content for class discussion and journal responses. Collaborative learning is emphasized in the Working Together feature that concludes each chapter. Instructors teaching in learning and career institutes will find this feature especially useful in helping students master job-related skills. Some teachers will want to take advantage of what the Web has to offer the writing student. The authors have developed The Writer's Online Workplace (http://www. thomsonedu.com/english/scarry/) for this purpose. The Exploring Online feature provided before the end of each chapter directs students to this website for chapter-specific links to relevant online quizzes, handouts, and other online resources. The website also contains online activities and a glossary for each chapter. Whatever vision an instructor has for the classroom, the complete writing program offered in *The Writer's Workplace* will act as a flexible resource for students of writing.

Using the General Syllabus

Many composition instructors use both a general course syllabus and a more detailed course outline to provide students with a clear understanding of the requirements for the class. The advantage of using a general course syllabus is that it allows teachers to provide students with a concise overview of the goals and general requirements of the course, grading and plagiarism policies, and important information such as class meeting times and the instructor's office location and hours. Many colleges consider the syllabus to be a legal document, which sets forth a contractual agreement between instructor and student. For this reason, it is important that all policies, goals, and requirements listed on the syllabus are within the guidelines for the particular institution. New instructors will want to check with a mentor on these specifics before handing out syllabi to students.

Sample Syllabus

Basic Composition
ENEX 100, Section 24
Fall 2006

Insturctor: Instructor Name Office: Liberal Arts 220
Classroom: Liberal Arts 100 Office Hours: Th 2–5
Class Time: T/Th 12:40–2pm email: instructor@college.edu

REQUIRED TEXTS.   *The Writer's Workplace with Readings*, *Sixth Edition* by Sandra Scarry and John Scarry; available at the UC Bookstore

COURSE GOALS.   English 100 is designed to give students a foundation in the principles of college-level writing. Students will work on all aspects of the writing process, from prewriting to proofreading. Attention will also be given to the mastery of grammar and to the critical reading of selected essays. By the end of the semester, students should be able to construct clear and grammatically correct sentences and paragraphs, leading to the creation of a successful college essay.

COURSE DESCRIPTION.   Students in this course will be introduced to the steps of the writing process, and will engage in writing exercises, journaling, grammar study, critical reading, and other activities to develop skills for clear and effective writing. By the end of the term, students will have a substantial portfolio of their own writing and will have mastered the skills necessary for writing successfully at the college level.

COURSE REQUIREMENTS.

- Two short essays, to be typed and handed in on or before deadline
- One in-class essay
- Proficiency exam (administered on the last day of class)
- Numerous in-class writing exercises
- Journal
- Active participation in class. You and your classmates—for the duration of this course—are a community of writers. You are expected to participate in discussion and respond to each other's ideas and writing in a manner that is productive and diplomatic.
- Attendance. Because your participation in class is a major part of your grade, attendance is vital. More than three unexcused absences will negatively affect your grade in this course.
- At least one conference with me to discuss your writing progress

GRADING.   Students enrolled in English 100 are graded by the traditional letter-grade system: A, B, C, D, F, or are given NCR for no credit. Receiving NCR does not affect grade-point average; however, it is reserved for students who have worked unusually hard, attended regularly, and completed all assignments, but whose skills are not at a passing level at the end of the semester. final grades will be based on the quality and improvement of your writing (two essays, numerous in-class assignments, and journal); your attendance and participation in class; and your adherence to deadlines.

ENGLISH 100 PROFICIENCY EXAM.   To receive credit for English 100 students must successfully pass the team-graded English 100 Proficiency Exam, which consists of a portfolio containing one formal paper written over the course of the semester and the final essay exam administered on the last day of class. However, the final letter grades of passing students will be assigned by the classroom instructor.

PLAGIARISM POLICY.   Plagiarism occurs when a writer appropriates or passes off as his or her own the ideas or writings of someone else. Intentional plagiarism is stealing. In the academic and professional writing communities, passing off someone else's creative or intellectual property as your own is an actionable offense under the law. Similarly, the University severely punishes students who intentionally plagiarize. A student who plagiarizes may receive a failing grade for the plagiarized paper, or for the course, or he or she might be expelled from the university. Furthermore, plagiarism is extremely easy to detect.

Customizing Your Course: Developing a Course Outline

Because *The Writer's Workplace* is a flexible resource, instructors can easily tailor their courses to best meet the needs of their particular students and classes. The following course outlines represent only a fraction of what is possible in terms of structuring a course using *The Writer's Workplace* as the primary classroom text. However, each of the provided outlines represents some of the more common approaches to using the text. The sample outlines provided here assume a sixteen-week semester, with classes meeting twice a week. These can be altered as needed to accommodate six-week summer terms or courses on the quarter system. Many instructors develop the course outline (some refer to it as the detailed syllabus) not only for their own organizational purposes, but to supply a week-by-week version of the outline so that students feel clear about their assignments. The two course outlines provided here are organized according to the following pedagogical principles:

- Course Outline 1: Skills Emphasis Incorporating Collaborative Prewriting and Writing Activities
- Course Outline 2: Rhetorical Emphasis Incorporating Developmental Skills as Needed

Sample Course Outlines

Course Outline 1: Skills Emphasis Incorporating Collaborative Prewriting and Writing Activities

This class outline has been designed for a course that emphasizes developmental skills, along with a reading and writing component to encourage critical thinking skills. The exit exam for such a course usually requires students to produce a writing sample that demonstrates mastery of basic English grammar skills as well as overall writing competence. This includes the use of a variety of sentence structures and clear presentation of ideas.

To construct a syllabus that uses this approach, the instructor needs to decide the grammar topics to be covered and how best to incorporate reading and writing activities that will improve students' critical thinking skills. The use of journals, portfolios, reading assignments on relevant topics, and occasional collaborative activities in prewriting or peer review, will keep the course a lively and engaging experience. Instructors may have the option of teaching the rhetorical modes or of organizing the writing by theme. *The Writer's Workplace* has a wealth of material that allows both approaches.

Students using this syllabus should be encouraged to use good study skills. Preparation for class should include previewing each chapter, including studying the chapter objectives, boxed definitions, rules, and charts.

Instructors may want to check the textbooks regularly to make certain students are doing the assignments conscientiously. A percentage of the final grade may be based on assignment completion. It's a good idea to have students keep their writing assignments in a portfolio for submission at the end of the course.

WEEK 1

T   Introduction to the course and explanation of the syllabus
A diagnostic writing will be administered
Homework: Preview Chapter 1

R   Chapter 1: Gathering Ideas for Writing
In-class Activity: Surveying Student Attitudes About Writing
Homework: Read from "The Diary of Latoya Hunter" and do Activity 1
(Journaling Assignment #1)

WEEK 2

T   Chapter 2: Recognizing the Elements of Good Writing
In-class Activities 1, 2, and 3
Homework: Activities 4 and 5

R   Chapter 2: (continued) Voice, Unity, and Coherence
Homework: Read Working Together for Chapter 6, What is a Fair
Salary?; Consider the discussion questions for Journaling Assignment #2

WEEK 3

T   Chapter 3: Finding Subjects and Verbs in Simple Sentences
Homework: Exercises 2, 6, 9, 12, 14, 16

R   20 Minute **QUIZ** from Mastery Tests (Finding Subjects and Verbs)
Chapter 3 continued: Parts of Speech
Homework: Working Together (Crossword Puzzle)

WEEK 4

T   Quiz returned
Chapter 4: Making Subjects and Verbs Agree
Homework: Exercises 2, 5, 7, 9, 11

R   20 Minute **QUIZ** from Mastery Tests (Subject and Verb Agreement)
In-class freewriting
Homework: Read "How to Mark a Book" by Mortimer Adler (in Further
Readings) and respond with Journal Assignment #3

WEEK 5

T   Quiz returned
Chapter 5: Understanding Fragments and Phrases
Homework: Exercises 6, 9, 12, 15

R   20 Minute **QUIZ**: Identifying phrases
In-class reading and discussion: "Summer Reading" by Michael Dorris (in
Further Readings)
Homework: Journaling Assignment #4 based on class discussion

WEEK 6

T   Quiz returned
Chapter 6: Combining Sentences Using the Three Methods of
Coordination
Homework: Exercises 2, 5, 7, Test 4

R   Chapter 6: (continued)
Homework: Chapter 15, Group 1, Exercises 1, 2; Group III, Exercises 5,
6; Group VI, Exercises 11, 12; Memorize the list of coordinating conjunctions and adverbial conjunctions.

WEEK 7

T   Chapter 7: Combining Sentences Using Subordination
Homework: Exercises 2, 5, 8, 9, Test 4

R   Chapter 7: (continued)
Homework: Memorize the list of subordinating conjunctions

WEEK 8

T   Review: Mastery Tests
Homework: Study for midterm exam

R   **MIDTERM EXAM**

WEEK 9

T   Chapter 13: Capitalization and Punctuation
Homework: Exercises 2, 5, 8, 11; Test 2

R   Midterm exam returned and discussed
Homework: Respond to Working Together Chapter 7, "A Hard Lesson,
Learned Door to Door"; Use the discussion questions for ideas for Jour-
naling Assignment #5

WEEK 10

T   Chapter 16: Working with Paragraphs: Topic Sentences and Controlling
Ideas
Chapter 17: Working with Paragraphs: Supporting Details
Homework: Chapter 16 Exercises 4, 7, 10, 13, 17

R   20 Minute **QUIZ**: Topic Sentences and Controlling Ideas
In-class reading: "Neat People vs. Sloppy People" by Suzanne Britt (in
Further Readings)
Homework: Chapter 17 Exercises 2, 5, 8

WEEK 11

T   Chapter 17: Working with Paragraphs: Supporting Details
Homework: Read "A Day at the Theme Park" by W. Bruce Cameron (in
Further Readings)

R   In-class writing: Freewrite describing a place
Homework: Read student essay "Going to School Behind the Iron
Curtain" (in Chapter 26)

WEEK 12

T   Chapter 14: Choosing Words that Work
In-class reading of student essay, "Bad Weather" and Activities 1, 2, and 3
Homework: Exercises 2, 5, 7, 9

R   Chapter 20: Developing Paragraphs: Description
In-class writing: Description of a place
Homework: read "Salvation" by Langston Hughes (in Chapter 28)

WEEK 13

T   Chapter 19: Developing Paragraphs: Narration
View DVD "Salvation" by Langston Hughes; followed by discussion of
narrative elements
Homework: Chapter 11 Irregular Verbs, Exercises 1, 2, 3, 4, 5, 6; Test 4
Prepare brainstorming list for a narrative about a childhood experience

R   In-class writing: narrative of a childhood experience (bring brainstorming
list)

WEEK 14

T   Chapter 18: Developing Paragraphs: Illustration
Study of a model essay, "Darkness at Noon" by Harold Krents
Homework: Write one or more paragraphs, developing your ideas by us-
ing examples (choose from topics suggested in class)

R   Chapter 18 (continued): Exercise 8, brainstorming and in-class writing
using examples
Homework: Read "I'm a Banana and Proud of It," by Wayson Choy
(in Further Readings)

WEEK 15

T   Chapter 24: Developing Paragraphs: Definition, Classification
Discussion of "I'm a Banana and Proud of It"
In-class writing using definition
Homework: Chapter 9 Exercises 1, 2, 4, 5, 8

R   Peer editing of semester writing.
Homework: Chapter 15, Group II Exercises 3, 4; Group IV Exercises
7, 8; Group V Exercises 9, 10

WEEK 16

T   Peer review of writing
Review: Mastery Tests

R   Semester portfolios due
Exit Exam administered

*By the end of the term, students using this course outline should have the
following writing assignments completed and ready to turn in as part of their
portfolios:

- 5 journal assignments
- 1 freewriting assignment (on description)
- 1 description (2nd draft)
- 1 narration
- 1 illustration
- 1 definition
- any other in-class or homework writings

Course Outline 2: Rhetorical Emphasis Incorporating Developmental Skills as Needed

This class outline has been designed for a course that emphasizes paragraph development and includes a thorough grounding in basic sentence skills. The exit exam for such a course would most likely consist of writing several paragraphs using different rhetorical modes along with taking a multiple choice test of 50 or so questions on basic sentence skills.

To construct a syllabus emphasizing this approach, the instructor will need to decide how many of the modes can be realistically taught within the time period. Another issue to consider is whether or not the students will work entirely on paragraphs, or if essay writing will also be included. This course outline gives students the opportunity to complete two full essay assignments. Furthermore, a plan that includes the practice of basic skills needs to be a regular part of the syllabus, especially if these skills are a part of the final exit exam criteria.

Students using this syllabus need to come to class having previewed the chapter to be presented on that day. They should study the chapter objectives, the boxed definitions and charts, and any other important examples in the chapter. Instructors need to check the textbook regularly to make certain students are doing the assignments conscientiously. A percentage of the final grade should be given to assignment completion. All writing assignments should be kept in a portfolio for submission at the end of the course.

Unit 1: Introduction to Writing

WEEK 1

T   Introduction to the course and explanation of the syllabus
A diagnostic writing will be administered
Preview Chapter 1

R   Chapter 1: Gathering Ideas for Writing
In-class collaborative activity: Surveying Student Attitudes About Writing
Homework: Activity 1 (Journaling Assignment) and Activity 2 (Focused Freewriting)

WEEK 2

T   Chapter 2: Recognizing the Elements of Good Writing
Subject, Purpose, Audience
Homework: Read "How to Mark a Book" by Mortimer Adler (in Further Readings) and determine subject, purpose, and audience

R   Chapter 2: Recognizing the Elements of Good Writing
Voice, Unity, and Coherence
Homework: Read "No Comprendo," by Barbara Mujica (in Further Readings) and describe how she creates voice, unity, and coherence

Unit 2: Developing Paragraphs

WEEK 3

T   Chapter 16: Working with Paragraphs: Topic Sentences and Controlling Ideas
In-class writing, topic sentences
Homework: Exercises, 4, 7, 10, 13, 17

R   20 Minute **QUIZ** from Mastery Tests: Writing the Topic Sentence
Chapter 3: Finding Subjects and Verbs in Simple Sentences
Homework: Exercises 2, 6, 9, 12, 14, 16

WEEK 4

T   Quiz on Topic Sentences returned
Chapter 17: Working with Paragraphs: Supporting Details
Homework: Exercises 2, 5, 7

R   Chapter 3 (continued)
Chapter 4: Making Subjects and Verbs Agree
Homework: Chapter 3, Exercise 18; Chapter 4, Exercises 2, 5, 7, 9, 11

WEEK 5

T   Chapter 18: Developing Paragraphs: Illustration
Homework: Exercises 5, 6; Exercise 3 (Illustration paragraph, to hand in)

R   20 Minute **QUIZ**: Parts of speech and subject-verb agreement
Chapter 5: Understanding Fragments and Phrases
Homework: Exercises 6, 9, 12, 15

WEEK 6

T   Quiz on parts of speech and subject-verb agreement returned
Chapter 20: Developing Paragraphs: Description
Homework: Exercises 2, 4, 6, 9, 13; read "Dream Houses" by Tenaya
Darlington (in Further Readings)

R   Discussion of reading
20 minute in-class descriptive writing (from Model Paragraph assignment
#1: Description of a Home; students may bring brainstorming list)
Chapter 14: Choosing Words that Work
Homework: Exercises 2, 5, 7, 9

WEEK 7

T   Chapter 19: Developing Paragraphs: Narration
Homework: Exercises 2, 5, 8, 10

R   20 minute in-class narrative writing (from Model Paragraph Assignment
#4: Narrative of a Frustrating Situation; students may bring brainstorming
list)
Chapter 6: Combining Sentences Using the Three Options of Coordination
Homework: Exercises 2, 5, 7; Test 4

WEEK 8

T   Chapter 21: Developing Paragraphs: Process
Homework: Exercises 2, 4; write a process paragraph on one of the suggested topics (to hand in)

R   Process paragraph due
Chapter 7: Combining Sentences Using Subordination (understanding clauses)
Homework: Exercises 2, 5, 8, 9; Test 4

WEEK 9

T   **Midterm exam**: 50% writing paragraphs using rhetorical modes, 50% skills assessment

R   Chapter 13: Using Correct Capitalization and Punctuation
Homework: 2, 5, 8, 11; Test 2

WEEK 10

T   Return and discuss Midterm Exam
Homework: Read "Neat People vs. Sloppy People," by Suzanne Britt (in Further Readings)

R   Chapter 22: Developing Paragraphs: Comparison/Contrast
Discussion of Reading
In-class writing: Exercise 6
Homework: Exercise 10

WEEK 11

T   Chapter 23: Developing Paragraphs: Cause and Effect
In-class collaborative assignment: Working Together on Rosa Parks
Homework: Exercises 2, 8

R   20 minute in-class cause and effect writing (from Working Together discussions; students may bring brainstorming list)
Chapter 8: Correcting Fragments and Run-ons
Homework: Exercises 3, 5; Test 4

WEEK 12

T   Chapter 24: Developing Paragraphs: Definition, Classification
In-class reading and analysis: "I'm a Banana and Proud of It" by Wayson Choy (in Further Readings)
Homework: Write a paragraph using definition or classification, choosing from suggested topics

R   20-minute **QUIZ** on Fragments and Run-ons
Chapter 9: Choosing Correct Pronouns
Homework: Exercises 1, 2, 4, 5, 8; Test 4

Unit 3: Structuring the Essay

WEEK 13

T   Chapter 25: Moving from the Paragraph to the Essay
Discussion of thesis statement, parts of the essay, transitions
Chapter 26: Following the Progress of a Student Essay
Collaborative in-class assignment: Discuss the development of the student essay from brainstorming through the final draft
Homework: Write a one-page analysis of the changes that the student writer made, comparing the freewriting with the final essay. In what ways did the writer change the essay?

R   Quiz on Fragments and Run-ons returned
Chapter 28: Narration

Reading out loud: "Salvation" by Langston Hughes (in Further Readings)
Homework: brainstorming and choosing a topic for essay #1 (narration)

WEEK 14

T   View DVD of "Salvation;" discussion of narrative elements
       Chapter 10: Working with Adjectives, Adverbs and Parallel Structure
       Homework: Write a short narrative essay

R   Essay #1, Rough Draft due
       In-class collaborative assignment: peer editing
       Homework: Read "The Ugly Truth About Beauty," by Dave Barry (in
       Chapter 30)

WEEK 15

T   Essay #1, Final Draft due
       Discussion of "The Ugly Truth About Beauty"
       Chapter 30: Writing an Essay Using Comparison/Contrast
       Chapter 11: Practicing Irregular Verbs
       Homework: Exercises 1, 2, 3, 4, 5, 6; Test 4; brainstorming for essay #2

R   Chapter 12: Mastering Verb Tenses
       Homework: Chapter 12 Exercises 2, 4; Test 4; Write a short
       comparison/contrast essay

WEEK 16

T   Essay #2 Due
       Practicing Mastery Tests

R   Semester Portfolios due; **Exit Exam** administered

Incorporating Journals into Your Curriculum

Introducing the Journal

Assigning journal writing for your students is a means of helping them develop the "habit of writing." Ideally, students who use a journal will become more comfortable with writing and with doing so on a regular basis. The journal can be especially useful in a developmental composition course, utilizing students' creativity in the development of their skills and giving them a place to write freely without having to worry about mistakes.

Chapter 1 introduces students to the journal as a prewriting technique, making the beginning of the term an ideal time to get students started on their own journals. Encourage students to keep their journals in separate spiral-bound notebooks or in separate sections of the notebooks they use for class notes. Explain the importance of the journal in the development of their overall writing skills, and stress that the journal will be a constant companion throughout the course. The object is to encourage students to take the journal seriously from the first day and to let them know that they will be graded on the way they have used the journal by the end of the course.

A journal can be many things for students—a place for brainstorming, recording thoughts or experiences from their personal lives, or responding to readings and discussions from class. Because the journal is an idea-generating device, you do not want to regulate the kinds of thoughts and feelings that students may wish to put into it. However, a little structure is better than total freedom when it comes to giving guidelines to students. It is advisable to expect students to produce specific journal assignments on a regular basis—weekly journal assignments ensure that students are keeping up the "habit" of writing and feeling clear about what is expected from them. Additionally, you may wish to give students an approximate number of pages you expect for their journals by the end of the term. Again, the goal is to provide structure and direction while leaving the content up to them. The Chapter Guides in Part 2 of this manual contain weekly journal assignments, which are integrated with the topics of each chapter in *The Writer's Workplace*, giving students the opportunity to reinforce the chapter skills they are learning in creative ways. All journal assignments listed in this manual are also collected in Appendix C for your ease of use.

Pitfalls and Solutions to Using the Journal

Despite the fact that journals are often used as a successful and integral part of developmental composition courses, some instructors abandon the journal early in the semester or early in their professional careers due to several common but tenacious problems.

One of the most persistent difficulties is that students often remain perplexed as to the types of entries they should be writing in the journal throughout the term. It is not unusual to collect journals at mid-semester and find entries beginning as follows: "I'm still not really sure what I'm supposed to be writing, but here it goes. Jennifer and I had a fight last night and I still feel bad...." If an instructor has not been specific as to the nature of the entries students should produce, he or she may be in the uncomfortable position at the semester's end of trying to grade journals filled with unfocused student writing, not to mention knowing far more about students' lives than is appropriate for an authority figure. Giving weekly journal assignments, specifying page count expectations, and collecting journals more than once in the semester will alleviate these problems.

Another pitfall that instructors often face is the lack of guidelines for grading or judging the journal, making it difficult to convince students to use it and take it seriously. In addition, there seems to be no easy way to collect journals in order to grade them. Toting thirty to sixty spiral binders across campus is often daunting, if not impossible. These issues can be remedied with a clearly considered grading and collecting system. If you are specific about your expectations and plan carefully, you will be successful using the journal in the classroom setting.

Grading the Journal

The most difficult aspect of incorporating the journal into a composition course is finding a grading system that is fair but does not impede students' creativity. There are several possible grading methods. Find one that is easiest for you to execute, achieves consistent results, and maintains a high degree of objectivity. To avoid the unpleasant job of carrying armloads of notebooks to the car or office, the following three methods are designed to be accomplished in class while students work together in groups.

Point System

Perhaps the easiest, and fairest, journal grading method uses a point system. Students receive a certain number of points for aspects of their journals, and the total is then either entered in your grade book as a percentage, or converted into the letter grade corresponding to that point range. The most important parts of their journal work will be weighted the most heavily. An easy example of a 100-point scale might be:

- Journal Length (30 pages or more): 25 points
- Completion of Assigned Journal Activities: 50 points
- Creativity and Coherence of Writing: 15 points
- Legibility: 10 points

Grading for Completion

Another grading method counts pages of work done during the semester, taking into account the size of each student's handwriting. The following rubric—for a course requiring 30 pages of journal writing — might be used to grade for completion:

- 30 or more pages: A
- 25–29 pages: B
- 20–24 pages: C
- 15–19 pages: D
- Under 15 pages: F

Grading for Content

A third method takes into account content rather than quantity. Have the students mark 20 pages of their finest journal work with Post-It notes or have the students photocopy and submit the pages to you in a folder. You would then judge their work as you would an essay, for signs of in-depth work, progress, creativity, and coherence.

Tips on Using the Journal Assignments

The journal assignments included in this manual strive to help students exercise similar skills to the ones they are learning in *The Writer's Workplace*, while providing them with enough freedom to explore ideas and topics on their own. Some journal assignments are closely integrated with the topics and exercises in the book while others have little or no direct connection to the textbook. How you decide to focus your students in their journal writing and how you decide to organize your course will determine which journal assignments will be most useful for you. With an eye toward integrated learning, each Chapter Guide in Part 2 of this manual offers suggestions for weekly journal assignments. If assigning specific journaling work to correspond to given chapters or readings seems too rigid for your students, you may wish to leave the choice of assignment up to them and simply make a general requirement that they complete a certain number of the journal assignments by the end of the term. For your convenience, all the journal assignments are collected in Appendix C.

Incorporating Collaborative Learning into Your Curriculum

Capitalizing on Student Knowledge and Creativity

Students come into the classroom with skills, life experiences, and creativity that can enhance the composition classroom. Collaborative learning is a way to capitalize on what students have to offer while simultaneously empowering them to take an active role in their own learning. Given the right balance of direction and freedom, students can become effective teachers to their peers. Learning to work effectively in groups will also help students gain confidence in their abilities to communicate, think critically, and add their voice to the academic community. Instructors integrate collaborative learning into their classroom in a variety of ways, including:

- breaking classes into small groups for discussion;
- assigning groups for class presentations;
- using peer evaluation to "workshop" student rough drafts;
- and using peer groups to edit and proofread student final drafts.

Using the "Working Together" Component in Each Chapter

The Writer's Workplace makes collaborative learning an integral part of the book's writing program by including a section called Working Together at the close of each chapter. Each Working Together encourages students to put into practice—in a group learning situation—the skills learned in each chapter. These activities encourage critical thinking and ensure cumulative learning. Beyond this, the Working Together component enables students to gain an appreciation for the ideas of others and gives them the confidence to voice their opinion and work in groups, all skills that will benefit them in the workplace and in life. Some of the activities offered in the Working Togethers include:

- taking a survey;
- summarizing a class discussion;
- developing a résumé;
- writing a restaurant review;
- reading a selection about Rosa Parks and making a list of short-term and long-term effects of her actions;
- brainstorming for examples;
- using outside sources to write a comparison/contrast essay;
- and discussing an editorial for its ability to persuade.

Collaborative learning can be used as a touchstone too. Many ideas generated from small group discussions will find their ways into student journals or may spark a student's imagination and lead to a topic for an essay. The Portfolio Suggestion that follows each Working Together allows teachers to extend the classroom collaborations into assignments students may continue at home. For teachers working in learning and career institutes, the Working Togethers will be an important part of their course. In recognition that many students have an interest in career issues, many of the Working Togethers focus on topics that are work-related, giving students insight into issues of the workplace and helping them master job-related skills.

Peer Evaluation and Workshopping

Once students have working drafts of essays or assignments, peer response and feedback can become a crucial component to the writing classroom. Dividing students into pairs or groups in which they respond to each other's work not only enables the development of subsequent drafts, but also brings class members together, allowing students to take charge of their own learning and act as teachers themselves. Peer groups and workshops can decenter the classroom in important ways, redirecting focus from the teacher as the person in the room holding the "answers," and thus empowering students to see themselves as valuable and integral to the learning process.

Organizing and structuring workshops will be crucial to their success. Student writers tend to be anxious at first about the workshop process. Giving written and oral feedback about writing is not a familiar role for many beginning writers. Setting specific goals and providing students with evaluation worksheets will go a long way toward making peer workshopping a valuable classroom tool.

Structuring Workshops

Peer workshops can be structured in a variety of ways. The two most common involve dividing students into pairs based on writing ability and putting them into small groups, which allows greater room for discussion. However you decide to structure this aspect of the workshop, students should come to class with enough copies of their drafts to pass out to the members of their group. You may also ask students to bring in an extra copy for you to have on hand during the workshop. Because students will need some direction about workshop etiquette and expectations, at least in the early stages, it is a good idea to move from group to group, offering advice or providing help as needed. Having a copy of each student's draft will allow you to provide specific comments as you circulate among the groups.

Peer Evaluation Worksheets

Asking students to provide written responses to peer work will ground student writers in the goals and expectations of the workshop. A written analysis of peer work will sharpen students' critical thinking skills, hone their abilities as editors, and help to illuminate the recursive nature of the writing process. Workshop evaluation sheets engage students to do just these things. Evaluation sheets might ask students to find and underline the thesis statement, choose their favorite passage, or identify any run-on sentences. A number of evaluation worksheets—both for peer workshops and for instructor evaluation of student work—can be found in Appendix D.

Setting the Tone for Successful Workshops

As with any classroom activity, peer workshops are most helpful when the environment is a healthy mixture of criticism and praise. Student writers are often wary of being too critical of their peers and often err on the side of praising their fellow writers. While all writers need encouragement, workshops will become a disservice to student writers if advice about improving the work is not able to be voiced. On the other hand, some students may launch into devastatingly honest evaluations of their peers. This can be equally unhelpful. A few rules of thumb about workshop etiquette will help students strike the right balance.

Beginning the workshop process with an anonymous piece of writing is often a good way to get students comfortable with discussing and analyzing student work while at the same time giving the instructor the opportunity to set the right workshop tone. Material for these "mock workshops" can be drawn from the work of previous students. Do remember to black out the student's name before photocopying the piece for the rest of the class.

Another method of ensuring a smooth workshop is to ask the writer whose work is being discussed to remain silent during the discussion. This may be uncomfortable for students at first, but there are good reasons for this rule. At the draft stage, writers are often unsure about what they have or have not communicated through their writing. Encouraging students to truly listen to the responses of their peers will allow them to discover what struck readers as honest and engaging or which portions of their piece came across as confusing or unconvincing.

Having students read each other's essays out loud can also go a long way toward creating a positive workshop environment. For the writer, hearing his or her own essay out loud can be a powerful experience. Oral readings also tend to illuminate which portions of the text may need additional work. Having students read the work silently and make marginal notes is also an effective way to begin a workshop, but can sometimes cause group discussion to get off to a slow start. Beginning a workshop with an oral reading can often ease the transition and pave the way for lively classroom discussion.

Grading and Responding to Student Writing

Responding to Writing Assignments

Every instructor develops a personal style in regard to responding to student writing. Comments and marginal notes on student work are an instructor's way of coaching, teaching, and developing a rapport with students through the work itself. Many instructors give students a handout of proofreading marks (found on the inside back cover of the textbook) at the beginning of the term so that students will have a clear understanding of any textual markings such as carats or delete symbols. Being clear about one's comments on student work and setting out one's grading criteria in the syllabus and course outline will clarify expectations, ensure fairness, and minimize student complaints. If you are new to teaching, your mentor or department chair should be able to provide you with copies of graded essays that have been used in the preceding semesters. Otherwise, ask a colleague to share with you student papers he or she has kept from past semesters. Students appreciate seeing both extremes—the exemplary A paper and the failure paper. Ideally, they should also see copies of essays that have received grades of B, C, and D. Even though the student work may be end-of-the-semester examples, sharing these examples will go a long way toward showing students what the writing course will be about and what the expectations will be.

Assigning grades to student writing and developing a response style require finding the right balance between praise and criticism. Beginning writers often become discouraged when they get their writing assignments returned only to find them riddled with red pen and marginal comments. Instructors need to bear this in mind when grading student writing, especially in the beginning of the semester when grammar issues may abound. It is a good idea, in other words, to choose one's battles. Marking every punctuation error in an essay may be less effective than marking every punctuation error in a single paragraph and then writing in one's comments that the student needs to work further in this arena. Focusing one's attention on the areas that need the most work will allow students the opportunity to work on specific writing problems rather than feel overwhelmed by how much their grammar and writing need to improve. In the same way, the paragraph of instructor comments given on the last page of student essays will be more helpful to students if the criticism is peppered with some positive comments.

One way to ensure that students are paying attention to instructors' comments is to ask students for revisions of their work. Not only will revisions help them take charge of their own learning, but will set standards more effectively than assessing students with low grades that they cannot fix themselves.

Using Student Portfolios

Many colleges are now requiring first-year writing students to turn in portfolios of their work at the end of the semester. Portfolios are often used for assessment purposes, helping departments to set program-wide standards. But many instructors make use of portfolios as a way of assigning individual grades and as a way of encouraging students to assess their own work. Asking students to gather and organize all the writing they have done over the course of the semester often results in students realizing just how much work they have accomplished. With this in mind, many instructors assign a self-assessment as part of the portfolio requirement. You might ask students to describe the experience they have had with the writing process, or you may ask them to analyze their own essays in their portfolios in terms of the guidelines you choose.

Here are a few ways of approaching the portfolio in the writing classroom:

- Students hand in all the work they have done over the course of the semester along with a self-assessment of their writing.

- Students hand in a selection of what they consider to be their best work done in the course along with a self-assessment explaining how they determined what work to include.

- Students hand in the major assignments of the course with one substantial revision, along with a self-assessment describing their revision process.

There are many other variations, and instructors may tailor the portfolio assignment to the specific goals and expectations of particular courses. Whatever model you decide to use with the portfolio in your classroom, students will benefit from gathering, organizing, and assessing their own work; and as an instructor, the portfolio will give you all the tools necessary for assessing your students their final grades.

Incorporating Student Conferences

With the demands of current teaching loads that many instructors face, one-on-one time with students can feel like an impossible pedagogical tool to put into practice. However, individual conferences give students a place to discuss their writing concerns and ask questions they may not feel comfortable asking in the context of the classroom. Conferences also give instructors the opportunity to articulate individualized goals for students. Making time for students one-on-one also goes a long way toward developing rapport with each and every member of the class.

Conferences of 20–30 minutes seem to work best. It is important that students bring writing with them to the conference. Asking students to bring in a draft of a current assignment will ensure that time spent conferencing is used wisely. Some instructors find conferencing such an important part of their pedagogy that they cancel classes for one week in order to make time to see every student one-on-one. This can be an especially effective way of scheduling conferences, especially if students are asked to do extra work that week, such as bring a first draft or a revision to the conference itself.

Grading Rubrics

Decisions about grading should be firmly rooted in your philosophy about writing. Grading criteria should be clearly set out in the syllabus and course outline. Some instructors grade using rubrics that give numerical values to set aspects of writing assignments. A number of rubrics that use this method are available for your use in Appendix D of this manual. Some instructors prefer to use a holistic grading process, which assesses student writing without assigning letter grades. This can be an especially effective way of grading student writing at the beginning of the term, when students are curious about how they are doing but instructors are trying to emphasize that writing is a *process* and thus try to wait a number of weeks before assigning letter grades. A holistic grading rubric is included in the following section on Writing Proficiency Exams. Whatever your approach to assigning grades, here are a number of things to keep in mind as you develop your syllabus and course outline:

- You are going to administer a grade at finals.
- You must judge as fairly as you can all the aspects of a student's work and competence.
- Whenever you grade a student's paper, you may have to defend your grading decisions to that student.
- You want to be as explicit and detailed as possible, not just at the beginning of the semester but at all the points in between, including the juncture where you might have to counsel a student about the fact that it is in his or her best interest to drop the course.
- You may find yourself in a position of being asked to justify a grade you've given a student to a supervisor or dean.
- You will want to clarify your decision on a contested grade as much as you can in writing to convince an administrator, parent, student, or yourself.
- You want to convince students that your class is manageable and that they understand the demands as printed in your syllabus.
- You want to be certain that your standards and assessment match those of your colleagues in your department.

In summary, your grading policy should be written in clear and precise language. It should be spelled out in more ways than one. References to grading should be frequent. Your policy should be elucidated and meted out fairly so that there is no question or confusion.

Writing Proficiency Exams

Preparing Students for the Exam

Many colleges and universities use writing proficiency exams as a way to place students in writing courses and in order to assess student progress. Exams often produce a fair amount of anxiety for students. For instructors teaching in institutions that administer writing proficiency exams, preparing students adequately for taking timed writing tests will be a component of the course curriculum. Diagnostic essay exams and the use of in-class writing assignments will alleviate a good deal of student anxiety concerning writing under pressure. You may want to share the following with students before they take the exam:

10 Things Students Should Know About Proficiency Exams

1. It would be rare for a student to have made it through both college and life without having to prove his or her writing competence on a surprise topic or choice of topics.
2. Students should prepare for this possibility on proficiency exams in order to minimize anxiety.
3. Students should understand that readers know that all writers write differently, and that the exam will probably not force them into a rhetorical mode or particular design.
4. Almost all writing needs to have many supporting details and examples, must make a point, and must have a clear thesis sentence that answers the topic.
5. Students should check their work as they write to make sure they are staying on topic.
6. Freewriting, outlining, brainstorming, and clustering can all usually be done on scratch paper.
7. Although they will not have the chance to revise at home, students are usually allowed to use a dictionary.
8. Worldwide, the timed student essay is considered a valid measure of student writing development.
9. Writing performance is an effective measure of whether students have mastered and can apply the instruction that they have received in class.
10. Proficiency exams are almost always graded by more than one instructor.

A Sample Rubric (Holistic Grading)

The following rubric can be easily adapted to your class or department needs. Many colleges and universities have established holistic entrance and exit exams for writing and ESOL students. Rather than being assessed the standard letter grades of A through F, students are given a numerical score on a scale of 1 through 6 (some colleges use a grading scale of 1 through 4).

By using an even number of possible scores, faculty are forced to make tough judgments between essays that would normally fall into the "C" category and decide if those essays were, in fact, essentially upper-level "C's" (competent) or lower-level "C's" (not competent). In team grading situations, each essay is usually blind-read by two faculty members. If the scores differ by more than two scoring levels for a particular essay, a third faculty tie-break reader is brought in to score the essay. There are many models of holistic grading, and each department will design the one that best fits its student population. Sample Grading Rubric: Using a scale from 1–6 where 6 is the highest score a student can receive, a breakdown of general criteria for each score might be as follows:

A SCORE OF 6.   The essay provides a well-organized response to the topic and maintains a central focus. The ideas are expressed in appropriate language. A sense of pattern of development is present from beginning to end. The writer supports assertions with explanations or illustrations, and the vocabulary is well suited to the context. Sentences reflect a command of syntax within the ordinary range of standard written English. Grammar, punctuation, and spelling are almost always correct.

A SCORE OF 5.   The essay provides an organized response to the topic. The ideas are expressed in clear language most of the time. The writer develops ideas and generally signals relationships within and between paragraphs. The writer uses vocabulary that is appropriate for the essay topic and avoids oversimplifications or distortions. Sentences generally are correct grammatically, although some errors may be present when sentence structure is particularly complex. With few exceptions, grammar, punctuation, and spelling are correct.

A SCORE OF 4.   The essay shows a basic understanding of the demands of essay organization, although there may be occasional digressions. The development of ideas may be sometimes incomplete, but a basic, logical structure is apparent. Vocabulary is generally appropriate for the essay topic, but at times it is oversimplified. Sentences reflect a sufficient command of standard written English to ensure reasonable clarity of expression. Common forms of agreement and grammatical inflection are usually, although not always, correct. The writer generally demonstrates through punctuation an understanding of the boundaries of the sentence. The writer spells common words with a reasonable degree of accuracy.

A SCORE OF 3.   The essay (or paragraph) responds to the topic and shows some structure. The main idea is discernible and is developed, not merely repeated. The writer uses informal language occasionally and records conversational speech when appropriate academic prose is needed. Vocabulary is limited. The writer signals relationships within paragraphs. Syntax may be rudimentary and lacking in variety. The essay has some grammatical problems, or because of an extremely narrow range of syntactical choices, only occasional grammatical problems appear. The writer may not demonstrate a consistent understanding of the boundaries of the sentence. The writer occasionally misspells common words.

A SCORE OF 2.   The essay begins with a response to the topic but does not develop that response. Ideas are repeated frequently, or are presented randomly, or both. The writer uses informal language frequently and does little more than record conversational speech. Words are often misused, and vocabulary is limited. Syntax is often tangled and is not sufficiently stable to ensure reasonable clarity of expression. Errors in grammar, punctuation, and spelling occur often.

A SCORE OF 1.   The essay suffers from general incoherence and has no discernible pattern of organization. It displays a high frequency of error in the regular features of standard written English. Lapses in punctuation, spelling, and grammar often frustrate the reader. Or, the essay is so brief that any reasonably accurate judgment of the writer's competence is impossible.

Chapter Guides for *The Writer's Workplace with Readings,* Sixth Edition

Using the Chapter Guides

The chapter guides that follow are designed to provide instructors with additional tools and methods for teaching each chapter of *The Writer's Workplace*. Each chapter guide provides:

- a brief overview of the chapter and its goals;
- helpful ideas for approaching and using each chapter;
- and additional assignments for students including in-class activities, journal and other writing assignments, and responding to readings.

The in-class activities build on the material and activities found in the textbook, opening the door for collaborative learning and dynamic classroom discussion.

For those instructors making use of the student journal as a core requirement of their composition courses, the journal assignments provided for each chapter will ensure that students are producing focused writing in their journals. Also, many of the journal assignments correspond directly to chapter material, thus making the journal an opportunity for integrated learning. Many of these assignments can be used as more formal writing assignments to be done in class or for homework.

Instructors will find the activities labeled Responding to Readings especially helpful in integrating writing skills with those of critical reading. These activities make active use of the generous selection of essays found in the Further Readings section of the textbook, unless otherwise noted.

All of the additional assignments are collected in Appendix B, Collected Assignments, for your convenience.

Part 1: An Invitation to Writing

Chapter 1 Gathering Ideas for Writing

Using This Chapter

Students are introduced to the stages of the writing process in this first chapter, with attention given to prewriting techniques such as journaling, brainstorming, freewriting, clustering, and outlining, to name a few. Students learn techniques for gathering information, such as conducting surveys, through the chapter activities.

Journaling and other prewriting techniques are crucial to the development of ideas. After carefully going through each of the activities in the chapter, you may want to ask your students to keep their own journals as part of the requirements for the course. Journals help to keep students in "the habit of writing" and provide a place for students to think critically about what they are learning in class. At this stage it is important for students to feel encouraged to ask questions and offer opinions.

Additional Assignments

IN-CLASS ACTIVITY.   Bring in selections from famous writers' diaries and journals (either copy for all of the students or read aloud). After reading the journal entry, read a selection from that writer's creative work. Good examples for this would be Virginia Woolf's diaries and a selection from *To the Lighthouse* or John Cheever's diaries and the ending to his short story, "The Swimmer." Other famous diarists include Anais Nin, Sei Shonagon (*The Pillow Book*), Samuel Pepys,

Sylvia Plath, and Benjamin Franklin. A good resource for this activity would be *The Poet's Notebook: Excerpts from the Notebooks of 26 American Poets* edited by Stephen Kuusisto et al. (Norton, 1997). No matter which examples you decide to use, students will surely appreciate being able to study actual examples of the journal in action.

JOURNAL ASSIGNMENT.   Create a one-page cluster on the word "summer."

JOURNAL ASSIGNMENT.   List all the items you would put in a time capsule to be opened in the year 2100. Explain the significance of each item and why you chose it for the time capsule.

RESPONDING TO READINGS.   Read "On Writing" by Stephen King. King tells us in this piece that he has enjoyed a wide variety of books over the years. Reflect in writing about the books or other texts (comics, magazines, etc.) that have been a part of your reading life up until this point.

Chapter 2 Recognizing the Elements of Good Writing

Using This Chapter

The elements of good writing—subject, purpose, audience, voice, unity, and co-herence—are introduced in this chapter. Through reading student examples and following the chapter activities, beginning writers will gain an appreciation for how these elements work together to create effective pieces of writing.

Finding each one of the elements of good writing in any text is a crucial part of learning to read critically. You may want to use this chapter as an opportunity for students to read a variety of short pieces—advertisements, newspaper articles, grocery lists, etc.—in order to hone their skills in critical reading. The Writing As-signments below are designed with this in mind. Because many college writing courses stress the importance of using a more formal voice in academic writing, you may want to make particular use of the sample paragraphs leading to Activi-ties Four and Five. (see the handout in Part 4 of this manual for the original ver-sion of the paragraph given in Activity Five.) It is also interesting to note that many students often confuse the terms "unity" and "coherence." The in-class activity below will help them make the distinction between these two elements.

Additional Assignments

IN-CLASS ACTIVITY.   *Exercise in Coherence*: Have students underline every log-ical connector or transitional word or phrase in the sample paragraph given in the section on coherence in Chapter 2. Ask them what they think is lost by deleting these words. Often, they will easily get the point. *Exercise in Unity*: Draw a large umbrella on the board or on a transparency. Within the umbrella, write a topic sentence such as "Stress can cause many problems in a student's life." Tell stu-dents that only people who belong to that topic sentence can stand under the umbrella, and then give them supporting details, one at a time, and ask if these details belong under the umbrella or outside (in the rain). This is just one quick visual device to help them relate "umbrella" to "unity."

WRITING ASSIGNMENT.   *Analyze an Advertisement*: Find an advertisement in a current magazine and analyze it in terms of its subject, purpose, audience, voice, unity, and coherence. Pay attention to both the written and the visual text. Write a few sentences for each element, describing to the reader what visual or verbal cues helped you determine the audience, purpose, and other elements. Hand in a copy of the ad with your written assignment.

WRITING ASSIGNMENT.   *Analyze Television Commercials to Discover Audience*: Set aside one hour every night for three nights to watch television, making sure you are watching at the same hour every night. Make note of each advertisement during the hour—what products are being advertised and what target audience or audiences do you think the ads may be aimed at? At the end of the three days, write a paragraph about your findings. Is there a specific audience or audiences these ads are trying to reach? How did you determine audience from watching and taking note of these advertisements? How did the time of day that you watched the television play a role in your research?

RESPONDING TO READINGS.   Read "Why Don't These Women Just Leave?" by Elaine Weiss. Determine the subject, purpose, audience, voice, unity, and coherence of this essay. Pay particular attention to the issue of audience. To whom is this essay addressed? Why?

Part 2: Creating Effective Sentences

Chapter 3 Finding Subjects and Verbs in Simple Sentences

Using This Chapter

Without the ability to locate the subject and verb in every sentence, students cannot possibly comprehend major usage errors such as run-ons and fragments. Chapter 3 provides a wide range of activities in locating subjects and verbs in simple sentences. The chapter includes finding subjects in simple sentences, sentences that begin with prepositional phrases, sentences that begin with *here* and *there*, sentences with an understood "you," and sentences that contain appositives. In addition, the chapter covers finding action verbs, linking verbs, and helping verbs. Students also learn to identify the parts of speech.

Because this chapter marks the beginning of the set of chapters focusing on grammar, instructors will want to emphasize the importance of grammar comprehension with attention to the exercises in the textbook while keeping students engaged with lively in-class activities and the use of readings to illuminate grammar topics.

Additional Assignments

IN-CLASS ACTIVITY.   Divide the chalkboard in half and list all of the parts of speech on each half. Choose any reading from the textbook, toss a coin to see which team goes first, and then the first team works to find the subject and verb of the first sentence of the chosen reading. If their answer is incorrect, the question goes to the other team. If neither team gets the answer correct, the first team to correctly identify another part of speech within the same sentence receives a point. Then go on to the next sentence until ten sentences or twenty minutes have expired—whichever comes first. The winning team should get a small prize. Candy or a reduction in that night's homework are incentives that often work well!

JOURNAL ASSIGNMENT.   Write about the role public libraries could play in a person's life. What role have they played in your own life? You could describe the building itself, memories of checking out your first book, or the books that you remember being most important to you. What role do libraries play in your life today?

RESPONDING TO READINGS.   Read "The Paterson Public Library" by Judith Ortiz Cofer. Underline the subjects and circle each verb in paragraphs 1–3.

Chapter 4 Making Subjects and Verbs Agree

Using This Chapter

This chapter covers subject-verb agreement on many levels. It discusses the problem of subject-verb agreement with pronouns, with verbs *do* and *be*, with hard-to-find and hidden subjects, with group nouns, with indefinite pronouns, with compound subjects, and with unusual singular and plural nouns.

One of the common difficulties students face when working through this material is having to come to terms with their own dialectical idiosyncrasies—the standard English "she does" may sound overly formal, strange, or simply wrong to a speaker whose own dialect dictates "she do." As an instructor, be sensitive to these differences while remaining firm in terms of the necessity that all students master the material and use the standard forms for written assignments. When devising exercises or additional material to accompany this section, remember that each exercise should employ the simple present tense since it is the only tense that forces the writer to pay attention to subject-verb agreement.

Additional Assignments

IN-CLASS ACTIVITY.   Bring in a 10-minute videotape of a sporting event. Have students practice being sports announcers giving a play-by-play account of the action. If the technology is not available for video, give directions to several students to mime a specific action while a panel of students gives a moment-to-moment account of what they are doing. Keep track of any mistakes that students make in subject-verb agreement and discuss these mistakes when the exercise is over.

IN-CLASS ACTIVITY.   Have the class visit a campus commons or community center. It is important that students are able to witness many people doing different activities. Have students write for fifteen minutes about all of the activities they see using the present tense. Upon returning to class, have students exchange papers and look for subject-verb agreement errors.

JOURNAL ASSIGNMENT.   Write about a physically strenuous activity that you have experienced. You may want to discuss a sporting event, a difficult hike, or any other demanding activity. Describe the event in detail as if it is happening right now, using present tense verbs.

RESPONDING TO READINGS.   Read the first two paragraphs of "Should Women Go Into Combat?" by Catherine L. Aspy. Rewrite the paragraphs in the present tense taking care to avoid mistakes in subject-verb agreement.

Chapter 5 Understanding Fragments and Phrases

Using This Chapter

Now that students have a good grasp of subjects and complete verbs, they are expected to identify incomplete sentences and correct them by supplying missing elements. Chapter 5 helps students identify fragments, distinguish the types of phrases, and gain practice in correcting sentence fragments.

Because fragments are common in conversation and are standard fare for advertisers, students often have trouble identifying them. Those students who were encouraged to "write the way they talk" in order to help them overcome their fears of writing often find they have particular trouble distinguishing fragments from complete sentences. Using advertisements to teach this chapter will make students well aware of the presence of fragments in their everyday lives.

One might ask why the book has two chapters that cover fragments. The reason may not be obvious since most books cover the fragment in one chapter. Chapter five covers fragments as phrases. Since many students may enter the course with very little idea of what constitutes a phrase, this chapter carefully lays the foundation for understanding these sentence groups. Without this foundation, discussions about clauses and phrases in complicated fragments will be largely unproductive. Once students understand phrases and then move on to the types of clauses (independent and dependent), they can begin to understand the more complicated fragment that may have a variety of phrases and dependent clauses but no independent clause. This type of fragment truly demands a sophisticated analysis on the part of the student. One of the major goals of the entire grammar foundation of Part 2 is to bring the student to this point: tackling the analysis of a complicated fragment.

Additional Assignments

IN-CLASS ACTIVITY.   Magazine advertisements are filled with sentence fragments. There are several reasons for this—fragments can be emphatic, they stand out from sentences because they are unusual or even irritating, and they can create a conversational tone. Find an assortment of ads that contain fragments and give several ads to each group. Have the groups identify all of the fragments in the ads. Then have students change each fragment into a complete sentence. Next, have the groups analyze the difference the complete sentences make on the overall tone of the ad. When the groups have had sufficient time to work, have them present their findings on one or two of the ads to the rest of the class.

JOURNAL ASSIGNMENT.   Write about the activities you have enjoyed during the summer that aren't a part of your life during the rest of the year.

RESPONDING TO READINGS.   Read "Summer Reading" by Michael Dorris. There are five sentence fragments in Dorris' essay. Find all of them. Then turn each fragment into a complete sentence.

Chapter 6 Combining Sentences Using the Three Options for Coordination

Using This Chapter

Students will be encouraged to attempt more complex sentences as they proceed through *The Writer's Workplace*. The first step toward this goal will be taken in Chapter 6 as students learn ways to combine sentences using coordination.

Students who tend to write short, choppy sentences will benefit the most from this chapter, but all students will receive valuable training in using commas and coordinating conjunctions correctly, as well as using semicolons and adverbial conjunctions.

At this stage you would do well to introduce several concepts that will become increasingly important as students gain writing confidence. First, not all short sentences should be joined using coordination—only sentences of equal importance and those that contain related ideas. Encourage students to leave other types of short sentences alone for the time being. Second, the use of the appropriate coordinating conjunction is a crucial logical and meaningful link. Have students take special care to use the best conjunction in each case and to avoid overuse of "and." Third, semicolons should be used sparingly. Some students discover early on that semicolons are the easiest answer to every coordination question and begin to overuse them.

Additional Assignments

IN-CLASS ACTIVITY.   Provide class groups with a list of short choppy sentences that relate to the same topic. The groups must create a "paragraph" that sounds good and makes sense by combining the sentences appropriately. You may wish to specify that students use all of the methods of coordination at least once; or you may wish to hone their critical skills by leaving the choice up to them, and then ask them to articulate the reasons for their choices.

WRITING ASSIGNMENT/RESPONDING TO READINGS.   Read "No Comprendo" by Barbara Mujica and write a short summary of the piece, making sure to focus on all the writer's main points.

Chapter 7 Combining Sentences Using Subordination

Using This Chapter

One of the most difficult concepts for students to master is that of dependent and independent clauses, yet much of future writing success hinges on the ability to distinguish between the two. Chapter 7 will help students learn the difference between independent and dependent clauses, ultimately teaching them how to use subordination to form complex sentences.

If you find students hitting a wall right away, review the parts of speech and all of the different types of phrases, showing the difference between an incomplete verb in a participial phrase and a complete verb in the clause. In some cases, you may have to review locating subjects and complete verbs as well. After students have worked through the exercises in the chapter, have them use a reading from the textbook to identify the independent and dependent clauses. The In-Class Activity below is designed with this in mind.

Additional Assignments

IN-CLASS ACTIVITY.   As a class, read "Darkness at Noon" by Harold Krents (in Chapter 27). Go through it slowly to identify dependent and independent clauses. When students experience difficulty, help them identify and eliminate all of the prepositional phrases to get to the basic sentence. Give them the answer if they continue to be confused.

IN-CLASS ACTIVITY. Have students bring in their versions of the paragraph given in Test Two. Provide students with the handout of the original found in Part 4 of this manual. As a class, analyze how American writer James Thurber combined ideas. Have students compare Thurber's choices with their own.

JOURNAL ASSIGNMENT. Harold Krents describes his difficulty in finding a job in his essay "Darkness at Noon." What are some of the challenges that job seekers face?

RESPONDING TO READINGS. Read "Summer Reading" by Michael Dorris. Find five examples of sentences that use coordination to join more than one idea. Rewrite those five sentences using subordination. Read Dorris' sentences and your own versions. Which do you think sound better, and why?

Chapter 8 Correcting Fragments and Run-Ons

Using This Chapter

The Writer's Workplace simplifies the topic of run-ons by using it as a general term to describe "and" run-ons, fused sentences, and comma splices. Students commonly have difficulty distinguishing between the different types of usage errors, so this grouping will make your job easier by letting you stress the concept rather than the terminology.

It may work well to review the basics of Chapter 6 on the three options for coordination before beginning Chapter 8. Instructors working through this chapter may want to have students evaluate their portfolios or writing assignments produced up to this point, looking at their own work or the work of their classmates for fragments and run-ons.

Additional Assignments

IN-CLASS ACTIVITY. Have each student exchange work with another student in class. Have students closely examine each other's work for fragments and run-ons and then have them provide solutions for fixing problem sentences.

IN-CLASS ACTIVITY. Have students write down a story you are about to tell them. They are to transcribe your story word for word. Proceed by telling a rambling story in which most of your sentences are connected with "and." When you have told the story twice (exactly the same way both times), ask students to look over their version and eliminate run-ons by using the three methods of coordination and subordination. When they finish, have several read their finished products aloud.

JOURNAL ASSIGNMENT. Write about your feelings on the current interest in all types of cosmetic surgery. To what extent should people alter their real or perceived flaws?

RESPONDING TO READINGS. Provide students with a copy of the freewriting example from Appendix A of this manual. Have students fix the fragments and run-ons.

Chapter 9 Choosing Correct Pronouns

Using This Chapter

Students will be ready to begin fine-tuning their grammar skills by Chapter 9, which covers pronouns and case and pronoun-antecedent agreement. The chapter also covers the use of *who* and *whom*.

Practice with pronouns is the best way for students to make sure they are grasping this material. The chapter exercises will give students ample opportunity to practice pronoun agreement.

Additional Assignments

IN-CLASS ACTIVITY.   Create a deliberately confusing paragraph in which it is impossible to tell the antecedents of the pronouns. Write this paragraph on the board. Have students fix the pronouns so that the paragraph makes sense.

JOURNAL ASSIGNMENT.   Choose a human interest story that is currently in the news. If you were the subject of the story, how would you handle the situation?

RESPONDING TO READINGS.   Students that have completed the chapter's Working Together will be fascinated to read the article written for *Harper's Bazaar* (October 2000, page 328), which follows the story of Princess Meriam Al Khalifa's first months in America, including her marriage in Las Vegas with the wedding supper at Taco Bell. Now that students have read further on this subject, they will be well prepared for writing a response that considers some of the rich themes suggested by this news story.

Chapter 10 Working with Adjectives, Adverbs, and Parallel Structure

Using This Chapter

This chapter covers the comparison of adjectives and adverbs, commonly confused adjectives and adverbs, misplaced and dangling modifiers, and parallel structure.

Many students will need convincing that mistakes in these areas mark a writer as inexperienced in both academic and business writing. To stress the importance of the material, instructors may want to bring in examples of resumes or other job-related documents that suffer from a lack of parallel structure. Another teaching tool for this chapter could be humorous examples of dangling modifiers.

Additional Assignments

IN-CLASS ACTIVITY.   Bring in newspaper headlines that have gross (and often funny) dangling modifiers or find examples of dangling modifier bloopers in magazines (*Reader's Digest*, for example). Have students work on fixing the errors.

JOURNAL ASSIGNMENT.   Write down your observations about someone you know who has grown up without one of his or her parents. From your perspective, how has it affected this person's life?

RESPONDING TO READINGS.   Read "Where Have All the Fathers Gone?" (in Chapter 31) Make an outline of the essay, making sure to use parallel structure.

Chapters 11 and 12 Practicing Irregular Verbs and Mastering Verb Tenses

Using These Chapters

It is hardly an overstatement to say that the key to fine writing is the careful use of verbs. In Chapters 11 and 12, students will address all essential aspects of verbs: tenses, passive and active voices, regular and irregular verbs, and the subjunctive mood. They will also learn to identify incorrect verb forms and shifts in verb tense.

Explaining the time sequence of complex verb tenses is a challenge for any instructor. Don't hesitate to map out sentences containing complicated sequences of tense on a time line. Have students come to the board and map out a sentence from the book. Reiterate the meaning of the various tenses, and show them how even complicated tenses show up in casual speech. Make it a goal to teach students to write all of the tenses of one regular and one irregular verb by the end of the unit.

Additional Assignments

IN-CLASS ACTIVITY.   Ask for a student to volunteer to tell the class about some incident that has occurred recently. The rest of the class should listen and list the verbs used by the student. Are the verb tenses used accurately and consistently?

JOURNAL ASSIGNMENT.   Go through the list of irregular verbs listed in Appendix C. Make your own personal list of the verbs you consider most important for you to learn.

RESPONDING TO READINGS.   Read "Unforgettable Miss Bessie," by Carl T. Rowan. See if you can find the twenty irregular verbs given in the past tense form or past participle form. Write down the base form, past tense, and past participle of each verb.

Chapter 13 Using Correct Capitalization and Punctuation

Using This Chapter

This chapter covers ten basic rules for capitalization, eight rules for comma use, three uses for the apostrophe, four uses for quotation marks, three uses for the semicolon, four uses for the colon, and the correct use of dashes, parentheses, and underlining/italics.

Because you will be covering a great deal of material, you may wish to hand out study sheets (or copies of transparency masters) of the basic information you will be covering for students to follow along. You will not need to spend much class time on capitalization after covering the ten rules, but you might try giving a spot quiz to see if the students are absorbing the material. You will need to spend time on rules for commas and uses for quotation marks. The information on semicolons will mostly be a review from Chapter 6 on coordination.

Additional Assignments

IN-CLASS ACTIVITY.   First, tell students the following short made-up story: A man and woman meet at the local Wal-Mart and fall instantly in love. Unfortunately, the man is there to buy a few items for his flight home to another state or a foreign country. The woman is there because she needs directions to the nearest medical center. After finishing the story, have students get into groups to write their own versions of the story, packed with name brands, geographical locations, and dialogue. Have each group write a clean copy to submit for an activity grade.

JOURNAL ASSIGNMENT.   Write your impressions of the last memorable event you attended. For example, you could write about a movie, lecture, concert, or reading.

RESPONDING TO READINGS.   Read "The Changing American Family" by Alvin and Heidi Toffler. In paragraphs 1, 9, 10, and 17 explain the reason for each capitalization that occurs other than at the beginning of a sentence.

PART 3: Understanding the Power of Words

Chapter 14 Choosing Words That Work

Using This Chapter

This first chapter of Part 3 in the textbook introduces students to the complex issue of word choice. Topics covered include connotation and denotation, the use of appropriate language for formal writing, and the use of words rich in meaning.

As long as we are working within our own vernacular, we are all intensely attuned to the connotations and inflections of spoken and written speech. You may wish to exploit this fact if you find that students find the idea of connotation and word choice a foreign concept.

Additional Assignments

IN-CLASS ACTIVITY.   Write the following paragraph on the board or show it on the overhead projector:

> The small child turned the bowl of pasta over on the floor and sat down in it. Her mother was not happy about the child's action. After speaking loudly to the child, the father got something from the sink to help pick the pasta off the floor. The child spread the food across the floor and smiled.

Ask students to go through the paragraph sentence by sentence and change neutral words and phrases into words and phrases that give a negative connotation to the child's actions.

JOURNAL ASSIGNMENT.   Poet Wallace Stevens wrote a poem entitled "Thirteen Ways of Looking at a Blackbird" in which he attempted to get closer to the idea of a blackbird by writing about it in every sense he could think of—some of the descriptions abstract and spiritual, some of them concrete. Think about an object, animal, person, or concept that is interesting and mysterious to you. Write down as many thoughts and perceptions that you can about your subject. Be creative and don't avoid the weird—Stevens didn't! Number your perceptions. *To make this assignment even more effective, bring in the poem and read it together as a class.

JOURNAL ASSIGNMENT.   Affix a photo of a person from the newspaper, a magazine, or your personal album to your journal. First, describe the person with words that have a positive connotation, making him or her as appealing and attractive as possible. Next, write a description of the same person using words with a negative connotation.

RESPONDING TO READINGS.   Read "Dream Houses" by Tenaya Darlington. Identify the metaphors and similes the writer uses to describe both her new and old houses. Why is her use of these devices effective? How does she enrich the meaning of the essay by using these metaphors and similes?

RESPONDING TO READINGS.   Read "A Day at the Theme Park" by W. Bruce Cameron. Find the words or phrases with negative connotations in the descriptions Cameron uses. In each case, change the word or phrase to one of neutral or positive connotation. How do these changes affect the piece as a whole?

Chapter 15 Paying Attention to Look-Alikes and Sound-Alikes

Using This Chapter

Chapter 15 covers the important topic of look-alikes and sound-alikes, grouping words into manageable units for study, and dealing extensively with some of the most frequently confused words, such as *lie* and *lay*.

Some of the most common problems students need to work on are the differences between their/there/ they're, to/too, then/than, and its/it's—to name just a few. Consider giving quizzes to make certain students are absorbing the information.

Additional Assignments

IN-CLASS ACTIVITY.   Have students look up the word "loose" in the dictionary. Have them make a list of the different kinds of information they find out about this word. Then have students compare with each other how many different items they have found.

JOURNAL ASSIGNMENT.   Why should a person try to build a bigger vocabulary? What do you think some effective methods might be of increasing one's vocabulary? Find five words that are new to you in the dictionary and add them, along with their meanings, to your journal.

RESPONDING TO READINGS.   Read your college catalogue's position on plagiarism. Paraphrase the policy, being careful not to plagiarize yourself!

Part 4: Creating Effective Paragraphs

Chapter 16 Working with Paragraphs: Topic Sentences and Controlling Ideas

Using This Chapter

This chapter covers four basic but easily confusing concepts: What exactly is a paragraph? What is a topic sentence? Where is the topic in a topic sentence? How can you tell the controlling idea of a topic sentence? Students will also learn how to distinguish between a title and a topic sentence, an activity that gives instructors the opportunity to discuss sentence fragments and how to convert fragments—or titles—into complete sentences.

When presenting paragraph basics such as initial indentation, capitalization, ending punctuation, etc., do not neglect to mention that the block format is also quite common. However, the indented paragraph is still considered standard. You may discover that the most efficient way of teaching the paragraph is by examining what the paragraph is not.

Additional Assignments

IN-CLASS ACTIVITY.   Show the class current headlines from newspapers. Then have them convert the headlines into complete sentences. If the sentences do not yet contain a controlling idea, lead them through the steps needed to create one or more controlling ideas. Then have students identify the controlling ideas in headlines from letters to the editor. You may want to copy one letter to be looked at by the entire class, having them identify the topic sentence in each paragraph.

JOURNAL ASSIGNMENT.   Choose a favorite holiday. In three paragraphs, persuade the reader that this holiday is the most important one of the year. Make sure each paragraph contains a topic sentence.

RESPONDING TO READINGS.   Read "Neat People vs. Sloppy People" by Suzanne Britt. Underline the transitional words and phrases used by Britt. Do you think she has provided enough? Too many? In paragraphs 6 through 12, put a double line under each topic sentence and jot down the controlling idea in the margin.

Chapter 17 Working with Paragraphs: Supporting Details

Using This Chapter

Few instructors will complain about an overabundance of detail in student essays. It is for this reason that the lesson on supporting details should be reinforced in a variety of ways. Chapter 17 helps students identify supporting details and distinguish between the topic sentence and its supporting details. The chapter also offers exercises to help make supporting details specific.

The concept of supporting details is rarely easy for students, but quite often several students in the class will realize breakthroughs in their writing when this concept suddenly becomes clear. You may first try to read a paragraph in which the language is decidedly vague. Beware: some students, probably under the spell of your oratory skill, will think the writing is good! See if you can change their minds by reading the same paragraph again, but this time supplied with plenty of detail.

Additional Assignments

IN-CLASS ACTIVITY.   Have students bring to class the assignments in which "vague" or "not specific enough" has been written in the margins. If this is not feasible, the instructor can provide paragraphs containing vague writing. Have students alone or in groups write the paragraph/s over by including lots of supporting details. This gives students an opportunity to incorporate everything they have learned in Chapter 16 with the newer information about supporting detail. A good way to wind up this exercise is to have groups of students read their paragraphs aloud so that everyone can hear all of the possibilities.

JOURNAL ASSIGNMENT.   Are you a neat person or a sloppy person? Do you wish you were neater or slo**ppier? Why or why not?**

RESPONDING TO READINGS.   Read "Neat People vs. Sloppy People" by Suzanne Britt. Underline examples of good supporting details in the essay. Does Britt use better details in describing the habits of neat people or sloppy people? Explain the differences. Why do you suppose the author made those choices?

Chapter 18 Developing Paragraphs: Illustration

Using This Chapter

The illustration paragraph is the workhorse paragraph—it can be employed for many writing occasions. For students, it can also be considered the "training" paragraph. It gives them an opportunity to control their writing by recognizing the need for further examples to prove a given topic sentence. Chapter 18 covers the topic of illustration by providing students with an understanding of what illustration is, where a writer finds examples, and three ways writers use illustration.

Making use of readings is especially useful for teaching this chapter. Discovering how other writers use illustration will be key to student success in this area.

Additional Assignments

IN-CLASS ACTIVITY.   Ask the class to choose a writing topic and put the topic on the board. Give students the following illustration paragraph structure and ask them to write eight sentences employing the structure.

- First Sentence: Make a claim about your topic that needs to be proven (Topic Sentence or Main Idea).
- Second Sentence: Give one good reason that claim is true (First Major Detail).
- Third Sentence: Give a specific example that explains or clarifies that reason (Minor Detail supporting Major Detail).
- Fourth Sentence: Give another good reason that your claim is true (Second Major Detail).
- Fifth Sentence: Give a specific example that explains or clarifies the second reason (Minor Detail supporting Major Detail).
- Sixth Sentence: Give your last and best good reason that your claim is true (Third Major Detail).
- Seventh Sentence: Give a specific example that explains or clarifies your last, best reason (Minor Detail supporting Major Detail).
- Eighth Sentence: Write a neat, concluding statement that sums up your position.

*If you have your students use this chart several times, their writing will begin to sound better to them. It is an excellent way to build their confidence before working with more complicated patterns.

JOURNAL ASSIGNMENT.   Choose a saying or cliché that you find interesting. First explain what the saying means in general and then give at least three examples to illustrate how this saying has applied to your own life. A few examples of sayings or clichés are:

- Never let the sun go down on your anger.
- Don't judge a book by its cover.
- Necessity is the mother of invention.

RESPONDING TO READINGS.   Read "My Daughter Smokes" by Alice Walker. Walker tells her story in a series of anecdotes. Reread her essay and mark the anecdotes that you find the most effective. Are there any that surprise you? Which ones are most effective? What are some of the sensory images that Walker uses?

Chapter 19 Developing Paragraphs: Narration

Using This Chapter

Students' favorite rhetorical form is often narration. This chapter will cover the most important aspects of narration: how to make a point with the narrative, how to arrange events chronologically, and how to use appropriate transitions.

In order to help the students understand what makes a good narrative, you may want to bring in short stories, or even short, short stories, to let students get a feel for what makes the narrative work (or fail). In addition, you may wish to take this opportunity to discuss direct and indirect quotation. You will also want to discuss the difference between showing (scene work) and telling (exposition). A common problem with beginning drafts of narratives is that students forget that *something must happen* in order to for a story to become a narrative. Students tend to write narratives in which nothing happens, creating vignettes instead of true narratives. Getting involved in helping students to choose their topics will go a long way toward alleviating this problem.

Additional Assignments

IN-CLASS ACTIVITY.   Ask a student to volunteer to tell a story to the class. It could be true or fictional. Set a time limit. Use this story to discuss the basic elements of narration. Ask students to decide whether or not they think the story was true or not. On what did students base their decisions?

JOURNAL ASSIGNMENT.   Cut out a photo from a magazine or newspaper and affix it to your journal. Create a narrative from the photograph, explaining what you think is going on in the picture, and describing what may have happened just before the picture was taken and what happened just afterward. Write about the details of the picture using sensory descriptions.

RESPONDING TO READINGS.   Read "My Daughter Smokes" by Alice Walker. Walker discusses various moments in her life and in the lives of her father and sister, some in sequence, but all with large stretches of time between them. On a separate piece of paper, plot out a timeline of the different moments of her story and compare this to the organization of these moments in the essay. Why do you think Walker chose to tell her story in the way that she did?

Chapter 20 Developing Paragraphs: Description

Using This Chapter

This chapter builds on Chapter 19 with an in-depth discussion of description. Students will learn to recognize and create a dominant impression through word choice and will learn how to identify and create sensory images. Attention is paid to ordering descriptions spatially and writing descriptive paragraphs step by step. Using sensory images is emphasized in the writings offered in the chapter, which describe such varied topics as a condemned building, a specific time of day, and the various seasons in Jamaica.

Many instructors notice that students enjoy the discussion of descriptive writing more than any other rhetorical pattern. Keeping this in mind, if you find that your class enjoys the section on description, try to bring descriptive exercises to class from time to time to help them further the skill. No other form of writing is quite as important for them to master because of its emotional appeal and versatility. Take this opportunity to bring to class a varied selection of readings from novels, essays, and poetry.

Additional Assignments

IN-CLASS ACTIVITY.   Have students bring in their favorite paragraphs from novels or short stories of their choice. Read them aloud and discuss the aspect of description in each selection.

IN-CLASS ACTIVITY.   Have students write for fifteen minutes at the beginning of class about the present moment—the chairs, people, marks on the board, quality of light, what can be seen from the window, etc. Tell them to write sharp, exacting detail. When they have finished, you may want to go over the details they noticed. Which details seemed the "sharpest"?

JOURNAL ASSIGNMENT.   Practice description and focused freewriting by sitting in a room of your home and describing everything in the room exactly as it looks to you from your perspective.

RESPONDING TO READINGS.   Read "Dream Houses" by Tenaya Darlington. Go through the essay and circle words that seem particularly descriptive. Which descriptions seem the "sharpest" and why?

Chapter 21 Developing Paragraphs: Process Analysis

Using This Chapter

In this chapter students will be given a working definition of process, they will have to identify whether or not a written process is complete, and they will learn to pay attention to logical sequence and to employ transitional words and phrases. At the end of the chapter they will be asked to write several types of process paragraphs based on models.

When discussing process with students, it is a good idea to talk about the range in which this mode is used in everyday life: writing recipes, giving advice on how to get a baby to sleep through the night, giving a pedestrian directions to the post office, and putting together a children's toy, to name just a few.

Additional Assignments

IN-CLASS ACTIVITY.   Provide groups with a set of overly general directions to a common task and have them revise for unity and clarity, making sure to fill in the steps that were omitted.

JOURNAL ASSIGNMENT.   People today are especially concerned about security and personal safety. Do you consider yourself a risk taker, a cautious person, or somewhere in the middle? Write about the ways that you consciously protect yourself.

RESPONDING TO READINGS.   Read "Advice to Parents: How to Communicate with Your Teen" (in Chapter 1). Write your own process piece, giving advice to a person you know well on how he or she could improve communication skills with someone.

Chapter 22 Developing Paragraphs: Comparison/Contrast

Using This Chapter

Students will address more complex structures in the Comparison/Contrast section. After a discussion of the basic principle behind the pattern, students will get practice in choosing and narrowing two-part topics. Then they will analyze the differences in the point-by-point and block methods and learn to recognize them in sample paragraphs. Students will also learn about appropriate transitions and compose sample paragraphs step by step.

The greatest difficulty you may face as an instructor in presenting this material is that students often choose to compare two topics with blatantly obvious similarities (vanilla bean ice cream and French vanilla ice cream), and contrast topics with readily obvious differences (living in the desert as opposed to living by the ocean). How do you impress upon students that readers are interested in the surprising insight, the unusual take? Your involvement as students choose their topics will ensure that students are off to the right start.

Additional Assignments

IN-CLASS ACTIVITY.   Work together as a class to compare buying a house to having a baby. Topics that seem dissimilar at first will emerge as having a lot in common: both having a baby and buying a house take about a year from start to finish; the rosy glow of pregnancy and deciding on a home may turn to fear and pain when delivery and closing costs occur, etc. After this exercise is complete, have the students challenge you by trying to come up with a two-part topic that is so dissimilar they cannot imagine any similarities being drawn between the two. Prove them wrong—this is the perfect opportunity to discuss analogy!

JOURNAL ASSIGNMENT.   Write about your current or future occupation. Compare and contrast the positive and negative aspects of the job.

RESPONDING TO READINGS.   Read "Dream Houses" by Tenaya Darlington. Outline Darlington's essay in terms of comparison and contrast. Does she employ a block format or a point-by-point format? Decide whether the other format would have been more or less effective for her essay and explain your answer.

Chapter 23 Developing Paragraphs: Cause and Effect

Using This Chapter

Students will learn to think more analytically about causal relationships in Chapter 23, which covers finding causes and effects in paragraphs, separating the cause from the effect, looking for the causal relationship, thinking about underlying and immediate causes and immediate and long-term effects, using transitions, and writing both cause and effect paragraphs step by step.

Instructors often find that students have some trouble distinguishing cause from effect—it is no wonder since the effect of one event can become the cause of another event. In other words, you would do well to keep a broad view of causal relationships rather than attempt to simplify your explanation, which could serve to further confuse. Stress that when you discuss cause and/or effect, it is relative to a specific issue or event. You might also want to mention that there are multitudes of causes so minute that they are impossible to label as such but they are every bit as real as the identifiable causes, and are called influences. Effects are equally numerous, but it is easiest to identify those we can readily measure and see.

Additional Assignments

IN-CLASS ACTIVITY.   Have students get into groups to analyze the many causes of a particular social issue. The groups should produce between twenty-five and forty causes. Then have the groups rank the causes in order of importance. Finally, have the groups decide which of these causes were immediate, underlying, and remote influences. When they have completed this assignment and the class has had a chance to compare notes, have the group work on the effects of the same issue. Students may wish to use the list to formulate their own cause and effect paragraphs. See the handout on Sample Topics for Persuasive Essays in Part Four for a list of topics you may want to discuss.

JOURNAL ASSIGNMENT.   In what ways (positive or negative) do you believe your environment has affected the person you have become today?

RESPONDING TO READINGS.   Read "Requiem for a Champ" by June Jordan. Decide whether the reading deals with causes or effects or both. Explain your answer in writing.

Chapter 24 Developing Paragraphs: Definition and Classification

Using This Chapter

Being able to clearly articulate a definition is an essential skill for the analytical thinker. Students will be asked to define words and concepts in this chapter in several ways: by putting terms into larger classes, by identifying their characteristics, by giving examples, and by negation. Impress upon students that during political debates or any other argument, each side must "define their terms." Holding a debate in class and taking note of any vague or ill-defined words will illustrate the importance of this rhetorical mode.

The second method of developing ideas presented in this chapter is classification. Use the concrete example of how "movies" could be classified (found in Part 4 of this manual) to help students understand the relevance of classification.

Additional Assignments

IN-CLASS ACTIVITY.   Have students sit with their desks in a circle and present an issue to be discussed. Instruct the students to voice their opinions on the issue. Tell the students to listen very carefully to what the others are saying; if any statement seems vague, students should demand that the speaker define his or her terms. Take the discussion very slowly at first so that nothing is missed. If the conversation gets heated, make notes of vague terms on the board and discuss the terms when the discussion concludes.

JOURNAL ASSIGNMENT.   Take several minutes to think about the types of people with whom you attended high school. Then write down four or five descriptive categories to which these people belonged. Once you have established these categories, go back and develop a definition for each category.

RESPONDING TO READINGS.   Read "I'm a Banana and Proud of It" by Wayson Choy. Choy defines himself through ethnicity/ethnicities. How do you define yourself?

Part 5: Structuring the College Essay

Chapter 25 Moving from the Paragraph to the Essay

Using This Chapter

In the opening discussion about essay writing, students are led through the entire writing process in order to produce the college essay: choosing a topic; distinguishing the controlling idea of a topic sentence; identifying and defining a thesis; brainstorming; selecting and organizing material; writing the rough draft; developing an idea in a paragraph; revising the rough draft for unity and coherence; editing the second draft; and preparing and proofreading the final copy.

It is a good idea to focus on the first half of the process at this stage. Lead students through writing process activities that help them see the connection between topic and narrowed thesis. You may want to mention that brainstorming in search of a topic is as important as subsequent brainstorming since it generates interest in the writing task and eliminates common and mundane topics from the outset.

Additional Assignments

IN-CLASS ACTIVITY.   Turn to Part 6 of the textbook, Further Readings for the College Writer. Study each of the introductory paragraphs and discuss the variety of approaches. Which ones seem particularly effective?

JOURNAL ASSIGNMENT.   Make a list of topics discussed in class so far this semester that you would be interested in writing about further. Choose one of these topics and brainstorm about how you might develop this idea into a full essay.

RESPONDING TO READINGS.   Read "The Changing American Family" by Alvin and Heidi Toffler. Go through the essay and determine how the authors achieved coherence by using transitional expressions, repeated words, and appropriate use of pronouns.

Chapter 26 Following the Progress of a Student Essay

Using This Chapter

In this chapter, students will both observe the progress of a student essay and develop an essay of their own. The entire writing process, from brainstorming and freewriting through draft development to peer editing and proofreading, is illustrated in the sample piece. The step-by-step and hands-on approach of both watching an essay develop while composing one at the same time is the real strength of this chapter. The rough and final drafts of the student essay in Appendix A will give students further insight into how a final draft emerges from the writing process.

Additional Assignments

IN-CLASS ACTIVITY.   Photocopy and distribute to students the rough draft and final draft of the student essay "Witness," located in Appendix A of this manual. Have students read both drafts. Then place students into groups in which they can discuss the changes the writer made between the rough and final drafts. Discuss the changes the writer made, paying particular attention to the reworking of the introduction and conclusion.

JOURNAL ASSIGNMENT.   Brainstorm in your journal about the ways in which the belief system of your parent or parents or those who raised you has impacted your life.

RESPONDING TO READINGS.   Read the student essay "Leibovitz Revealed" by Yarrow Allen-Hickey, found in Appendix A of this manual. Discuss the essay in terms of its thesis, topic sentences, supporting details, and the development of its ideas.

Chapter 27 Writing an Essay Using Examples, Illustrations, or Anecdotes

Using This Chapter

In this chapter, students will learn to distinguish among the types of illustrations that writers employ—whether from personal experience, hypothesis, research, or surveys.

It is fair to say that most students will feel quite comfortable with examples from their own experience. Therefore, while not excluding that resource, it is important to expose them to the other types as painlessly as possible. Ideally, you might present a single issue and ask the class to provide support for it in each of the four ways. Afterward, ask students which types of illustration seem to be the most effective in proving the stance of the author. The firsthand experience, due to its compelling nature, almost always wins. However, if you ask which type of example *ought to be* the most persuasive, students will often say research. This chapter and the discussion that the material generates can provide an excellent launching point for introducing ideas about persuasive writing.

Additional Assignments

IN-CLASS ACTIVITY.   Send students to the library to gather statistics on a topical issue, such as the statistics on drunk driving in their home state in the past year. Then students work together to create a paragraph built on statistical illustration.

JOURNAL ASSIGNMENT.   Look back over your day so far. What examples can you give of enjoyable moments? What examples can you give of unpleasant moments?

RESPONDING TO READINGS.   Read "Requiem for the Champ" by June Jordan. Mark each occurrence in which the author employs an example, extended example, illustration, or anecdote. When you finish, go back and try to identify which type the author relied upon the most.

Chapter 28 Writing an Essay Using Narration

Using This Chapter

Students will be required to expand the narration skills they have acquired in previous coursework in Chapter 28. Important points covered in the chapter include analyzing the writer's strategies, gathering information, and achieving coherence.

   Now that students are more familiar with the narrative mode and are ready to write essays using this mode, you might want to provide this checklist for students to use before handing in their rough drafts:

- Does the narrative contain a coherent beginning, middle, and end?
- Is there a point to the story? Does something happen or change?
- Are there enough supporting details to make the story seem real?
- Is there dialogue? Does it seem natural? Is it in the correct format?

Additional Assignments

IN-CLASS ACTIVITY.   Gather class examples of childhood experiences that left profound impressions. List them on the board and, as a class, discuss the ways in which these experiences lend themselves to the narrative mode.

JOURNAL ASSIGNMENT.   Write about a childhood experience that has left a profound impression on your life.

RESPONDING TO READINGS.   Have students read "Memories from 7th Street" by Treyson Hopkins, found in Appendix A of this manual. What is the main point of this narrative? What makes this narrative compelling?

Chapter 29 Writing an Essay Using Process Analysis

Using This Chapter

Developing an entire essay using process analysis demands a topic that is complex enough to warrant an essay-length piece of writing. Instructors will want to focus on the model essay provided in the chapter, "How to Ace a Job Interview" in order to study how the writer presents his advice. Paying particular attention to the introduction and conclusion will be especially helpful since students will learn well from a writer who is able to lead the reader into his material and interjects humor into his conclusion.

Additional Assignments

IN-CLASS ACTIVITY.   Open up classroom discussion to the ways in which process plays a role in our daily lives. Have the class divide up into three groups: those who are decisive, those who cannot make up their minds about the simplest things, and those who fall somewhere in the middle. Put two situations on the board and have students discuss the processes they might go through to make a decision. Have the groups compare notes.

JOURNAL ASSIGNMENT.   Present the sequence of how you mastered an important skill. Address your writing to someone who does not have this skill and who is trying to learn it. Explain the steps in careful detail. Anticipate any difficulties the person may face, and encourage that person by describing any difficulties you had in learning this skill.

RESPONDING TO READINGS.   Locate an instruction manual for an appliance or piece of equipment you have in your home. Analyze the text. Is it clear and easy to follow? Does the manual cover all the important steps necessary to set up or use the appliance? How could the manual be improved?

Chapter 30 Writing an Essay Using Comparison/Contrast

Using This Chapter

Chapter 30 builds on earlier learning about comparison/contrast by having students explore topics and read a model essay on a given topic. Other topics covered in the chapter include selecting and organizing material, writing and revising the final draft, and proofreading the final copy. Instructors may want to have students write an outline of the same two-part topic first using the block method then using point-by-point. Ask students to analyze both structures and decide which is a better approach for the given topics. One of the most challenging tasks you can present to students is to have them write a comparison or contrast of two written works (any genre works well).

Additional Assignments

IN-CLASS ACTIVITY.   Hand out copies of two paragraphs that you deem suitable. Have students read the paragraphs, identify the topic sentence in each, and write three-sentence summaries. Have students get into groups and discuss their opinions and eventually come up with a basic outline for comparing or contrasting the works. Ask students to write a three-paragraph comparison or contrast for homework, or, if time permits, in the remaining class period.

JOURNAL ASSIGNMENT.   What are some of the products or objects you used to have that are no longer manufactured or are now obsolete? Write a comparison of then and now. Which objects do you prefer?

WRITING ASSIGNMENT.   Find accounts of the same newsworthy event that appeared in two different newspapers, and investigate the manner in which this event is reported. Analyze the differences between the articles in terms of the use of language, the phrasing and size of the headlines, the choice of accompanying photos, and so forth. Does either of the articles persuade the reader to a certain position by outright statements of opinion, or more subtly by using non-verbal cues? Quote directly from the articles and don't assume that the reader of your paper will be familiar with the articles.

RESPONDING TO READINGS.   Read "The Ugly Truth About Beauty" by Dave Barry (in Chapter 30). Compare how much time you spend on your appearance to how much time other members of your family spend. Do you or other members of your family fit the stereotype that Barry describes?

Chapter 31 Writing an Essay Using Persuasion

Using This Chapter

Chapter 31 guides students through the writing of the persuasive essay, giving them guidelines, model essays, and possible topics for student essays using this mode.

Most classes enjoy debating issues. Take advantage of this fact if you have a lively class when you begin the unit on persuasion. However, verbal debate tends to be much easier than written argument. Whenever you have sufficiently debated an issue in class, have students spend 10 to 15 minutes writing about the points that were discussed during the debate. You may even wish to have students freewrite on a given issue before the debate begins. Two handouts in Part 4 of this manual will be especially helpful in teaching this chapter: Logical Fallacies and Sample Topics for Persuasive essays.

Additional Assignments

IN-CLASS ACTIVITY.   Photocopy the "letters to the editor" section of your local newspaper and distribute copies to the class. Have students get into groups and discuss the methods of persuasion for each letter. Are any of the writers using verbal attacks or threats? How do those methods of argument affect the persuasiveness of the letter? *You may want to photocopy and distribute the handout on Logical Fallacies, located in Part 4 of this manual. After you have gone over each logical fallacy, have students re-read the letters to the editor, looking for logical fallacies.

JOURNAL ASSIGNMENT.   Choose three or four ads from magazines that are part of a political or marketing campaign. Analyze the persuasive techniques employed in the campaign. Describe the ads in detail, and address both the verbal and visual aspects. Is the campaign persuasive? What methods of persuasion does the campaign use?

JOURNAL ASSIGNMENT.   Convince someone you care about to stop smoking, drinking, or doing any other unhealthy habit (watching television? dieting too often?) Persuade him or her by using reasons, facts, and statistics about the effects of the habit.

RESPONDING TO READINGS.   Read "Why Don't These Women Just Leave?" by Elaine Weiss. Regardless of your personal opinion on the matter, see if you can write an essay taking the opposite stance.

Chapter 32 Other College Writing: The Research Paper and the Essay Exam

Using This Chapter

Chapter 32 prepares students for two of the staples of college writing: the research paper and timed essay exams. Looking for sources, conducting research, incorporating and documenting sources, and setting up a timetable are just some of the topics covered on the research paper. The chapter also prepares students for timed writing such as exit and proficiency exams by providing them with strategies for answering in-class essay questions and giving them a refresher course on thesis statements.

All students need practice writing within time limits to force them to organize material and make choices quickly. Students will find these skills valuable in all areas of their college careers. After working through the unit, give students several short, timed writing assignments. Many colleges and universities require students to take an exit exam to test proficiency in college composition. Instructors teaching in schools requiring the exit exam will want to use this chapter to prepare students adequately for the upcoming test.

Additional Assignments

IN-CLASS ACTIVITY.   Put the following topic on the board and allow students a specific amount of time in which to respond: The Internet: How It Has Changed Our Lives. Afterward, discuss with students how they approached the topic, what prewriting techniques they used, and how they organized their material.

IN-CLASS ACTIVITY.   Give your class the sample exit exam question located at the end of Appendix A in this manual. After students have developed their own responses to the question, pass out the sample student exit exam also located in Appendix A. Have students go through the sample essay and analyze how the student writer organized his material. Open up discussion about how their essays compared to the sample essay. Did everyone organize his or her essay in a similar way? What kinds of topics seemed to work best?

JOURNAL ASSIGNMENT.   Read a letter to the editor in your local newspaper. Decide what research the author of the letter has done in order to make his or her claim. Was enough research done, if any? Research the topic yourself and write down your findings. After doing your own research, did your opinion change on the matter?

RESPONDING TO READINGS.   Read "Should Women Go Into Combat?" by Catherine L. Aspy. Discuss the specific research the writer has done to produce this essay. Does the research seem well-balanced?

Instructional Essays

Collaboration in the Developmental Writing Classroom

By Dick Harrington

PIEDMONT VIRGINIA COMMUNITY COLLEGE

Two Related Breakthroughs

During my twenty-nine years of teaching writing, two related discoveries have transformed my pedagogy: writing-as-a-process and collaboration—collaboration among peers and my own collaboration with my students. As *The Writer's Workplace* illustrates, in composition classes instructors now coach students through successive stages of revisions, helping them develop habits that improve all dimensions of their writing, from ideas to punctuation. The classroom has become a workshop. Students learn primarily by reading and discussing texts in progress, collaborating with the teacher and with one another.

Stages of Writing

As in learning a sport or a musical instrument, it's useful to focus attention on certain elements at a given time and to attend to others later. With plenty of allowance for individual differences, I encourage students to view and practice writing in four broad, recursive stages: EXPLORING, DRAFTING, EDITING, and PROOFING. EXPLORING involves whatever precedes drafting: reading, note taking, cogitating, freewriting, clustering, or whatever works. DRAFTING establishes intention, voice, development, arrangement—the big picture. EDITING refines word choice, imagery, rhythm and flow of sentences, other points of style. PROOFING verifies convention (or intentional deviation) in grammar, usage, mechanics, documentation, and format. These stages are the foundation for meaningful collaboration with me as the teacher and with peers.

Stages and Collaboration

Whether in developmental or college composition, learning and applying a regimen for each stage of the writing process engages students constructively with works in progress and enables students to develop awareness of audience—of how tone and other choices affect readers. They learn to talk about writing and therefore to think about it, with different emphases at each stage. They discover their own strengths and weaknesses, and they learn by example, seeing how others approach writing. They build genre awareness from the ground up. This kind of learning fosters responsibility and independence, particularly independence from the teacher, and allows students to take possession of their writing, spend more time on it, and generally experience greater success and satisfaction as writers. For all of this to develop, students must usually make quite an adjustment in their concept of roles in the classroom, both theirs and the teacher's. At the beginning of a semester students may expect the instructor to do most of the work during a class period, filling them up with what they need to know. For students to adapt and to contribute more in class it's essential for the instructor to adapt by encouraging students to participate more frequently.

Instructor Moves to the Side

To teach writing as a process and to employ peer work groups requires a profound shift in pedagogy and therefore in roles. In the traditional college classroom the instructor is the central figure, the most animated participant, and the hardest worker, lecturing, questioning, assigning, responding, and grading. Many students remain passive even when apparently listening and taking notes. In the collaborative classroom all students participate actively and indeed do most of the work. Each group becomes its own microcosm of the writing world. For this to happen, the instructor must move to the side and commit to student independence, to giving up control, to living with what may seem like chaos. At first, students feel incapable of helping one another or even of following the regimen for each stage, especially the DRAFTING stage. Although I do sit in on groups to coach them as they learn the regimens, as much as possible I let them be, trusting in the value of their ongoing engagement with texts in progress—mostly without me. I prepare students thoroughly for the regimen of each stage, allowing plenty of time for each session, orchestrating but not controlling their discovery of how the group process works. While students work in groups, I mainly sit by myself, working on course-related matters and observing from a distance, awaiting signals for consultation. It's taken me a long time to adjust to this role of relative unimportance. Recently in a class just a few weeks old, as I walked among the groups to see if there were any questions or problems, they were so engaged that not one student looked up even to smile. Although my ultimate goal is for students not to need me, the reality of being ignored – however appropriately–takes some getting used to.

My Developmental Courses

My developmental courses begin with several introductory classes devoted to orientation, to the course, to group work, to getting acquainted, and to practical lessons in writing-as-a-process. On the first day, students take seats at small tables and find themselves already in groups of four or five facing one another rather than facing the front. Unless I see a problem with groups so selected, I let them remain as they are. Early in the course they engage in brief, purposeful group activities to get to know one another and to begin working together cohesively. They exchange phone numbers and consider times to meet outside of class if necessary. We discuss writing as both a solitary and social activity, and I stress the necessity of hard work alone, such as reading, note taking, thinking, and producing good working drafts. I refer students to the bold, extra-large type in the course description and schedule, signaling the most important deadline of all: the class when the working draft of Paper 1 is to appear, without fail, no matter what, for presentation to the group. The course depends on such preparedness, good working drafts typed on a word processor with copies for the group.

After several days in the classroom, we meet in a reserved section of the computer lab for an introductory session on word processing and then several sessions of drafting and redrafting. The first paper assigned is a short essay on a social and/or personal issue developed from students' own thought and experience. While working at the keyboard, students can call me over for consultation about DRAFTING issues such as a main purpose, voice, development, and arrangement. I encourage students to overlook surface features and concentrate on rereading and thinking through their drafts. When ready, students print out a draft and sign up for a mini-conference in the lab. I skim the draft and coach them in rethinking and revising. By the scheduled deadline they produce a working draft for presentation to their peer group. Already they should be developing awareness that a draft for presentation to the group is not merely a freewrite, but the result of several hours of writing, coaching, rethinking, and rewriting.

Responding at the Drafting Stage

Responding at the DRAFTING stage requires the ability—and will—to comprehend whole drafts and help the writer see the big picture. Many developmental students must struggle very hard to read globally and respond constructively. To do so, they need time and in many cases privacy. I used to have students respond orally after listening to the draft read aloud and then reading it silently. The more I've observed and inquired about students' areas of difficulties with this procedure the more clearly I've understood their problems in comprehending a draft read aloud. I now have students take home the drafts and respond in writing, following the same prompt they will later use when responding at the moment. This same prompt helps writers respond to their own drafts, too, and prepares them to understand and consider the responses of others. An example of this prompt follows. At the next class meeting, the writers collect the responses to their drafts, read them thoughtfully, without conversation, and make notes toward revision. After perhaps half an hour, each writer gets five minutes to sum up and discuss his/her plans for revision. Early in the course, I request copies of responses, so that I can skim them and offer coaching where necessary. Because students are curious about the responses to their drafts, they tend to keep busy, although temptation lurks to converse all along. I want them to read silently and think on their own, so I foster relative quiet for that first half hour. When a group strays from appropriate behavior, I signal them from where I'm sitting or sit down with them and, preferably with humor, entice them back to the fold. Once, early in the term, after an immature, disruptive group continued to defy my enticements, I wrote to them on a big piece of paper and laid it face up on their table: "Act like adults or get out now." Once they realized I take this stuff seriously and expected them to, they transformed themselves into students and had a successful semester.

The prompt for the DRAFTING stage (originally adapted from Peter Elbow's "Giving Movies of Your Mind" and from his distinction between criterion-based and reader-based responding) is designed to promote spontaneous, natural conversation by which the writer gains insight about strengths and weaknesses, and feels enthusiasm for rewriting:

Prompt for the Drafting Stage

1. Tell your experience of the draft — what it says and how it affects you. Intention? Audience? Tone? Arrangement? Development?
2. Tell what strikes you as effective — ideas, phrases, images, etc.
3. Tell what you'd like to know more about.

Note: See the big picture. Neglect style, grammar, usage, mechanics, format, and other points treated later.

The first step in the regimen, by far the most lengthy and demanding, may incorporate the other two steps. The responder iterates the main intention of the piece and how it comes across as the piece develops. The response is a summary of both the draft as such and of the responder's thoughts and feelings in experiencing it. Addressing the writer directly, the responder creates connection with the writer and with what the writer is saying, even in areas where the draft breaks down. Telling what is actually there in the draft, what seems struggling to be there, and what the responder experiences helps the writer envision a likely focus and often the language with which to express it. Telling what seems especially effective helps the writer know what to build upon. Telling what the responder would like to know more about helps the writer sense what readers need to know or are interested in knowing. Throughout the process, responding as a reader reading seems much more helpful than giving advice.

Much of what the writer gains from a response comes not from advice, but from the language and feeling of the responder. Generative energy develops between responder and writer, and the writer imagines possibilities for rewriting. One word or phrase used by the responder may create an opening to insight. For this to happen, the writer must think intently, seeking ideas about rewriting. It's especially important to highlight whatever makes the writer feel defensive. Usually feelings of defensiveness are a sign of the writer's wanting to reject a truth being revealed. Later, that information may become essential in rewriting. Especially group members who are prone to defensiveness must train themselves to accept and consider whatever responders say. Following is an example of a working draft and reader-based response using the prompt for the DRAFTING stage. The student writer, S. J., is composing an essay on a social and/or personal issue, developed from her own thought and experience.

A Sample Draft by S. J.

Family Problems

Crack Cocaine been in our neighborhoods for more than ten years. The talk about crack have quieted down but the usage of the drug have only gotten worse, harming the life of those that uses it or be around it.

Crack stay inside the body for less than a week but it may stay a habit for many years. Crack have become a drug stronger and more addictive than any other drug on the streets. It take less time to become addicted to crack than any other drug. Crack have been the reason our society must deal with the crime wave that is sweeping our nation. We don't only have to worry about the addicted one. We also must worry about the ones that are dealing.

Crack is a hard drug to cure yourself from. Most addict usually relapse over and over again. Most crack addict return to smoking because they feel that there is nowhere for them to turn to. Often family members let them think that no one know what they are doing, so they continue using drugs.

Crack have taken over my family in more ways than one. The only thing that crack has done for my family is torn it apart. I have had to bail family members out of all kinds of trouble. If they were to use their minds as much as they use the drug, they would not be getting in so many mishaps.

In my family there has been a bad drug problem. My family don't have to worry only about the drug user, we also have to worry about the drug dealers in the family. When you have drug users and dealer's in one family things can get very hard to deal with. Most of the time we must worry about whether some of our family members will make it home alive or unharmed.

When a family member is on drugs it is sometimes hard to believe it. It may be because your don't want to believe what is going on. You may notice that a family member is acting funny or starting to steal things from around the house.

At first you may not want to say or do anything about it, but we all know that something must be done about the drug problem.

I have gotten to the point that I will not trust my children with my uncle. I'm afraid that he might neglect them in some way. He is into drugs real bad. Most of the time I don't trust him in my house. I'm afraid that he might steal something from me.

When you have a dealer and user in the same family they both usually watch one another back, so that no one will find out what is going on. The dealer will give the drug to the user so that no one in the family will find out there are selling drugs. The addict will take the drug because most of the time it is coming free. Sometime this can end up as a big problem. The dealer must keep account for what he have giving away. If not the person that he is selling the drugs for will take the payment out on the dealer.

There was this time when my cousin was selling drugs and my uncle was the addict. My cousin would give my uncle the drugs he wanted so that he wouldn't go back and tell that he was selling drugs. My uncle started getting used to my cousin giving him drugs. One day my uncle couldn't find my cousin so he decided to go in the bed room and just take the drugs he wanted. My uncle didn't realize that my cousin would get in trouble for that.

My cousin knew who had taken the drug but there was nothing that he could say or do. The next day when my cousin got home he told us that he had been beaten up by some guys who didn't like him. I knew what had really happen to him.

My family try to act like they don't know what is going on but they do. A few years later my cousin was sent to prison. He was charged as a drug Kingpin and sentenced to thirty-six years. My uncle is still in and out using drugs all the time bringing his family down more and more each time he spend his pay check and get into trouble.

Solving this drug problem must start within the home. Families need to try to help one another with there problem and stop over looking it.

A Sample Reader-Based Response (Written) to S. J.'s Draft

J. D. Telling Her Experience of the Draft, What Strikes Her as Effective, and What She Wants to Know More About

I feel the main idea of your paper is how dangerous crack can become and how it affects the family. It was very interesting to see how crack can work from within a family out into the community. You point out and clearly show how crack can affect family member's trust and how it breaks down the family unit. For example, when you mention how your cousin gave your uncle crack, for free, in order not to be exposed to the family. I can empathize with you on why you would not trust certain family members and how this could harm your family. I feel you develop the paper nicely and show what crack is and bring in how it effects the family. I definitely see your point on how drug abuse has started at home and treating the problem needs to begin at home, as well.

I found your paper to be very interesting and felt very connected with you when you talked about how it has affected your life and family. I certainly can see you would like to see the problem stopped and agree that families need to help each other. I was able to follow your paper and clearly see where it was going. Personally, I feel you were very courageous to write about this topic and how you bring out your family. It seems that you really want to help make a change and wish you luck. I enjoyed reading your paper and it did touch me, as far as, making me aware of how crack can hurt a family.

My Analysis of J. D.'s Response to S. J.'s Draft

As a novice responder, J. D. does a good job of identifying and recounting the main purpose and effect of the draft. I like how she connects with the writer, addressing S. J. directly, revealing how the draft touches her as a reader and teaches her about cocaine in families. I like how she focuses on the big picture, as instructed, and neglects any mention of editing or proofreading issues. I like how she recalls a specific example from the text to illustrate what seems effective. Apparently, she feels satisfied with the scope and coverage of the piece, because she doesn't mention anything she'd like to know more about.

In helping J. D. learn to respond even more constructively, I focus on two elements:

1. As she summarizes the piece and recounts her experience of it, I want her to reveal the arrangement of parts as well as the means of development, and help the writer see how the introduction and body might focus the reader's attention more directly on the main purpose.

2. I want her to use the language of the prompt more deliberately so both responder and writer know whether she is telling her experience of the piece, or telling what strikes her as effective, or telling what she wants to know more about. While it's fine to intermix the three elements rather than divide them artificially, I want the responder to consider each element deliberately and to respond specifically. Recounting her experience of the piece should include audience and tone, which J. D. doesn't mention. Telling what strikes her as effective should involve saying back, often word for word, the outstanding passages. Telling what she wants to know more about should involve deliberate consideration of the scope and coverage of the piece. In this instance, J.D. should acknowledge directly that the piece feels complete.

Need for Teacher Intervention

Her response reveals the need for teacher intervention at the DRAFTING stage—to coach each group in responding and to coach the writer in learning what to do with peer responses. J. D.'s response well identifies the main purpose and spirit of the piece (although I want her to see that the piece primarily recounts the effects of drug use on the family; while prevention of drug use may need to begin in the family, the primary intention of the piece is not to develop a solution). Given such responses and coaching, S. J. can learn to reread her draft, imagine reader expectations from the opening sentences, decide whether her introduction establishes the intended purpose, and revise more deliberately. Ideally, J. D.'s response helps cause the writer S. J. to think for herself, "Aha, the effect of cocaine on families is my main intention, isn't it? Now I see what I need to work on to focus and unify my piece."

Such Responding Is Hard and Takes Lots of Practice

To provide ideal responses, students need considerable coaching, practice, and concentration. It's difficult for some to articulate the primary intention of even a published article. Doing so for a working draft sometimes requires locating evidence of a primary intention that is only partially realized or ambivalent.

I discuss this challenge—grasping main ideas—as part of the lifelong process of developing ourselves as readers and thinkers. In the struggle to read globally and respond constructively, they improve their reading comprehension, learning over time to see the big picture rather than smaller elements. Ultimately (as E. D. Hirsch once mentioned in a seminar) students can write only so well as they can read their own writing. And of course, as they freewrite their responses at home (or in the computer lab), they gain practice in expressing themselves on paper, and they develop abilities needed for responding extemporaneously later in the course and in college composition. At first, some students, especially the self-conscious or shy, may feel uncomfortable communicating what feels like criticism. As they develop this ability, they learn to reveal a draft's shortcomings honestly—but diplomatically and constructively—from their perspective as readers. The writer learns to consider what each group member says. Students learn that even the least accomplished or perceptive group member may provide useful information. They also come to understand that writing need not and cannot be just a leap in the dark. It's a process of rewriting.

Responding Orally at the Drafting Stage

Later in the course, as students improve their ability to read globally, ideally they can begin to respond orally at the moment rather than taking drafts home and writing their responses. I say "ideally" because I've tended to postpone such expectation until college composition (even there, students need to practice by writing responses at home). A good intermediate step is for them to read the drafts at home and then to respond orally in the next class period after the writer reads once aloud. In an oral session at the DRAFTING stage, the writer reads the draft aloud once at a natural pace while other group members follow along and make notes on their copy. Then they take a few minutes to read silently and make more notes. The member to the left of the writer responds orally for two minutes, using as a guide the prompt for the DRAFTING stage. In turn, each group member responds likewise for two minutes, regardless of how much others' responses are repeated. A monitor keeps time and helps keep members on track. With practice, groups can cover four shorter papers in a class period (if I don't talk too much at the beginning). The writer listens, makes extensive notes, and keeps quiet, quelling the urge to justify a passage criticized or to talk about the subject. I emphasize writing down whatever feels uncomfortable, living with it for a while, and then deciding whether revision is appropriate.

At the start of class when the working draft is due for oral presentation and responses, students set a copy on my desk and give each group member a copy. While they work together, I skim each draft looking for focus, development, and arrangement. I usually bracket the main idea/intention and supporting points as I go and then at the end summarize the idea/intention. If the draft seems adequate as a draft, I return it to the writer without suggestions, trusting the group process to generate thoughtful revision. If the draft feels inadequate as a draft, lacks focus, is undeveloped, or seems disorganized, then I usually outline what's there and suggest what might need to happen during rewriting in order to fulfill the apparent intention. Because I intervene only when I see real problems, the groups tend to maintain independence from me. They don't negate group responses, expecting that I'll present "the real truth." This boundary is essential—as is my intervening when appropriate. By the end of the hour, I've usually read and returned all the drafts, and the groups have usually completed their responses and note taking. One or two students will usually seek help from me in resolving conflicting responses. Sometimes I help best by clarifying their options and saying, "The decision is up to you, the writer." Other times I reveal what seems an effective choice.

Redrafting and Editing

Now it's the solitary job of each student to consider our sometimes conflicting responses, to rethink and rewrite as much as is needed for presenting at the next class a draft that is better focused, better developed, better arranged, and more consciously edited. Accomplished mainly with the ear and eye, EDITING refines the style or character of a piece. I want them to understand that good writing engages readers and pleases us aesthetically, like music. The notes work together to create one purposeful effect. While students have no doubt edited some along the way, they have attended mainly to the big picture. Now they consider each word, each phrase or image, each sentence, each cluster of sentences, each paragraph—all in relation to the focal intention. I model the EDITING process and provide practice in reading the text aloud and responding to the writer's stylistic choices. To help attune their eyes and ears, I suggest reading into a tape recorder and then listening while editing. Students who do so often report astonishment at what they discover.

In the class period devoted to EDITING, they provide a copy for each group member (but not for me). They divide the class period into four units of about twelve minutes, one for each writer. The writer reads one paragraph aloud and then awaits responses, which don't involve a set prompt or order. Responders are encouraged to bring up anything that nags at them: a vague generalization in the opening, a cliché, a seemingly highfalutin Latinate noun, inappropriate choppiness of rhythm. The group tries not to rewrite but to help the writer see where refinements of style might be appropriate. For one thing, the writer needs to learn by doing. For another, a group might spend the whole time bogged down in one sentence. The writer makes notes, especially about observations that feel uncomfortable. When that writer's time is up, the group moves on to the next member's paper, even if not completed with the former. During such EDITING sessions, students tend to work appropriately for the whole period because the task is well defined, practical, engaging, and challenging. Many seem fascinated, never having attended so deliberately to stylistic choices in relation to purpose and effect. They learn to notice and articulate how choices affect them. At the end of the period, they now face the solitary job of applying what they have learned to the refinement of their paper. After doing so, they proof it as best they can and make whatever changes seem necessary, in preparation for the class period devoted to proofing.

Proofing

The Scarry text offers practical lessons on common proofing problems, and I've found that as students produce successive revisions and work in groups, they tend to employ and build on their tacit knowledge of language, which is usually much greater than they or we realize. Many surface errors are the result of inattention rather than ignorance. As students attend to their own texts and the texts of others, they make more and more corrections of nonstandard forms and come to grasp and apply more and more conventions of college writing. They identify what they don't know, such as the distinction between lie and lay, and they explore how to learn such distinctions (*The Writer's Workplace*, handbook, dictionary, grammar check, spell check, conversation with group members or me). They also learn that different readers have different expectations or preconceptions about "correctness," that proofing choices depend partly on intention and audience, not on set rules. Some students have been taught "Never use *I*" or "Never use contractions," while others have been taught to use *I* when referring to themselves or to use *don't* to help establish a conversational interaction with the reader, even in fairly formal writing.

If there is enough time, the writer presents the whole paper to the whole group for PROOFING. My students prefer doing so because they get more eyes and ears involved. To save time, however, I often have them work in groups of two, each with a copy. One partner reads the piece aloud naturally but slowly. Both try to keep their eyes and minds focused on each successive element, listening and looking for "errors." Some sentences have to be reread and reexamined. Either partner is encouraged to bring up whatever might be a problem, the point being to engage in conversation about proofing issues that will help each writer learn what to look for and how to make corrections in the future. If the partners can't resolve an issue by discussing it or by consulting the handbook, a raised hand brings me to their table for a consultation. Sometimes I can resolve a question directly: "Yes, you do need a comma there to prevent misreading." Other times I'm moved to say, "It depends. Journalists leave out the comma before *and* in a series, while academic writers include it. I prefer its inclusion because it sets off the elements clearly. Your main concerns are to be consistent throughout your paper and to make choices that don't call attention to themselves. Since right now you're focusing on college writing, I recommend including the comma before *and* in a series." The best students, because they raise so many proofing issues, will sometimes take a whole class period for two papers, first the one partner's and then the other's.

The writer keeps a master copy and is the only one who writes on it, deciding whether or not to make a suggested change or correction, assuming full responsibility for the text. Students learn and remember more by thinking about and writing the suggested change. Also, they would in effect be cheating if someone else, including me, actually made corrections for them, instead of raising issues for discussion and learning. During PROOFING sessions students tend to stay focused because — as with the ending sessions–the work is well defined, practical, engaging, and challenging. When students do stray, I can usually bring them back by approaching them and saying in good humor something like "Here come the writing police." I must say that in both developmental and college composition, such PROOFING sessions have transformed my job of reading "finished" papers. After the second or third paper of the term in developmental, it's not unusual for me to have to mark as few as five or six items in a paper, a comma here, a capital letter there. It's a pleasure to read and respond as a reader rather than as a marker. Of course, some students may require even more intensive intervention than the PROOFING sessions and the systematic lessons in *The Writer's Workplace* can provide.

The "Finished" Paper

Now students make all necessary refinements in form and then in the next class period submit the paper for my evaluation. Unlike some of my colleagues in the profession who are rightly determined to de-emphasize grades, I do put a "grade" on each "finished" paper. It lets students know where they stand in an imperfect academic world where grades are the norm. It also serves as an incentive to rewrite for a higher grade. At my college, developmental courses are graded *Satisfactory* or *Unsatisfactory* (essentially *Pass* or *Fail*). Sometimes I'll write, among other comments, "An excellent paper, S if you correct the one comma splice and prove to me you understand the principle." Often the student will say to the group, "I still don't understand this comma splice thing. Can you help me?" And of course what happens is the whole group explores the issue.

Much for the Teacher to Learn

I began by asserting that writing-as-a-process and peer work groups constitute the two most important breakthroughs in my twenty-nine years of teaching. Some crusty, seasoned colleagues dismiss such notions out of hand: "Just more educational fads," they mutter, "nothing more than the swing of the pendulum." I would argue, conversely, that we're developing these concepts and practices from substantial, documented observations of how writers actually work. Unlike most beginners, seasoned writers expect to rewrite. Writers develop habits of revision that enable discovery, revelation, and refinement. Writers also employ trusted readers whose responses help to validate or redirect the writing. We're also becoming aware that learning to write is something like learning a sport. Students need coaching and training, but most of all, they need to get out there daily and play the game. If you don't like the sports analogy, then consider sculpting. The sculpting class is a workshop in which the teacher demonstrates principles, students work on their own pieces, and all engage in ongoing critiques of works in progress. The more I learn about coaching students as writers writing and readers responding, the more I value this pedagogy and the more I realize I'm just beginning to understand its possibilities. It puts students at the very center of what we have always wanted them to master.

Portfolios as a Part of the Developmental Writing Classroom

BY Patricia I. Mulcahy-Ernt, Ph.D.

UNIVERSITY OF BRIDGEPORT

As teachers of writing have changed the focus of their instruction from a product-orientation to a process-orientation, the attractiveness of portfolios as both an instructional tool and an assessment tool has increased in developmental writing classrooms. Deciding on the use of portfolios, however, is analogous to making a New Year's resolution for a complete body make-over: if you want good results, you cannot make a halfhearted effort; likewise, once you make the total commitment, you will see a substantial change not only in the outcome but in your everyday routines. So, if you are contemplating using portfolios, you may want to ask some critical questions. What is the best use of portfolios for my classrooms? How can I use portfolios for instruction as well as assessment of students' writing? What are some of the benefits as well as drawbacks in using portfolios?

Portfolios as a Process Approach

To begin, using portfolios for both instruction and assessment incorporates a process approach. In other words, the focus is on the development of students' writing in various stages and forms, rather than the finished product. Although one definition of portfolio use, common to artists and writers, is the collection of their best pieces, representing the expertise and versatility of the artist, the alternative and more widely used version of the portfolio in the developmental writing classroom is the collection of work over time, representing the student's growth as a writer. By definition, a portfolio is a systematic collection of student work (Valencia, 1991; Popham, 1995). As a collection of snapshots of student work, a portfolio has examples of a student's progress and achievement, showing how over time the student has changed and matured in different aspects of writing. These artifacts of student work constitute a representative sample of the depth and breadth of the student's performance.

Due to the link between a process approach to writing and the use of portfolios as snapshots of student work in the various phases of the writing process, portfolios have a natural niche in the developmental writing classroom. As an assessment tool, the instructor can evaluate the student's progress, based on the student's actual work situated in the actual writing contexts. In contrast to other forms of assessment, the power of portfolios is that they are considered authentic, especially in light of the writing tasks the students are requested to do and the context of instruction (Valencia, 1991). In other words, the tools for assessment are grounded in the same tasks that are used for instruction. Unlike other forms of assessments that are not aligned with instruction, portfolios are considered a more valid, naturalistic type of evaluation.

However, the worth of using portfolios is not just as an approach for evaluation but as an approach for instruction. The dynamic properties of a portfolio system emerge when an instructor adopts a portfolio approach for instruction. To do so, an instructor designs classroom instruction that allows for planning, drafting, conferencing, revision, reflection, and student choice, which are often part of a writing classroom. For example, not only does the student choose writing samples for inclusion in a folder of student work, but both the instructor and student participate in individual conferences to discuss the student's progress; records of these conferences are included in the student's portfolio. The student also participates in peer conferences; records of these conferences also become part of the portfolio. When the student revises a paper, the revision, especially in contrast to the original paper, is included in the portfolio. Throughout the semester, however, the student may decide to substitute a revised "best piece" after a series of revisions. Included in the portfolio may be the student's own writing reflections that promote a metacognitive awareness of the writing process and the student's own individual growth as a writer. Unlike more traditional types of assessment that depend on performance on one type of task, such as a multiple-choice test or essay test, a portfolio system approach relies on multiple measures gained through the processes of conferencing, revision, student choice, and self-reflection; the final grade includes these multiple measures of growth collected throughout an entire instructional period rather than a single score gained on one assessment given during a single-setting exam period.

Using portfolios as a process approach for both instruction and assessment contains a number of implicit assumptions about writing, instruction, the participation of students, the role of the writing instructor, and the role of assessment. First of all, the process of writing is linked to the other language arts processes; students learn how to improve their writing by sharing their ideas with others, discussing their writing, reading the work of others, and incorporating the feedback of peers and mentors in their own work. Second, assessment is aligned with instruction and shows the ongoing efforts of students in a variety of writing tasks and contexts; particularly for the field of writing, portfolios can indicate the planning, drafting, conferencing about, revising, and publishing of a student's piece of writing. Rarely is this process captured in other evaluation tools. Third, students as writers and readers become part of the process of writing instruction along with the instructor; since peer feedback helps students learn about writing to communicate to an audience, the peer conference summaries can also be included in the portfolio. Due to this emphasis, writing becomes a social, collaborative activity, rather than an isolated, solely independent one. In this sense, students are stakeholders in the instruction-assessment process, unlike more traditional formats. Fourth, the role of the writing instructor shifts to that of a mentor, a coach, a trusted confidante. The feedback that the student receives, as well as the manner in which it is communicated to the student, can make a significant difference in building a student's self-confidence in writing ability; it can motivate a student to take risks, to try new styles and patterns, to view another's writing in a new light. Therefore, individual conferences between the student and instructor become part of both the instructional as well as assessment approach. However, evaluation of a student's work is formative, focusing on the emergence and process of the writer. Often, instructors using a portfolio approach will write descriptive notes about a student's performance so that the student's writing strengths are also noted as well as areas for improvement; or, conference notes may be specific to a focused area for development, such as writing for a stylistic effect. The instructor's role also shifts from a traditional classroom lecturer to one that requires redesigning the classroom for peer discussion, for the use of writing tools for revision, and for collaboration among teachers and students. Finally, if portfolios are implemented in a writing program across a series of courses, careful planning among administrators and instructors needs to occur so that decisions about the contents of the portfolio, the assessment of the portfolio as a whole, and the final ownership of the portfolio are made before portfolios are used for the whole curriculum.

Decisions About Using Portfolios for Instruction and Assessment

In a developmental writing classroom the integration of a portfolio system depends on three key stages: planning, implementation, and evaluation. During the phase in which the instructor plans to use a portfolio system, several key decisions about the purpose of the portfolio, the contents of the portfolio, and the ownership of the portfolio need to be made.

Purpose

In any good assessment approach the purpose of testing and evaluation needs to be clear. In other words, what needs to be evaluated? Why? Typically, the case for the inclusion of portfolios in a developmental writing classroom is that they show the student's growth in writing over time; samples of the student's own writing are the focus for both instruction and assessment. Hopefully, the purpose of testing and evaluation are in alignment with instruction. In other words, the benefit of using portfolios is that the processes of planning, drafting, conferencing, and revision are exemplified in both instruction and assessment.

Contents

Deciding about the contents of the portfolio has important effects not only for instruction but also for assessment. The definition of the portfolio as a folder of the student's best pieces warrants a selective process in weeding out writings that the student no longer considers "best"; this focus keeps to a minimum the number of pieces that are included. In contrast, if the definition of a portfolio is to include a process perspective, showing how the student creates the "best pieces," then the quantity of items will be greater. In the latter case students will include examples of their planning, drafting, conferencing, and revising.

In a developmental writing classroom there are many feasible items for inclusion in a portfolio. Some of the more popular types of items are the following:

- Selected best pieces;
- Samples of different types of writing, such as narrative, expository, persuasive pieces; poetry; autobiographical pieces; letters; résumé;
- Examples of drafts, revisions, and edited manuscripts;
- Conference notes from both peer and teacher-student conferences;
- Self-evaluation summaries of the student's writing.

Since portfolios can be shaped to the contours of the writing classroom, depending on the types of writing tasks used, portfolios can include a variety of other representative works. If a student is involved in an in-depth research project, the writing portfolio could include samples of the student's field notes, such as personal interviews, observations, journal entries, outlines, and library research summaries. Portfolios also allow the use of multiple texts in various formats. For instance, depending on the writing task, portfolios can include works on computer, on videotape, in photographs, and in other media. This quality of portfolios provides a creative appeal to instructors who wish to provide an incentive to students to apply what they write to performance settings, such as a play.

In classrooms that focus on both developmental reading and writing, the portfolio can include students' responses to text, study notes, and vocabulary notes. Also, a portfolio can provide evidence how the student is applying literacy strategies in other classes; in other words, samples that show how the student is comprehending text and studying other disciplines may also be included in the portfolio to show how the student transfers acquired skills in the developmental classroom to other disciplines.

If the portfolio is used for long-range assessment, it may also include other types of tests that serve to provide normative data about the student's performance in relation to other students' performance. For instance, it is a widespread practice in many colleges to give students a writing test, typically for placement purposes. Therefore, as a baseline measure of writing performance, the student's writing test could also be included in the portfolio. Since students in developmental writing classes typically take a series of writing courses, then the student's portfolio could also travel with the student through those courses. Any final writing exams required by the college could also be placed in the student's portfolio. In other words, if a portfolio approach is adopted as a departmental policy for student evaluation, then the writing that the student completes during participation in a writing program can be evaluated through a long-range process. The benefit of this systems approach for evaluating students' writing is that there is naturalistic evidence of the student's progress and multiple measures of writing achievement. Thus, when portfolios are used to evaluate the student's writing through an entire program, rather than a single course, portfolios may include standardized test results to indicate performance in a variety of contexts. However, the inclusion of items in a portfolio, whether they are standardized test results or measures of naturalistic writing samples, should have a clear rationale in alignment with the goals of writing instruction.

Ownership

One of the attractions of a portfolio approach is that students take ownership for the contents of it, thereby having a voice in their own evaluation; through the process of selecting what is included in the portfolio, students are actively involved in both their instruction and assessment. Without a doubt, a portfolio is a testimony to a student's diligence, especially in the revision process, and the pride that the student takes in the creation of a portfolio is an important dimension in its success. However, since the portfolio collects evidence over time, it is often feasible to keep the physical folder and a copy of the student's work in the developmental writing classroom or writing lab so that the evidence is not lost. Yet, it is also important that the student has a personal copy of all of the portfolio works, has access to the portfolio, and has the authority to choose and discard work that is no longer characterized as best pieces. At the same time security for the contents of the portfolio needs to be maintained so that only the owner of the portfolio has access to it and that any standardized test scores are not lost.

To preserve the integrity of ownership of the portfolio, some instructors will hold an initial conference with the student to create a contract about the types of items the student will include (such as writing samples), the types of items that the instructor will include (such as conference notes), and the types of items the department will include (such as standardized tests or department writing tests). In this manner it is clear at the beginning of the semester who is responsible for completing and maintaining the various components of the portfolio. In some cases the student maintains complete control over the portfolio and is responsible for turning in the finished portfolio at the end of the semester.

Implementation

The implementation stage of using portfolios spans both classroom instruction and assessment. After the decision about where to physically keep the student folders is made and after the initial contract is negotiated with the student, the instructor uses the portfolio as a bank of the students' writings. Since the advantage of using portfolios is that they align with the natural flow in a writing classroom, the instructor can recommend that students include in their portfolios samples portraying their writing process.

However, one feature of portfolios that complements good writing instruction is the inclusion of instructor-student and peer conferences. Included in the portfolio can be samples that indicate an awareness of audience, style, tone, appropriateness, organization, voice, word choice (Tierney, Carter, & Desai, 1991); the effectiveness of each of these can be discussed through conferences. As a record of the conference, the instructor can design a checklist and summary sheet, noting the student's strengths and areas for improvement. (See Tierney, Carter, & Desai, 1991 for examples of checklists.)

Evaluation

The last phase of portfolio use entails evaluation. If the instructor has already clear-cut goals for instruction, then the assessment process should be in alignment. However, the challenge of portfolio assessment is to decide on what should be evaluated. The well-stocked portfolio has an enormous amount of data. One evaluation approach is to use holistic grading on the quality of the entire contents. A recommendation is to develop a rubric that clearly spells out different ranges of quality. In other words, what is an outstanding portfolio? Acceptable one? Weak one? Unacceptable one? Characteristics for each of these descriptors need to be clearly identified and communicated to the student during the instructional process. (See Tierney, Carter, & Desai, 1991 for examples of rubrics.)

Hopefully, the final portfolio grade is also part of formative evaluation. Since the student receives feedback about the writing samples created for the classroom (which are included in the portfolio), the final evaluation should be no surprise. Yet, in the spirit of consistency and collaboration the final portfolio evaluation should include solid descriptors of the student's performance. In this manner the student is able to learn how to improve writing performance.

Challenges in Using Portfolios

The astute reader will note that the implementation of a portfolio system is no small matter in the classroom. There are a number of challenges and drawbacks to portfolio use, among them are time, adequate resources, the availability of professional training, and the reliability of evaluation results.

Time

First, it takes not only a substantial commitment to using portfolios, but it also takes much time to develop a workable system for the classroom and even longer for a whole department. Some instructors have adopted a two-year plan for the development of their systems: the first year is to create the initial design and make a trial run of the use of portfolios, and the second year is to fine-tune the process.

Adequate Resources

Secondly, portfolios need a physical space to house their contents. A well-organized, accessible, and secure area, which should be in the proximity of the writing classroom, needs to be created. Student folders need to be purchased, some type of filing system needs to be created, and the physical storage of the portfolios needs to be available. Although this may not seem like a challenge to those working with small populations, in some colleges involving the participation of hundreds of students in freshman writing programs, this is no small matter. The alternative is for students to be responsible for their own portfolios.

Availability of Professional Training

In order for a portfolio system to work, instructors, administrators, and students, must be well-versed in those aspects influencing their role in the planning, implementation, and evaluation of portfolios. For example, instructors need to know how to design them for their own classrooms, how to create the appropriate instructional tools for student use, and how to evaluate their contents. Department administrators need to be aware of the commitment in time and resources that instructors and students make in creating a viable portfolio system. Also, students need to learn how to develop their portfolio, participate in its evaluation, and become part of a team of peer evaluators.

Reliability of Evaluation Results

Finally, as an assessment tool, the reliability of portfolios has been called into question (Popham, 1995). Psychometrically speaking, for a test to be reliable, it needs to give consistent results. Unlike standardized measures that are designed to give consistent, stable results, portfolios lack consistency. In other words, different evaluators can assign different grades. This is a concern among those who use portfolios; often the articulation of clear criteria for grading the contents of the portfolio has been cited as a first step in addressing this concern. However, without good training in evaluating writing and in evaluating portfolios, the merits of using a portfolio system are minimized.

In sum, as you decide on the worth of portfolios for your classroom, you are now in a better position to stick to your resolution, unlike making a New Year's resolution born out of guilt rather than felt need. Hopefully, as means to an end, your students will also enjoy the process and the outcome of your instructional decision-making, whatever you decide.

Recommended Readings

deFina, A. A. (1992). *Portfolio assessment: Getting started*. New York: Scholastic.

Farr, R., & Tone, B. (1994). *Portfolio and performance assessment*. Fort Worth: Harcourt Brace.

Gillett, J. W., & Temple, C. (1994). *Understanding reading problems: Assessment & instruction, 4th edition*. New York: HarperCollins.

Harp, B. (1996). *The handbook of literacy assessment and evaluation*. Norwood, MA: Christopher-Gordon.

Johnston, P. H. (1992). *Constructive evaluation of literate activity*. New York: Longman.

Popham, W. J. (1995). *Classroom assessment: What teachers need to know.* Boston: Allyn & Bacon.

Roskos, K. & Walker, B. J. (1994). *Interactive handbook for understanding reading diagnosis.* New York: Merrill.

Tierney, R. J., Carter, M. A., Desai, L. E. (1991). *Portfolio assessment in the reading-writing classroom.* Norwood, MA: Christopher-Gordon.

Valencia, S. W. (1991). Portfolios: Panacea or Pandora's Box? In F. L. Finch (ed.), *Educational performance assessment* (pp. 33–46). Chicago: Riverside.

Using Tutors in a Developmental Writing Class

By Karan Hancock and Tom Gier

UNIVERSITY OF ALASKA — ANCHORAGE

What Is a Tutor?

This seems to be a fairly straightforward question. A tutor is a person who has particular skill, expertise, or knowledge in a specific subject, content area, or discipline and who shares that skill, expertise, or knowledge with students one to one or in a group situation. Simply put, the goal of a tutor is to enable the person being tutored (the tutee) to acquire enough of the tutor's skills and expertise to become academically independent.

Why Are Tutors a Valuable Resource in the Class and the Writing Lab?

A tutor can be a tremendous resource because a tutor can do what the professor many times cannot do: give the student absolute undivided attention for an extended period of time and repeat, explain, define, and reexplain material or information when necessary. A tutor can lead a student through an assignment or a project step by step and point by point and then do it again if necessary.

Tutors are a valuable resource. Often a student experiencing difficulty will be more likely to seek help when needed if tutors are available. What student has not been just a little frightened of calling on a professor during office hours or before or after class to ask about an assignment that everyone else in class seems to understand? Many students find they are much more comfortable approaching a fellow student—a tutor—with a problem or concern.

Well-trained tutors seem to have a special knack for helping these students, too. Maybe it is just because the tutor is "closer" to the assignment or project—the tutor can probably very quickly remember and share his/her own difficulties with the same or similar assignment and thereby help take some of the stigma away by simply saying: "Yeah, I had trouble with this, too," or "I can see where you're having some difficulty."

What else can tutors do either in the class or the writing lab? The following are some general "tutoring do's." By no means is the list complete because every class, writing lab, and tutoring situation will have particular issues that cannot be delineated or anticipated. However, the list will give tutors, students (tutees), and professors a starting point.

Tutoring "Do's"

How can a well-trained tutor help in the class and/or writing lab? What are some of the things a tutor does?

1. A tutor appreciates and respects the uniqueness of each individual student and realizes that every tutee has strengths and weaknesses.

Karan Hancock and Tom Gier. "Using Tutors in a Developmental Writing Class." Used by permission of the authors.

2.   A tutor helps the tutee identify areas of strength. This gives both a good place to start. By identifying what the student already knows or can do, the tutor can more easily pinpoint and address any weaknesses.

3.   A tutor and the tutee next identify and address areas of weakness. If the student has difficulty with time management, it is going to be a waste of time to address topic sentences first. With the help of the tutee a tutor will be able to identify these areas of difficulty and then offer positive suggestions about how to best deal with them.

4.   A tutor asks appropriate questions that help the tutee identify just where the difficulty lies. "What do you understand the assignment to be? Explain it to me as you understand it." By ascertaining the tutee's level of understanding of the assignment, the tutor can then take the questioning further. Some additional questions might include:

"What can you do with the assignment right now?"

"What skills do you have that you can use to begin this assignment?"

"What skills do you think you need to review or sharpen before you can begin this assignment?"

"What is typically the first thing you do when approaching an assignment?"

"What is the most difficult thing for you about this assignment?"

"What is the least difficult?"

"How much time are you going to allot for the assignment?"

"Having talked about your difficulties, do you think this is going to be enough time?"

Answers the tutee provides to these and other questions will give the tutor a specific place to start and help him/her plan appropriately.

5.   A tutor makes diagnoses based on the information gleaned from the tutee and goes on to help the tutee overcome the identified areas of weakness while expanding on areas of strength. For example, if time management is identified as a problem area, maybe all that is needed is a review of the student's master schedule to help her/him see which pieces or blocks of time can be devoted to a specific class or assignment. If the initial discussion reveals that the tutee needs help in narrowing a topic then the work can begin there with a specific goal in mind. The tutee can then use the same questioning techniques to self-diagnose for other classes and other assignments.

6.   The tutor helps the tutee establish a positive attitude about a class or assignment. Some students do poorly in a class or on an assignment because they have no real interest in it or cannot see the relevance of it. The class or assignment is just something they have to get through. The tutee may never really come to "love" writing a research paper; but through the help of a tutor, a tutee may come to appreciate the process and why it was assigned.

7.   A tutor helps to foster positive self-esteem in the tutee. By helping the tutee acquire or polish skills and set reasonable, attainable goals, the tutor is helping the tutee learn to take charge and take responsibility for his/her own learning and academic success.

8.   A tutor expresses empathy, understanding, and respect for the tutee's difficulty. If a student has been away from the academic world for a while or is

new to the college/university setting, the tutor may need to start with dusting off long-unused "student skills" or even introduce the student to new student skills. A tutor may need to demonstrate how to use the computer that now takes the place of the card catalog in the library; which version of documentation style, MLA or APA, etc. is now required; how to format a computer for proper margins, etc.

A tutor may need to start by helping the tutee with very basic writing techniques: outlining, narrowing a topic, broadening a topic, political correctness in writing, subject-verb agreement, pronoun-antecedent agreement, parallelism, imagery, etc. With some students/tutees, it may be necessary to start with basic vocabulary skills, sentence structure, grammar, and punctuation. Within the class or writing lab, a tutor helps students recognize and address these types of difficulties.

9. A tutor shares with the tutee a variety of examples and techniques. Within the writing lab, a tutor can refer to any number of "process papers" to show the student exactly what is meant and expected by a particular professor. (It is especially helpful when the professor and tutor work together to have a file of examples to share with the tutee. These papers can exemplify just what the professor expects in a particular type of assignment.)

10. A tutor listens to what the tutee has to say and responds appropriately. Sometimes all a tutee needs is an opportunity to "talk through" a problem area or difficulty with someone else. Sometimes a tutee needs very specific help and can very succinctly ask for it; sometimes not. Sometimes a tutee needs a little pat on the back and a nod of encouragement. Sometimes the tutee comes to the tutoring session wanting help that the tutor is not able to provide; therefore, an effective tutor knows when and to whom the tutee should be referred.

This is a beginning list of some basic "Tutoring Do's." Each tutor working with the professor and writing lab should establish additional points as they specifically apply to their individual programs, settings, and students.

Tutoring "Don'ts"

It is important for tutors, professors, and tutees to realize that there are some things that do not fall into the scope of tutoring. As with the list of "Tutoring Do's," this list of general "Tutoring Don'ts" is just a beginning that can be expanded upon to fit the needs of the particular situation.

1. A tutor does not do the work for the tutee. A tutor's job is to help the student understand, begin, progress through, and complete the assignment. A tutor is NOT a ghost writer and does not do the assignment for the student.

2. A tutor does not tell the student how easy an assignment is or should be. Just because an assignment seems easy or self-explanatory to the tutor does not mean the tutee finds it so. If the assignment were easy why would the student be seeking help from a tutor? A tutor never belittles the difficulty a tutee may be having.

3. A tutor does not assume the role of a counselor. The tutor's role is academic, not psychological. Tutors are not trained counselors or therapists. This does not mean that a tutor cannot listen to a nonacademic problem — what it does mean is that a tutor should know when and to whom the student may be referred for appropriate help.

4. A tutor does not let the tutoring extend past the point of necessity. Some tutees seem absolutely unable to work on their own and seek continued tutoring when it really isn't necessary. An effective tutor will have given the tutee the skills and practice necessary to progress on his/her own and the independence to do so. If the tutee insists that the tutor is "the only one who can help me" or "I can't do it without you" then there may be a need for intervention by the writing lab supervisor or the professor.

5. A tutor does not take on tutees with whom he/she cannot be comfortable. If a tutor is not comfortable working with much older students, very young students, or any student with whom rapport cannot be easily established, then the tutor owes it to himself or herself and the tutee to realize that and recommend another tutor.

    An addendum to this is the tutor does not become personally involved with the tutee. It is crucial to maintain professionalism in the tutoring situation. There should be prescribed places to meet for the tutoring sessions, i.e., the writing lab, the classroom, or the resource center.

6. A tutor does not predict grades on projects or assignments.

7. A tutor does not criticize a professor's assignments, how assignments are graded, how a professor presents material, or how a professor tests. A tutor will help the student understand the grading criteria, assignments, etc. of professors and encourage the student to visit with the professor to go over the errors and shortcomings.

8. A tutor does not "fake" knowledge or expertise that he/she does not have. It is better to say, "I don't know that. Let's work on it together to find out" than to bluff one's way through something. This provides good modeling for the tutees by showing them that when tutors don't know an answer, they look it up.

9. A tutor remembers to praise the tutee and offer positive reinforcement and encouragement. The smallest step forward is just that: a step forward.

10. A tutor does not conduct the tutoring session as a one-way experience with information, directives, comments, and ideas coming only from the tutor. The successful tutoring session will be a two-way, give-and-take experience in which the tutor encourages questions, comments, and input from the tutee and expresses appreciation for the tutee's active involvement.

Responsibilities and Qualities of a Tutor

As with any job there are specific responsibilities and qualities that make the job and the person doing the job special. It is a given that the tutor will have the content area or discipline expertise that qualifies him/her to be a tutor in the first place and the tutor will have the desire to share that with the tutees. But having expertise and desire are only part of the equation. A successful tutor also has special qualities and responsibilities that must be factored in as well.

As with the lists of tutoring do's and don'ts, this is just a beginning list and the tutors, professors, and writing lab supervisors will want to add to and adapt it to meet their own special needs. What follows are some basic tutor responsibilities and qualities.

1. A tutor is ready before the tutoring session begins. If the tutoring is done in the classroom, the tutor must know what the topic of the day is, what is going to be covered, how it is going to be covered and what is going to be

assigned from it. The tutor must then work closely with the professor to ensure that they are both "on the same page."

If the tutoring is taking place in the writing lab, the tutor must be there before the tutoring session starts in order to get physically and mentally ready for the session: reviewing notes, texts, reference materials and getting the space ready for the tutee and the ensuing session. If the tutor has worked with a particular tutee before, the tutor should be ready to discuss and review the last session's work and the progress and/or difficulties the tutee has had since the last meeting.

If the tutor is working with a tutee for the first time, the tutor must be ready to ask appropriate questions to help diagnose the tutee's areas of concern or difficulty. The main responsibility of a first session is to establish positive rapport with the tutee.

How is this done? A tutor should greet her/his tutee with friendliness and a smile. Remember, the tutee is probably more than a little nervous! Don't just jump right into tutoring. Begin by asking the tutee's name, what other classes he/she is taking, etc.—in other words, make some brief small talk. But also keep in mind that this is a working session, not a social session.

The tutor then asks the tutee to describe as specifically as possible the area(s) of concern or difficulty, using appropriate questioning skills, not interrogation. The tutor is advised to take notes about what the tutee is saying. In fact, it is a good idea for tutors to keep a file or reference sheet for each tutee. This file could be as simple or as complex as the tutor wishes to make it. Some things to include would be: the tutee's name, class he/she is seeking help with, what the specific areas of difficulty are, what diagnoses the tutor makes, and what the tutor prescribes be done in as much detail as possible. It is also important to note what the tutee is going to do before the next session and detail what the tutee will bring to the next tutoring session. Of course, the tutor goes over these notes with the tutee to make sure the information is complete, accurate, and understood.

2. The tutor should make sure that both the tutor and the tutee ask questions and make comments as the sessions progress. It is not a one-way communication process. The tutor asks questions and explains and the tutee must be encouraged to do the same. Some tutees may be a little reluctant at first to join in the dialogue for any number of reasons, ranging from it not being the custom in their culture to being shy or embarrassed. If the tutee is reluctant, the tutor may help open the dialogue by asking the tutee to now explain the process back to him/her, to "teach" the tutor, or to summarize the session.

3. Tutors must be willing to take the sessions one step at a time and one thing at a time and not rush through or assume the tutee has specific knowledge. An entire essay cannot be written in one tutoring session, but the tutor can help the tutee write a good outline or topic sentence.

4. Tutors must know when to "sit back and be quiet!" Rapid-fire questions or instructions are not going to help the tutor or the tutee. It is the responsibility of the effective tutor to give the tutee "time to think through" an answer, idea, or instruction. An effective tutor realizes that silence can be an effective tutoring tool and understands when to use it.

5. At the end of the tutoring session, don't just say, "Well, time's up. See you next time." The tutor should take time to summarize what was done and accomplished during the session. A good way to do this is to ask the tutee to comment on or summarize the session. (This can be a way to draw out

the tutee who is reluctant to talk.) Be sure to jot these comments down on the tutee's reference sheet taking time to detail what the tutee will do or prepare for the next session. Again, make notes of what is discussed so that both tutor and tutee know and are in agreement. Make sure to end the session on a positive note by praising the tutee on his/her hard work and progress.

Other qualities of effective tutors:

1.   patient
2.   empathic, supportive, and nonjudgmental
3.   resourceful and flexible
4.   respectful of differences

Responsibilities and Qualities of the Tutee

What are some of the qualities and responsibilities of the tutees? These are very important to the ultimate success of the tutor/tutee relationship and should be discussed at the first session. Tutees must be aware of their role in the class and in the tutoring session and that they are responsible for their subsequent academic success or failure.

1.   Tutees must attend all class meetings. It is the tutee's responsibility to "acquire" the material in the first place. A tutor cannot possibly help if the tutee comes to the session saying: "I missed class the other day, so I don't know what we're supposed to do." This is especially crucial if the tutor is in the writing lab and not present in the class. If this is the case, the tutor should point out to the tutee that it is the tutee's responsibility to attend class, to be aware of what is assigned, due dates, etc. NOT the tutor's. If the tutor is present in the class, then it may be handled differently with the tutor explaining the assignment. However, the tutor is not the professor and the tutee should not ask or expect the tutor to repeat a missed lecture.

2.   Tutees must read class material, texts, handouts, supplementary material, etc., before attending class and before attending the tutoring session. The tutees should be encouraged to review their class notes daily.

3.   Tutees should come to the tutoring session prepared. After the first introductory session, there should be no reason for the tutee to come to a session without being ready to work and this should be very succinctly explained during the first session.

4.   Tutees should come to the tutoring session willing to be active participants. This is what often differentiates the tutoring session from the class setting. There is the opportunity in the tutoring session for real give-and-take participation that is not always present in the class.

Methods and Techniques

Tutoring is a challenging experience, and effective tutors will have at their disposal a variety of methods and techniques. Tutors will want to adapt and modify any method or technique to meet the individual needs of their tutees. Some techniques will be fairly straightforward, others involve a more circuitous approach, but whatever the approach, flexibility will be the cornerstone. Flexibility means that the tutor realizes that not all methods or techniques will be successful with all tutees and tries something else. Flexibility also means that the tutor realizes that some techniques or methods may not be appropriate to use with certain tutees and always takes into account the personal and cultural differences, comfort levels, and preferred learning styles, etc. when engaging the tutee(s).

When working with the tutee who needs minimal content area help, one of the most straightforward methods is simply letting the tutee start work. The tutor goes over the assignment with the tutee, ascertains that the tutee understands the directions and the requirements of the assignment and then lets the tutee begin work. The tutor must "check in" periodically with the tutee (i.e., every 15 minutes or so), to ensure that the tutee is still on target and asks if there are any questions or concerns, addresses those, and then goes on. This method lets the tutee have an anchor with the tutor while exploring the assignment on his/her own.

Some tutees will need more specific help. The tutor could, after diagnosing the areas of concern with the tutee, suggest a specific step-by-step approach. By delineating the process with the tutee, the tutor then leaves the tutee to work on point one. Example: when the tutee is working in a workbook the tutor would review the directions with the tutee; stand by while the tutee works through a few examples; check those examples and discuss them with the tutee; provide more examples; and let the tutee work on those examples for a specific period of time. Checking at the end of the allotted and agreed-upon time and reviewing with the tutee the work completed, the tutee will probably be ready to move to step two and so on.

Some may recognize this as a variation on successive approximation from general psychology class. Yes, it is, and it is an effective technique. By letting the tutee progress at his/her own rate through a process with success at each step as the reward, the goal of the desired end behavior can be reached without undue stress for the tutee or tutor.

It is not always possible, however, to give unlimited time to the acquisition of an end behavior or skill. A variation would be to piggy back skills and to address two or three skills at a time. Again, this can be done with a workbook in the tutoring session and supplemented with extra examples to be done by the tutee before the next session. At the next session, the homework is reviewed and discussed, and may be reinforced by asking the tutee to self-check with several more examples; and then move on. Any of these methods can easily be done one on one or while working with several tutees with similar difficulties.

Another method/technique that can be successful is a variation of role reversal. This is like the old adage: you don't really know something until you have to teach it to someone else. After the tutee has gained mastery of a particular skill or has overcome a particular area of difficulty, the tutor asks the tutee to "teach or tutor it back." This can give the tutee another way of looking at the skill and help instill a sense of confidence with the skill.

Yet another variation might be to ask the tutee what she/he thinks the first step might be in mastering a skill, the second step, third and so on. This can give the tutee a real sense that there is a process, as well as a scope and sequence to the skill while at the same time enhancing the tutee's critical thinking skills.

Other methods and techniques include game reviews which can be done one on one or in a group situation. A variation on *Jeopardy!* with a group of tutees can be a fun and very worthwhile review or exit activity. The tutees can actively participate by providing the "answers" to the categories (skill areas) the tutor provides. The tutees can then draw at random the "answers" and provide the appropriate question and an example.

EXAMPLE 1:

Category: Parts of Speech

Answer: "...tells what the subject is doing and when the subject does the action."

Question: "What is an action verb?"

Example: "Mac correctly answered the question."

EXAMPLE 2:

Category: Punctuation

Answer: "...joins two independent clauses whose ideas and sentence structure are related."

Question: "What is one use for a semicolon?"

Example: "Kacee wanted to go to the movies; Phoebe Anne phoned the theatre for the show times."

Whatever the methods or techniques the tutor uses, it is crucial for the tutor to have an understanding of individual learning styles. Is the tutee an auditory learner, a visual learner, or a hands-on learner? If the tutee is an auditory learner, the tutor may enhance the tutoring session by making audio tapes for the tutee. These tapes may have examples, directions, self-tests, reviews, etc. for the tutee to listen to, complete, and then discuss with the tutor as the session ending activity. The tutee could also make her/his own audio study or review tapes to enhance the class or tutoring activities. A tutee may benefit from talking through a writing assignment on tape, making a verbal/auditory outline or brainstorming session, then progressing to the writing stage.

If the tutee is a visual learner, it may be beneficial for the tutor to introduce the concept or idea of mapping to complement traditional outlining. Many tutees benefit from being able to draw a picture or diagram of an assignment before putting it into words. A simple example of this for writing an essay discussing three causes of the American Civil War might be: Step one: draw a train. On the engine put the topic, on the first train car indicate what is going to be discussed first, i.e., the first cause, on the second car the second cause, on the third car the third cause. Step two: go back and load each car with details that will support, explain, or identify. Step three: look at the couplings of the cars, how the cars are joined to one another. In other words, what is the transition from one car (paragraph) to the other? Step four: add on the caboose or the summary. A concept map does not have to be a work of art; it only has to be a useful tool to help get thoughts on paper so they can be seen and then written about.

If the tutee is a hands-on learner, a variation of the concept of mapping may be useful. Instead of drawing a picture, the tutee could use index cards or sheets of paper to write ideas on and then rearrange them. A hands-on learner may benefit from working on a particular area of interest in the tutoring session and then transferring that process to the class topic. For example, if a tutee is experiencing difficulty writing a paper on an assigned topic, it may be helpful to start with something the tutee enjoys, like a hobby. If the tutee can discuss the step-by-step process of something he/she enjoys, it is sometimes easier to translate that to something else.

When working with special needs tutees, the tutor must be aware of a variety of things that can have special bearing on the techniques and methods used. There are many types of special needs ranging from sight and hearing impaired to the older, nontraditional student, to the underprepared student. When working with sight-impaired students, for example, tutors could provide audio-taped exercises, activities, explanations and examples or enlarged print materials. The tutor must remember that detailed descriptions and specificity are crucial for the sight-impaired student; and the tutor realizes that more time may be needed to address skill areas and allows for this in the tutoring sessions.

When working with hearing-impaired tutees, the tutor will want to become aware of the proper procedure to use when working with the tutee and his/her signer. The tutor must be cognizant of the fact that he/she is working with and speaking with the tutee and to direct questions, answers, comments, and discussions to the tutee and not the signer. The tutor will want to use more visuals, diagrams, handouts, etc. and the tutor will provide a copy for the signer as well. The tutor should be aware of where she/he is sitting or standing in relation to the tutee—it is best to be across from rather than beside the tutee with the signer close beside the tutor.

Tutors are also advised that American Sign Language is a language, not just a system of signals, so some concepts do not translate easily. When a tutee is having difficulty it is crucial to have several variations, explanations or examples readily at hand to share with the tutee. Hearing-impaired tutees may read lips, so tutors should always be aware of possible "word filters" that can interfere: their head positions, back lighting, beards and mustaches, speaking very quickly, hands around the mouth, etc.

Mobility-impaired tutees may be working with a note-taker or writer so the tutor would want to take that into consideration when working with the tutee. Some tutees may require lap boards or special desks/tables in order to work most effectively.

The older or nontraditional tutee may need extra time to practice or at least dust off a skill that has not been used in a while, such as formal, academic writing or typing. The tutee may need time and encouragement to practice a newly acquired skill, such as using the computer.

Cultural differences are also factors to consider when tutoring. What may be perfectly acceptable in the tutor's culture may be just the opposite to the tutee—so when in doubt ask the tutee. "Shall I sit next to you or do you prefer that I sit across the table from you?" "You seem uncomfortable when I stand next to you while you are sitting and working. Is this inappropriate?" "Would you prefer to work with a female tutor (a male tutor)?" These may be appropriate questions to ask of any tutee when the tutor is in doubt.

Where can the tutor go for more information or additional resources concerning tutoring methods and techniques? Certainly the tutor should be aware of the help and support a professor can give. The writing professor may have instructor manuals, video or audio tapes, workbooks, exams, sample projects and assignments, a variety of textbooks, overhead transparencies, etc. that the tutor could use as tutoring adjuncts. A study skills professor may have similar material from his/her class that could be used to help address a particular deficit such as note taking or time management. A professor from another discipline may serve as a mentor to the tutor and offer particular insight about preparing written assignments for his/her particular discipline that the tutor could in turn share with tutees.

A very beneficial resource is other tutors. It is an extremely good idea for tutors to meet as a group to discuss and share ideas, concerns, problems, and successes. These meetings could be weekly or at least monthly. The tutor meetings could revolve around a specific topic or concern, for example: "How to tutor the reluctant tutee." This could provide tutors with a forum to share what has worked or what has not worked for them. The meetings could involve specific tutoring techniques such as role playing. Veteran tutors could assume the role of a reluctant tutee and novice tutors would take on the regular tutor role. By rehearsing in a role-playing situation, the novice tutors are given a chance to "try on" techniques and get immediate feedback from the veterans. Tutors can offer one another support, solace, advice, and reinforcement.

The tutor meetings could also include a guest speaker or discussion leader. The guest speaker could be a content area professor, a counselor, a coach, the tutor supervisor/trainer, a tutor from a different tutoring center or department on campus, a community leader, a member of the minority students affairs office or disabled student services, or one of the cultural organizations or clubs from campus.

Whatever the methods and techniques used, and the adaptations and variations made to them, the goal of tutoring is to help the tutee become a self-sufficient and successful student.

Recruitment

Where are the tutors to be found? Well, the answer may be surprising.

Perhaps the first place to start is right within the class. There are usually very skillful students in all classes who would be very good subject area tutors. They may be hesitant to come forward on their own, but the professor would certainly have an idea of who in the class might be an appropriate candidate after the first four or six weeks of the semester. If there are several sessions of the same class, the professor may want to recruit tutors from class A to tutor students in class B and vise versa. Former students are also good candidates to contact.

Professors may try recruiting from other classes in the department. Upper level writing students or graduate students might be the perfect candidates to tutor in the developmental or first-year writing classes. Students who are majors in disciplines other than English but who are English minors may be good prospects as are students majoring in disciplines that require good writing, for example, history or philosophy.

Schools or colleges of education may also be prime places to solicit tutors. Elementary or secondary education majors may welcome the opportunity to practice and hone skills, perhaps as part of a practicum course.

Existing tutoring centers on campus may have a surplus of tutors or underused tutors already trained and ready to go.

It is not uncommon to find retirees either on campus or in the community with specific skills who are more than willing to take on the role of tutor. A retired elementary or secondary school teacher, a retired English or writing professor, a former journalist, or professional writer may be a real boon to the tutoring community.

Specific student agencies on campus such as disabled student services or advising and counseling may be a source for tutors who already have specific tutor training in working with special needs students.

Cultural organizations or clubs on campus or in the community may be the place to seek tutors who have bilingual skills that would be beneficial.

Sororities, fraternities, or service organizations on campus may provide tutors as part of the group's community service commitment.

Athletic departments, departmental clubs, or organizations are also places to investigate.

Announcements may be aired on the college or university radio and/or TV station; as well as articles placed in the school and community newspapers. Additionally, notices can be placed on bulletin boards in the writing lab, classrooms, department offices, student center, counseling center, etc.

The next question is: "What about compensation?" Most tutors are volunteers but there are ways of expressing appreciation for their hard work when monetary compensation is not an option.

- Extra credit or independent study credit if tutors come from the class or from other classes in the department.
- Tuition waiver for the course: this, of course, would be dependent upon department or school policy.
- Textbook allowance for a course.
- Certifications of appreciation presented during the school's annual awards ceremony.
- Special recognition certificates or awards from the dean's office, department chair, and/or writing lab director.
- Inscribed plaque with tutors' names displayed in the department or writing lab.
- Articles in the school and community newspapers describing the tutors' contributions and a listing of their names.
- Announcements of appreciation on campus radio or TV and/or community stations.
- The opportunity to register early for certain department classes that tend to close or fill early.
- An end-of-the-semester party, luncheon, or dinner for tutors sponsored by the department or writing lab.
- A detailed letter of appreciation from the professor, department chair, and/or writing lab supervisor that the tutor can use as a reference letter or in a résumé or vita.
- Other possibilities include: special T-shirts, coffee mugs, tote bags, hats, discount arrangement with the bookstore or campus center, etc.

As with any job that is important but not recompensed, it is crucial for the workers, in this case, the tutors, to know that what they do is important, respected and appreciated.

Tutor Training

The people who become tutors have content area expertise, skill, or knowledge and a desire to share that expertise, skill, or knowledge; otherwise, why would they want to be tutors? What these tutors may be lacking are some specific "tutoring skills." Certainly these skills can be picked up by trial and error, but this may hinder and interfere with the tutoring process. It is especially important to train tutors in some specific tutoring skills before they actually start working with the tutees. Creating a packet of material for tutors is also helpful and allows tutors to revisit procedures and to look up answers they may have as they tutor.

What should tutor training include? The following is a list of topics and suggestions that the professors, writing lab personnel and novice tutors can adapt and modify according to the specific needs of the students served.

Tutors can be trained in the following tutoring skill areas:

1. Definition of tutoring and specific tutor and tutee responsibilities as defined by the department or lab. This includes tutoring ethics and the tutoring philosophy of the particular program or department.

2. Basic tutoring guidelines, i.e., where tutoring will be done, when it will be done, by whom, to what end, what will and will not be included, etc.

3. How to successfully begin and end a tutoring session (one-on-one and group sessions).

4. Tutoring "do's" and "don'ts."

5. Role modeling general student success strategies and behaviors. This includes modeling specific problem-solving techniques.

6. Appropriate goal-setting and planning strategies.

7. Effective communication skills; how to appropriately question the tutee; how to effectively lead a discussion or begin a discussion.

8. Active, effective listening skills; paraphrasing.

9. How to refer the student to another resource, agency, etc. and when it is appropriate to do so.

10. Critical thinking skills and how to incorporate them into the tutoring session.

11. Specific study skills to share with the tutees: textbook-reading strategies such as the SQ3R, Cornell note-taking system or other ways to take more effective class notes, test-taking techniques, concentration, memory improvement techniques, time management, outlining, stress management, basic library skills, vocabulary development, etc.

12. Characteristics of adult learners and different learning styles.

13. Cultural awareness and sensitivity as well as cross-cultural communications; gender and age difference awareness; awareness of special needs/abilities.

14. Diagnostic techniques.

15. Recordkeeping.

16. Group management skills; group dynamics and group interactions.

17. Assertiveness training.

18. How to deal effectively with problem situations.

19. How to structure the tutoring experience.

20. How to use different tutoring approaches and tools more effectively, for example: how to make and use overhead transparencies, how and when to use computer programs, how to make and use audio or video tapes, supplementary resources, etc.

21. How to use positive reinforcement and praise to instill a sense of accomplishment in the tutee.

22. How to train other tutors; supervisory and management skills.

This list may be expanded or shortened according to the needs of the particular class or writing lab, but it is important that the tutors have a minimum level of training before they actually begin tutoring. It is important for the tutors and others involved to realize that there is more to successful tutoring than content area expertise and a desire to share that expertise. Help with the tutor training may be readily available on campus from former tutors, study skills professors, other tutoring centers on campus, learning and resource centers, or advising and counseling centers.

Students enter schools and are introduced to many different types of academic tools: resource books, computer programs, maps, charts, diagrams, equations, definitions, and theories. It is important to also introduce the student to another very important and helpful academic tool: the tutor.

Recommended Readings

Gier, Tom, and Karan Hancock, eds. *Tutor Training Handbook*. Anchorage, Alaska: College Reading & Learning Association, 1996.

MacDonald, Ross B. *The Master Tutor: A Guidebook for more Effective Tutoring*. Williamsville, NY: The Cambridge Stratford Study Skills Institute, 1994.

Maxwell, Martha, ed. *From Access to Success: A Book of Readings on College Developmental Education and Learning Assistance Programs*. Clearwater, FL: H&H Publishing Company, Inc., 1994.

Maxwell, Martha, ed. *When Tutor Meets Student*. 2nd ed. Ann Arbor: The University of Michigan Press, 1994.

Myers, Lynda B. *Becoming an Effective Tutor*. Los Altos, CA: Crisp Publications, Inc. 1990.

Making a Case for Rhetorical Grammar

By Laura R. Micciche

Grammar makes people anxious, even—perhaps especially—writing teachers. Just as writing teachers dread when, our identities discovered, strangers announce that they had better "watch their grammar," we also recoil at the idea of teaching grammar, often considered a mind-numbing pedagogical task that offends our rhetorical sensibilities. In composition studies, grammar instruction is unquestionably unfashionable. It is frequently associated with "low-skills" courses that stigmatize and alienate poor writers while reproducing their status as disenfranchised. This association emerges naturally from teaching methods that present grammar as a fix-it approach to weak writing rather than, as Martha Kolln describes, "a rhetorical tool that all writers should understand and control" (*Rhetorical Grammar* xi). As a result, students' understanding of the tight weave between what we say and how we say it often gets short shrift as we reserve instruction on grammar for the very final stage of drafting.

In composition's disciplinary discourse (and perhaps in practice, though it's hard to know), teaching grammar and teaching writing are separate enterprises. While teaching style, the "extraordinary" use of language, is a familiar enough focus in disciplinary scholarship, teaching the "ordinary" use of language—grammar—is often constructed as ineffective because, it is widely believed, grammar knowledge out of context doesn't translate to grammatical correctness in context.[1] Further complicating the problematic place of grammar in writing instruction is the matter of what *kind* of grammar we're talking about. Often *grammar* is used in a way that assumes we all understand and agree upon its meaning—and, in fact, grammar referred to loosely seems to signify traditional "school grammar" and its focus on repetitive, decontextualized, drill-and-kill exercises. However, grammar has a range of referents (i.e., prescriptive, descriptive, rhetorical) that describe very different kinds of intellectual activities, differences that matter tremendously. These differences evaporate, reducing the issue of grammar instruction to a rather simple rejection of a banal practice, when we fail to specify just what kind of grammar we're rejecting.

My aim in this paper is to establish grounds for teaching grammar rhetorically and for linking this pedagogical effort to larger goals of emancipatory teaching. Teaching grammar is not *necessarily* incompatible with liberatory principles; binaries that suggest otherwise constrain our teaching and our thinking, solidifying and casting as unquestionable rehearsed assumptions about writing. The absence of a sustained contemporary conversation about grammar instruction at the college level does not eclipse the practical reality that nearly every writing teacher struggles with at one time or another: how to teach students to communicate effectively. And effective communication, which entails grammar knowledge, is essential to achieving many of the goals regularly articulated in composition studies. Chief among them are teaching students to produce effective writing that has some relevancy to the world we live in, to see language as having an empowering and sometimes transformative potential, and to critique normalizing discourses that conceal oppressive functions.

Rhetorical grammar instruction, I argue here, is just as central to composition's driving commitment to teach critical thinking and cultural critique as is reading rhetorically, understanding the significance of cultural difference, and engaging in community work through service-learning initiatives. Yet, teaching students grammar skills is rarely associated with the political programs that characterize our disciplinary rhetoric and is seldom linked with rhetorical education or the practice of cultural critique. Grammar instruction, in short, is decidedly not sexy but school-marmish, not empowering but disempowering, not rhetorical but decontextualized, not progressive but remedial.

I hope this study of rhetorical grammar will contribute to our collective thinking about the work of rhetorical education, its possibility and its promise. Donald Bryant, in "Rhetoric: Its Functions and Its Scope," offers an instructive description of the need for rhetorical education:

> If enlightened and responsible leaders with rhetorical knowledge and skill are not trained and nurtured, irresponsible demagogues will monopolize their power of rhetoric, will have things to themselves. If talk rather than take is to settle the course of our society, if ballots instead of bullets are to effect our choice of governors, if discourse rather than coercion is to prevail in the conduct of human affairs, it would seem like arrant folly to trust to chance that the right people shall be equipped offensively and defensively with a sound rationale of informative and suasory discourse. (291)

The construction of "informative and suasory" discourse includes knowing one's audience, responding appropriately to a particular situation, and drawing on relevant examples and illustrations. As I suggest here, it also requires an ability to communicate effectively, using grammatical devices that enable us to respond appropriately and effectively to a situation. Like Bryant, I believe that rhetoric—including rhetorical grammar—should occupy a place of "uncommon importance" in general education (291). While this emphasis is consistent with that of some ancient rhetoricians,[2] contemporary rhetoricians, by omission rather than vocal opposition, tend to construct grammar as outside the realm of rhetoric.

We need a discourse about grammar that does not retreat from the realities we face in the classroom—a discourse that takes seriously the connection between writing and thinking, the interwoven relationship between what we say and how we say it. In addition, we need to ask questions about the enabling work of grammar instruction alongside composition's view of writing and its instruction as social practices that have the potential to both reproduce and challenge cultural values, truths, and assumptions. Can grammar knowledge be conceived as extending the work of cultural critique? How might we teach grammar in a way that supports rhetorical education? I believe that the examinations of language made possible through rhetorical grammar pedagogy encourage students to view writing as a material social practice in which meaning is actively made, rather than passively relayed or effortlessly produced. In this sense, rhetorical grammar instruction can demonstrate to students that language does purposeful, consequential work in the world—work that can be learned and applied.

Rhetorical grammar as a way of thinking

Let no man, therefore, look down on the elements of grammar as small matters; not because it requires great labor to distinguish consonants from vowels, and to divide them into the proper number of semivowels and mutes, but because, to those entering the recesses, as it were, of this temple, there will appear much subtlety on points, which may not only sharpen the wits of boys, but may exercise even the deepest erudition and knowledge.
—Quintilian (in Murphy 29)

The chief reason for teaching rhetorical grammar in writing classes is that doing so is central to teaching thinking. The ability to develop sentences and form paragraphs that serve a particular purpose requires a conceptual ability to envision relationships between ideas. Such relationships involve processes of identification with an imagined or real reader and reflection on the way our language invites and/or alienates readers. The grammatical choices we make—including pronoun use, active or passive verb constructions, and sentence patterns—represent relations between writers and the world they live in. Word choice and sentence structure are an expression of the way we attend to the words of others, the way we position ourselves in relation to others. In this sense, writing involves cognitive skills at the level of idea development *and* at the sentence level. How we put our ideas into words and comprehensible forms is a dynamic process rather than one with clear boundaries between what we say and how we say it.

Of course, linking grammar and conceptual thinking is not the first thing that comes to mind when we think of teaching grammar. Usually, our minds go to those unending rules and exceptions, those repetitive drills and worksheets, perhaps even to diagramming sentences with a ruler, performing a quasi-scientific operation on language (one that I found particularly satisfying while in middle school). These are the hallmarks of formal grammar instruction, the deadening effects of which are widely known. A familiar argument against teaching formal grammar, particularly forceful since the rise of process pedagogies, insists that integrating grammar instruction would dangerously reduce time spent on higher-order concerns like invention and arrangement. Another argument contends that if students can't articulate their ideas in a comprehensible form, correct grammar does nothing to improve their writing. Both lines of argument rely on the faulty assumption that grammar instruction means only *formal* grammar instruction, the deadly kind that teaches correctness divorced from content and situation. Both lines of argument keep intact the binary that defines grammar instruction in opposition to composing and thinking, a binary that reproduces the notion that grammar-talk is most appropriate for the end stage of drafting.

When grammar is reserved for end-stage drafting, it is most often a version of formal grammar or "school grammar." The following passage, excerpted from the *Instructor's Manual and Answer Key to Accompany The Writer's Harbrace Handbook*, provides a familiar, though not an isolated, example of just what generates fear and paranoia in students and teachers alike:

> Once we diagnose and show students how to correct errors, then they must correct them consistently. Making comments about errors on drafts and then requiring students to turn in revisions provide immediate practice. However, only through subsequent assignments, however [sic], can we assess students' mastery over errors. Therefore, instructors and students should record errors, and instructors should hold students accountable for correcting those errors. (Winchell 21)

The orientation to grammar here is error driven and disciplinary, as evidenced in the description of efforts to "diagnose," "record," and "correct" errors. The goal is student "mastery over errors," resulting in self-conscious correction. Intentionally or not, the framework is one of finding and fixing errors rather than of active choice making for a purpose. Rhetorical grammar instruction, in contrast, emphasizes grammar as a tool for articulating and expressing relationships among ideas. The purpose of learning rhetorical grammar is to learn how to generate persuasive, clear thinking that reflects on and responds to language as work, as *produced* rather than evacuated of imperfections.

How we think and give shape to ideas is intimately tied up with the forms, patterns, and rhythms of spoken and written language. Thus, writing is profoundly reflective of the deep grammars that we absorb as inhabitants of a particular place and time. For this reason, when we reserve grammar-talk for the end of the drafting stage, I think we miss opportunities to discuss with students how the particulars of language use show us something about the way we figure relationships among people, ideas, and texts. Writing teachers need to be able to talk about how a well-coordinated sentence can keep your reader breathlessly moving with you, how techniques that create rhythm and emphasis heighten the feeling being conveyed, how subordination expresses relationships among ideas, how someone like Eminem uses repetition and power words—or words of emphasis—to create culturally relevant and, for some people, resonant stories.

More than a systematic application of rules, Mina Shaughnessy reminds us, grammar involves "a way of thinking, a style of inquiry," as opposed to "a way of being right" (129). For instance, we learn through Quintilian's excerpt above that *men* and *boys* are the subjects of education; his word choice reveals his "way of thinking" about who is entitled to an education. His male referents point to the real exclusion—as opposed to functioning as convenient place-holders for all people—of women and girls from the educational enterprise in the eighteenth century. When we broaden the goals of rhetorical grammar, it's possible to see how the intimate study of language it encourages has enormous potential for studying language as central to constructions of identity and culture. Rhetorical grammar enables such readings because it is "grammar in the service of rhetoric," which means that grammar is never divorced from ideological functions (Kolln, "Rhetorical Grammar" 29).

I am talking about rhetorical grammar as an integral component of critical writing, writing that at minimum seeks to produce new knowledge and critique stale thinking. One of the key operations of critical writing is that it locates an object of discourse in space and time, thereby placing it in a system of relationships. Joan Didion, in "Why I Write," describes this function when commenting on grammar's "infinite power": "All I know about grammar is its infinite power. To shift the structure of sentence alters the meaning of that sentence, as definitely and inflexibly as the position of a camera alters the meaning of the object photographed" (7). As Didion's comment suggests, grammar is a positioning tool, a way of framing and presenting ideas that influences how and what we see.

This shaping of meaning through writing is intimately connected with a writer's grammatical choices. Elizabeth Bruss illuminates this idea in her brilliant study of the discourse of literary theory, *Beautiful Theories*. She suggests that the rhetoric of grammar is an important factor in the construction and consumption of theoretical discourse, and it tells us something about the "mind" in the writing. She explains, "In reading theory, one often notes where the energy of the writing seems to have been expended—in lush diction or well-turned phrases, in the juxtaposition between sentences or organization of larger episodes. From this, one receives a first (if not always a lasting) impression of the power or delicacy of mind that informs the theory" (117). She notes that the "manipulation of syntax" in theoretical writing creates a "disturbing sense of disorientation," a point that nicely describes the way grammar and content work together in theoretical writing to disturb settled or "natural" ways of thinking (122).

Referring to language as "conceptual machinery," Bruss observes: "One comes to know the nature of this machinery through watching how it functions and using it for oneself, rather than by visualizing or possessing it as a set of properties" (131). Bruss's emphasis on *use* as a way to test and experiment with the possibilities of language informs my commonplace book assignment, designed for teaching rhetorical grammar. As demonstrated in the student writing samples in the next section, the study of rhetorical grammar encourages students to experiment with language and then to reflect on the interaction between content and grammatical form. While this approach entails study of sentence slots, structures like participial phrases and adverbials that add information to a sentence, and the difference between independent and dependent clauses, rhetorical grammar more generally requires students to think about the work these aspects of grammar achieve for a writer's message. In practical terms, as well as identifying a dependent clause, students are asked to construct a sentence with a dependent clause in it and to explain the discursive effects of subordinating one idea to another.

Among other things, I want students to consider how such a sentence-level choice might reflect configurations of power in a more general sense. Explaining how discursive practices signify more than technical skill, Michel Foucault writes, "Discursive practices are not purely and simply ways of producing discourse. They are embodied in technical processes, in institutions, in patterns for general behavior, in forms for transmission and diffusion, and in pedagogical forms which, at once, impose and maintain them" (128). To illustrate just how language practices are embodied in cultural institutions, I have asked students to read a variety of texts that bring this issue to life. Selections have included George Orwell's "Politics and the English Language," bell hooks's "Language," excerpts from Robin Lakoff's *Language and Woman's Place*, and James Baldwin's "If Black Language Isn't a Language, Then Tell Me, What Is?" In different ways, each reading offers students a framework for understanding how grammar and language practices are schooled and maintained in culture. In addition, we learn that grammar use can sometimes function as a form of resistance, a point that bell hooks discusses in relation to slave songs. She writes that the English in these songs "reflected the broken, ruptured world of the slave. When the slaves sang 'nobody knows de trouble I see—' their use of the word 'nobody' adds a richer meaning than if they had used the phrase 'no one,' for it was the slave's *body* that was the concrete site of suffering" (170). hooks argues that the syntax of the songs did not change over the years because "the incorrect usage of words" expressed "a spirit of rebellion that claimed language as a site of resistance" (170). hooks's essay, along with the readings named above, encourages my students to think about grammar as a crucial tool for both communication and the expression of identity. This way of thinking about grammar often challenges students' preconceptions about grammar as a rigid system for producing correctness, preparing them for the commonplace book assignment described below.

Getting close to language

I emphasize the rhetorical aspects of grammar by asking students to focus on connections between grammar and concepts such as audience and purpose, paying particular attention to grammar as an art of selection. I want students to consider how and why discourses take the form they do, seeing discourse as a production that involves work and intention and craft. In setting up a classroom study of grammar as rhetorically produced, I use Kolln's *Rhetorical Grammar* as the primary theoretical framework, supplemented by excerpts on figures of thought from Sharon Crowley's *Ancient Rhetorics for Contemporary Students*. My course[3] is based on the assumption that learning how to use grammar to best effect requires lots of practice and a good deal of exposure to varied writing styles. To this end, students maintain a commonplace book throughout the semester in which they imitate and record passages of their own choosing. In *Ancient Rhetorics* Crowley explains the history of commonplace books as follows: "In pre-modern times, most rhetors kept written collections of copied passages; these were called *florilegia* (flowers of reading) in medieval times, and **commonplace books** during the Renaissance and into the eighteenth century" (250; emphasis in original). She defines such a book as "a notebook kept by a rhetor as a storehouse of materials to be remembered or quoted" (335).

As I have conceived the commonplace book, students follow each entry with at least one paragraph of analysis in which they identify the work achieved by specific grammatical techniques in the passage. I ask students to look critically at writing by analyzing passages from their favorite authors, literature and textbooks they are reading in other courses, syllabi, Web-based texts, television advertisements, segments from presidential debates—in short, any text that students find interesting. I have two goals for the commonplace books: first, to emphasize the always entangled relationship between *what* and *how* we say something; second, to designate a place where students document and comment on their evolving relationship to writing and grammatical concepts. Both goals circulate around the idea that learning how to recognize and reflect on language as *made* and *made to work on* people's lives is central to being able to use language strategically.

Commonplace books encourage students to read and analyze texts as skillfully crafted documents that convey and perform different kinds of meanings—among them, aesthetic, rhetorical, and political. Students are able to tinker with language, seeing how it is crafted and directed rather than as simply "correct" or "incorrect." Thinking of language as correct or incorrect distorts it into an objective medium consisting of ahistorical rules and truths, obscuring the living quality of language. This aliveness—the changing, transforming capacity of language—is what makes the study of rhetorical grammar especially relevant and necessary. Rhetorical grammar offers a perspective on the way people purposefully use language to describe problematic or possible new realities. It presents students with a framework and a vocabulary for examining how language affects and infects social reality, as it also provides them with tools for creating effective discourse.

Understanding how language is made and then deployed for varying effects has the potential to highlight the important work of language in our culture. This goal is especially important at the present time, as political dissent is increasingly under suspicion, and the USA Patriot Act of 2001 threatens speech acts both within and beyond the classroom. An ability to examine closely and carefully the work of language could influence discussions of political texts in the classroom. For instance, in my fall 2002 Functional Grammar class, students analyzed the grammar of President Bush's speech to the United Nations on 12 September 2002. The speech, printed in the *New York Times on the Web*, sought to present evidence to the U.N. that would make a case for moving "deliberately and decisively to hold Iraq to account" for its harboring of weapons of mass destruction. In a large-group discussion, my students analyzed Bush's use of hedging, or qualification of claims. They noted the following language choices: "U.N. inspectors *believe* Iraq has produced two to four times the amount of biological agents it declared"; "United Nations inspections also reveal that Iraq *likely* maintains stockpiles of VX, mustard, and other chemical agents. . ."; if not for the Gulf War, "the regime in Iraq would *likely* have possessed a nuclear weapon no later than 1993" ("Bush's Speech"; emphasis added).

The students examination of hedging, demonstrated by Bush's word choice, evolved into a lively discussion about what counts as evidence in the context of declaring war; indeed, more recently, critics worldwide have begun asking questions about the "facts" regarding Iraq's weapons development program. This example is meant to suggest that rhetorical grammar analysis can form the basis for wider analyses of civic discourse, enabling students to hone in on the specific grammatical choices that give shape and meaning to content. While the following student applications of rhetorical grammar analysis do not take this sort of politicized focus, the close study of how grammar enhances and conceals meaning can certainly be applied in this way.

I ask students to make a variety of entries in their commonplace books. Recordings are entries that require students to record a passage of their own choosing and then analyze how grammar and content work together to convey meaning. In the following recording,[4] the student writer illustrates how language works on her as a reader. She records a passage from Washington Irving's "Rip Van Winkle." Rip comes down the mountain after being asleep for twenty years and is confused by the amount of time that has elapsed and by the figure, which turns out to be his son, who looks remarkably like Rip himself. "'God knows,' exclaimed [Rip], at his wit's end; 'I'm not myself—I'm somebody else—I'm somebody else—that's me yonder—no—that's somebody else got into my shoes—I was myself last night, but I fell asleep on the mountain, and they've changed my gun and every thing's changed, and I'm changed, and I can't tell my name, or who I am!'" In her analysis, this student writes,

> I think Irving does a great job of showing the puzzlement Rip Van Winkle feels when he comes down the mountain and doesn't know himself or anyone else. The use of dashes in this text is effective, which is sometimes hard to accomplish. If dashes are overused, the reader can get confused and have a hard time grasping the feeling the author is trying to convey. But in this passage, Irving uses dashes to help the reader understand how Rip is feeling. Rip is disoriented, confused, and he feels lost. The dashes break up his thoughts, and the reader can hear the panic he is feeling.
>
> The structure of the sentence also conveys the alarm Rip feels. As I read the passage out loud, I found that my voice got higher and I read faster as I got toward the end. The emphasis is put on the end of the sentence, and this lets the reader know that Rip is getting more and more upset as his thoughts go on.

This analysis explains how grammatical techniques intertwine with meaning to convey Rip's confusion. When the writer points out that the dashes help the reader to experience Rip's fragmented sense of identity, she demonstrates her ability to see that meaning emerges from the very specific marks a writer chooses. The writer's analysis offers a reading of how feeling is suspended in this passage, which creates, to borrow from Bruss, an "impression of the power or delicacy of mind" that shapes the narrative (117).

Other commonplace entries include imitations of a writer's form—not, it should be noted, imitations of content.[5] In these entries, the student writer must not only mimic the writer's syntax, but must also identify the specific effects created by the syntax. In an example from Brian's commonplace book, he begins with a quotation from Harper Lee's *To Kill A Mockingbird*. In this scene, Atticus, a lawyer, is questioning Mr. Ewell to determine why he failed to retrieve a doctor to examine his daughter who was allegedly raped. "'Mr. Ewell,' Atticus began, 'folks were doing a lot of running that night. Let's see, you say you ran to the house, you ran to the window, you ran inside, you ran to Mayella, you ran for Mr. Tate. Did you, during all this running, run for a doctor?'" In his analysis, Brian writes,

> Lee, through Atticus, uses parallelism to emphasize that Mr. Ewell seemed to be running everywhere. By beginning each clause with *you ran*, he adds emphasis each

time as he builds to the final point. Lee uses an asyndeton series style sentence to add emphasis to the final point. By using this type of series, there is no *and* used between each item in the series. This absence says to the reader that I could go on and on. This type of series is important in the underlying motive of the statement. Atticus is trying to emphasize that Mr. Ewell should have run for a doctor. By using the asyndeton series, he is saying that you ran here, you ran there, and I could go on and on pointing out where you did run, but the most important thing is that you didn't run to the doctor.

Having decided that Lee's passage is similar to "the kinds of speeches a coach might give his team for motivation," Brian creates the following imitation: "'Boys,' the coach began, 'this team has been doing a lot of scoring on us today. Let's see, they scored on a free kick, they scored on a header, they scored on a penalty kick, they scored on a cross, they scored on a nice shot. Did you, during all their scoring, score any of your own?'"

A similar attention to the grammatical work of a passage characterizes Chris's analysis of one passage in Kurt Vonnegut's *Breakfast of Champions*. Explaining Vonnegut's use of the word *charm* in a passage, Chris writes,

> In his definition, Vonnegut uses the word "charm" in one form or another six times within five sentences, and he uses the word "oodles" three times. He also uses the same basic sentence structure for the last three sentences. These repetitions convey the satirical nature of the explanation. That is, Vonnegut is mocking the word by over doing its definition. Rather than combining the subjects in the last three sentences and making one compound sentence, Vonnegut chooses to repeat the same sentence format three times in a row. This has the effect of enforcing each separate subjects place in the explanation. In this case the word comes out as being somewhat discredited. Vonnegut's point is that lots of people have charm and those who don't can usually fake it.

Drawing on descriptions of sentence structure and repetition that Kolln describes in *Rhetorical Grammar*, Chris shows us how Vonnegut reinforces the idea of the passage through grammatical techniques. He chose to examine Vonnegut's work because he had always admired it and wanted to get a better look at how Vonnegut creates such an effective tone. By requiring students to select texts to record or imitate in their commonplace books, this assignment can work well to get students to look closely at language that pleases or disturbs them. Students are pushed to think in unfamiliar ways about texts to which they have developed familiar responses. Or, in some cases, students analyzed texts that they come into contact with on a regular basis but never read attentively.

Getting close to a passage in order to reveal the technical processes that make it work forms the basis of another student's reading of Ambrose Bierce's story, "An Occurrence at Owl Creek Bridge." This excerpt, taken from a student's grammatical analysis paper,[6] was originally a recording in her commonplace book. In her discussion of Bierce's use of parallelism, she writes,

> Bierce masters this technique, and seems to understand the effects that it has on the rhythm: "The water, the banks, the forest, the now distant bridge, fort, and men— all were commingled and blurred" (86). To achieve parallelism, Bierce repeats "the," followed by a noun phrase, four times. He opts not to use it, though he has the opportunity, a fifth and sixth time—doing this may make the parallelism redundant or gratuitous. Bierce thoughtfully controls the rhythm of this sentence. The reader is

made to slow down where the word "the" appears—it takes more time to say "the water" than to say "water." Furthermore, the sentence gets progressively slower as we push through "the now distant bridge" and then are set free by the sleek, and fast flow of "fort, and men." This control of rhythm relates to control of emphasis, and thus drama. We emphasize the words following "the" simply because we slow down and have more time to absorb the image. Correspondingly, we pass over words without the "the" in front of them and do not have time to savor their meanings.

This writer's analysis highlights Bierce's use of momentum and rhythm to mirror the feeling of the passage. As I think her reading illustrates, the closeness to language encouraged by the commonplace book assignment requires students to dig around in the writing of others and really think about what makes it tick. This intimacy with the language of others can be an enormously powerful way to impress upon students that writing is made and that grammar has a role in that production. In addition, the commonplace book assignment offers a productive space where students document their sense of writing as reflecting intentional choices that have consequences.

While the examples I've included draw from literary texts, I want to note that my students have selected a variety of texts as the basis for commonplace book entries. These have included billing information accompanying phone bills and credit card bills, instruction manuals for appliances, text on food packaging, advertisements, textbooks, and syllabi. Whatever the textual source for entries, the model of rhetorical grammar pedagogy described here can be an asset to teaching practices that view analytical thinking as a necessary component of any socially engaged pedagogy.

Rhetorical grammar and empowering pedagogies

Composition scholars have yet to map out the potentially productive connections between rhetorical grammar and composition's disciplinary commitment to cultural difference and ethical rhetoric. What's notable about liberatory pedagogies of the 1980s and 1990s is not that they reject grammar instruction but that grammar is largely absent from their descriptions of critical education. The higher level concerns of liberatory pedagogies focused on creating social change by teaching students skills with which to challenge cultural norms (Berlin; Fitts and France; Luke and Gore) and by articulating teaching and writing as cultural practices that transmit and produce cultural meanings (Giroux and McLaren; Sullivan and Qualley). Internal analyses of composition's identity as a discipline have revealed the troubling working conditions and wages of part-time teachers (Schell); the gender, race, and class politics of composition studies (Bullock and Trimbur; Jarratt and Worsham); and the relationship between pedagogy and diverse student populations (Ashton-Jones; Severino et al.).

This body of work has profoundly shaped my intellectual and political orientation in composition studies, and I believe that its politicized dimensions can provide insights about teaching grammar as a study of how language does work *in* (and sometimes *against*) the world. Gary Olson's "Encountering the Other" offers a framework for considering this claim. Olson notes that composition studies has increasingly come to focus on "issues of gender, race, or 'contact zones'" as an ethical commitment to foregrounding "interaction with an Other" (92). Ethics, for him, deals with "how we balance our own needs, desires, and obligations with those of the Other" (92). This balancing act, which requires careful consideration of self/other relations, is relevant to grammatical choices that writers make because it is part of the conceptual work that we do as writers. We envision and construct an audience through diction, tone, and the selection of examples; and as writers we seek to reach across the space that separates us from our audience, using techniques that engender trust, establish credibility, and sometimes build connection.

A student in my sophomore-level Writing with Style course demonstrates how attention to grammatical choices dovetails with an understanding of self/other relations in his analysis of the grammar and style that typifies Malcolm X's writing. He argues that Malcolm X's use of "you" in "Not Just an American Problem but a World Problem" involves his African American audience in an intimate way:

> Speaking in the second person helps urge audience members to personally take responsibility for creating a political change and becoming active participants in the revolt for racial equality . . . . By constantly using words and phrases that signify "togetherness" to refer to himself and his audience, Malcolm urges African-Americans to organize and unify.

Throughout his paper, this student examines how grammatical choices reinforce Malcolm X's emphasis on black unity as a necessary component of meaningful social change, a focus that centers on the relations between the speaker and conditions in the world. Like other forms of textual analysis, grammatical analysis can yield engaged political and cultural insights about language as "the carrier of culture, the facilitator of humanity, and the most powerful of the means of social control" (Sledd 62).

Such insights form the basis of critical pedagogy, which reveals how language constructs and reproduces oppressive cultural discourses that naturalize inequality. For instance, Ira Shor describes critical pedagogy as a teaching method that "questions the *status quo*," and is consistent with democratic values, political activism aimed at eliminating inequalities, and efforts toward "desocializing" (3). Critical pedagogy, for Shor, entails a questioning "posture towards the construction of the self in society" (16), a model of inquiry that is also key to Krista Ratcliffe's conceptualization of feminist composition pedagogy. This pedagogy "foregrounds the functions of gender as it intersects with other categories (e.g., race, class, sexual orientation, nationality); as such, it attempts to empower real historical students, particularly real historical women students, by helping them to recognize their own politics of location and negotiate such positions" (58). This kind of cultural work associated with liberatory pedagogical efforts is not incompatible with analyses that foreground rhetorical grammar analysis. In fact, such analysis can enrich our understanding of how writers use language to construct identity—both that of self and other—and to position themselves alongside or in opposition to the status quo.

In a large-group discussion of Gertrude Stein's grammatical inventions and subversions, for instance, my students commented on the way Stein uses language to deconstruct prescribed subject positions. Stein, the students argued, constructs something like a new language, using repetition and alliteration of words to do the work of punctuation. She constructs herself as a builder of meaning who uses the conventional tools of language in unconventional ways. My students were interested in how Stein, rather than duplicating moves that characterize "good writing," uses language to assert her identity as a different kind of writer; in addition, they made links between Stein's disruption of language conventions and her disruption of sexual categories and desires (portrayed especially in *Tender Buttons*).

As I'm suggesting, rhetorical grammar analysis promises to offer students more tools for analyzing culture. Cultural studies scholars, according to Pamela Caughie, make "the construction of the subject in cultural institutions and social discourses central to their investigations" (111–12). Interdisciplinary approaches to cultural studies share a common goal of investigating "the complex ways in which identity itself is articulated, experienced, deployed" (Nelson et al. qtd. in Caughie 112). By looking at practices of representation in various discursive forms, cultural studies methodologies tell us something about the way desires are fabricated and reproduced in order to construct certain kinds of subjects. Rhetorical grammar analysis can work in concert with these goals by making available to students a vocabulary for thinking through the specificity of words and grammatical choices, the work they do in the production of an idea of culture and an idea of a people.

This insight is revealed not only in studies of grammar use but also in studies that make visible the cultural attitudes and assumptions informing grammar instruction itself. Miriam Brody's *Manly Writing*, for instance, examines gendered metaphors in advice texts from the Enlightenment through the twentieth century that liken good writing to manliness and virility. Brody's study reveals what she calls the "hidden curriculum" of writing instruction—a curriculum that, mirroring the shift from a rural to an industrialized culture, ennobled masculine virtues and repelled feminine "vice," or the arts of deception, emotion, and flowery language. Brody discusses early grammar texts, in which a "fusion of patriotic, linguistic, and gendered issues forged an ideology for an age that frankly and reasonably imagined itself as perfectible, if only young boys learned their mother tongue well" (96). In this context, Brody argues, writing was gendered as a male activity that signaled a boy's civility, intelligence, and cleanliness. In addition, grammar texts from the late-1700s and early-1800s compared writing to men's work, just as the increasing industrialization during the period was seen as male labor requiring strength, forcefulness, and muscular achievement. Brody contends that the grammar exercise was the method by which young boys learned their trade: "The grammatical exercise assumed that the student was like a master builder with words, which, like so many levers and bolts, became tools for production" (105). The simplicity and cleanliness of grammar exercises, while no longer gendered in the same way that Brody describes, continue to provide students with a sense of achievement and mastery and, perhaps most satisfying of all, finality. Yet, as many have noted, when correcting language outside a meaningful context, students and teachers alike are often frustrated by the lack of transfer from the exercise to the rhetorical situation (see note 1).

The point I want to emphasize is that grammar skill and instruction are linked to cultural attitudes, beliefs, and assumptions. But an absence of attention to grammar instruction prevents us from considering productive links. Instead, we adhere to a normalized reflex against teaching grammar in the context of writing instruction. David Lazere makes a similar point in "Back to Basics" when he questions leftists' automatic reflex against "basic skills" instruction. "Basic skills," for him, refers to a somewhat amorphous "factual knowledge" and to the more explicit "mechanical and analytic skills (including remedial instruction in reading and writing standard English)" (19). While he does not utter the g-word here, it seems that Lazere's focus on mechanical skills and Standard English is connected to teaching grammar. He finds that a lack of "basic skills and factual knowledge" among students and teachers creates obstacles "to autonomous critical thinking and to openness toward progressive politics," a point largely overlooked or simplified by leftist educators (9). By rejecting "basic skills" as dogmatically as conservatives endorse it, leftists err, Lazere contends, in failing to see that basic skills instruction "might be a force for liberation—not oppression—if administered with common sense, openness to cultural pluralism, and an application of basics toward critical thinking, particularly about sociopolitical issues, rather than rote memorizing" (9). Although the particulars of basic skills instruction are never made clear, Lazere poses a useful challenge to binaries that refuse to see skills instruction—including grammar instruction—as anything other than conservative and dehumanizing, a position that bespeaks the already achieved privileges of rhetorical skill and the cultural capital that accompanies it (see Delpit). The opposition between teaching grammar and teaching writing—which depends on an understanding of grammar instruction in the traditional, formal sense—limits and forecloses productive discussion about rhetorical grammar as a tool for supporting and extending cultural analysis.

Grammar competency has always been linked with social power or the lack thereof. As a component of written literacy, grammar knowledge often functions to "draw lines of social distinction, mark status, and rank students in meritocratic order" (Trimbur 279). In addition to its association with class markers that lock people into social place, grammar competency also raises difficult questions concerning second-language learners and the teaching of grammar as a skill (not a craft, an art, or a tool for cultural critique) that serves the dominant economic order (i.e., see Giroux). We can challenge these associations, exploring what it might mean to teach grammar in a way that promotes composition's goals to equip students to be active citizens of the worlds they inhabit. Rather than abandon grammar instruction, I'm suggesting that writing teachers seek avenues from which to revitalize practice, positioning rhetorical grammar as a necessary component of rhetorical education.

Acknowledgments

An earlier version of this paper was delivered at the 2000 NCTE Conference in Milwaukee. I want to thank Alice Gillam for introducing me to rhetorical grammar in her Teaching Composition seminar; thanks go also to Gary Weissman, Martha Kolln, and an anonymous reader for their generative feedback on earlier drafts. In addition, I want to acknowledge my graduate research assistant, Sean Memolo, who so carefully gathered and summarized research materials for this project. His assistantship was supported by the English Department at East Carolina University.

Notes

1. A number of studies questioning how formal grammar instruction translates into writing improvement have been influential in composition studies (Braddock et al.; D'Eloia; Hartwell; Hillocks; Meckel; Sutton; Tabbert). For useful reviews of this work, see Bonnie Devet, Susan Hunter and Ray Wallace, and Rei Noguchi.

2. On ancient rhetoricians and grammar instruction, see Gina Claywell, Cheryl Glenn, or Jon Olson.

3. In this section, I describe and draw examples from two different courses in which I taught the same material. One is Writing with Style, a sophomore-level course that I taught in spring 1999 while a graduate student at the University of Wisconsin-Milwaukee. This course integrated rhetorical

grammar study with issues of style, a pairing that reflects the frequent blurring of distinctions between grammar and style in composition scholarship (see Zemliansky).

The other course described in this section is a sophomore-level course entitled Functional Grammar, which I have taught during three noncontiguous semesters at East Carolina University since fall 2000. Like several of the linguists in my department, I teach the course as rhetorical grammar because this terminology highlights grammar as integral to persuasive speech acts. As an approach to studying language, however, rhetorical grammar shares several principles with functional grammar, including the idea that language *does* something, language use varies according to context, and learning grammar entails sentence-level and larger discursive-level knowledge. See Charles Meyer for a useful overview of functional grammar with specific attention to M.A.K. Halliday's functional theory of language.

4. I'd like to extend special thanks to those students who gave me permission to quote from their commonplace books; those whose names are not given wished to remain anonymous. All student writing appears here exactly as it was written.

5. Resources on using imitation exercises in the writing classroom are plentiful. For a sampling, see Robert Connors on rhetoric and imitation, Frank D'Angelo on "strict" and "loose" imitations, and Winston Weathers on "creative imitation."

6. Students wrote an eight-page analysis of the grammar of any text of their choosing. For more information on this and other assignments, visit the following links on my Web site: <http://personal.ecu.edu/miccichel/grammar02.htm> and <http://personal.ecu.edu/miccichel/2730.htm> and <http://personal.ecu.edu/miccichel/style.htm>. Send me an e-mail at miccichel@mail.ecu.edu regarding suggestions and/or comments about the ideas discussed in this article.

Works Cited

Ashton-Jones, Evelyn. "Collaboration, Conversation, and the Politics of Gender." *Feminine Principles and Women's Experience in American Composition and Rhetoric*. Ed. Louise Wetherbee Phelps and Janet Emig. Pittsburgh: U of Pittsburgh P, 1995. 5–26.

Baldwin, James. "If Black English Isn't a Language, Then Tell Me, What Is?" *Ten on Ten: Major Essayists on Recurring Themes*. Ed. Robert Atwan. Boston: Bedford, 1992. 321–24.

Berlin, James A. "Rhetoric and Ideology in the Writing Class." *College English* 50.5 (1988): 477–94.

Braddock, Richard, Richard Lloyd-Jones, and Lowell Schoer. *Research in Written Composition*. Champaign, IL: NCTE, 1963.

Brody, Miriam. *Manly Writing: Gender, Rhetoric, and the Rise of Composition*. Carbondale, IL: SIUP, 1993.

Bruss, Elizabeth W. *Beautiful Theories: The Spectacle of Discourse in Contemporary Criticism*. Baltimore: Johns Hopkins UP, 1982.

Bryant, Donald C. "Rhetoric: Its Functions and Its Scope." *Professing the New Rhetorics: A Sourcebook*. Ed. Theresa Enos and Stuart C. Brown. Englewood Cliffs, NJ: Prentice Hall, 1994. 267–97.

Bullock, Richard, and John Trimbur, eds. *The Politics of Writing Instruction: Postsecondary*. Portsmouth, NH: Boynton/Cook, 1991.

"Bush's Speech to U.N. on Iraq." *New York Times on the Web* 12 Sept. 2002. 12 Sept. 2002 <http://www.nytimes.com/2002/09/12/politics/12AP-PTEX.html>

Caughie, Pamela L. "Let It Pass: Changing the Subject, Once Again." *Feminism and Composition: In Other Words*. Ed. Susan C. Jarratt and Lynn Worsham. New York: MLA, 1998. 111–31.

Claywell, Gina. "Reasserting Grammar's Position in the Trivium in American College Composition." Hunter and Wallace 43–53.

Connors, Robert J. "The Erasure of the Sentence." *College Composition and Communication* 52.1 (2000): 96–128.

Crowley, Sharon. *Ancient Rhetorics for Contemporary Students*. New York: Macmillan, 1994.

D'Angelo, Frank. "Imitation and Style." *The Writing Teacher's Sourcebook*. 2nd ed. Ed. Gary Tate and Edward P. J. Corbett, New York: Oxford UP, 1988. 199–207.

D'Eloia, Sarah. "The Uses—and Limits—of Grammar." *Journal of Basic Writing* 1.3 (1977): 1–20.

Delpit, Lisa. *Other People's Children: Cultural Conflict in the Classroom*. New York: The New P, 1995.

Devet, Bonnie. "Welcoming Grammar Back into the Writing Classroom." *Teaching English in the Two-Year College* 30.1 (2002): 8–17

Didion, Joan. "Why I Write." *Joan Didion: Essays and Conversations*. Ed. Ellen G. Friedman. Princeton, NJ: Ontario Review P, 1984. 5–10.

Fitts, Karen, and Alan W. France, eds. *Left Margins: Cultural Studies and Composition Pedagogy*. Albany, NY: SUNY, 1995.

Foucault, Michel. *Language, Counter-Memory, Practice*. Ed. Donald F. Bouchard. Ithaca: Cornell UP, 1980.

Giroux, Henry A. *Teachers as Intellectuals: Toward a Critical Pedagogy of Learning*. Granby, MA: Bergin and Garvey, 1988.

Giroux, Henry A., and Peter McLaren, eds. *Critical Pedagogy, the State, and Cultural Struggle*. Albany, NY: SUNY, 1989.

Glenn, Cheryl. "When Grammar Was a Language Art." Hunter and Wallace 9–29.

Hartwell, Patrick. "Grammar, Grammars, and the Teaching of Grammar." *College English* 47.2 (1985): 105–27.

Hillocks, George, Jr. *Research on Written Composition: New Directions for Teaching*. Urbana, IL. NCRE/ERIC, 1986.

hooks, bell. "Language." *Teaching to Transgress: Education as the Practice of Freedom*. New York: Routledge, 1994. 167–75.

Hunter, Susan, and Ray Wallace, eds. *The Place of Grammar in Writing Instruction: Past, Present, Future*. Portsmouth, NH: Boynton/Cook, 1995.

Jarratt. Susan C., and Lynn Worsham, eds. *Feminism and Composition Studies: In Other Words*. New York: MLA, 1998.

Kolln, Martha. "Rhetorical Grammar: A Modification Lesson." *English Journal* 85.7 (1996): 25–31.

———, *Rhetorical Grammar: Grammatical Choices, Rhetorical Effects*. 4th ed. New York: Longman, 2003.

Lakoff, Robin. *Language and Woman's Place*. New York: Harper & Row, 1975.

Lazere, David. "Back to Basics: A Force for Oppression or Liberation?" *College English* 54.1 (1992): 7–21.

Luke, Carmen, and Jennifer Gore, eds. *Feminisms and Critical Pedagogies*. New York: Routledge, 1992.

Meckel, Henry C. "Research on Teaching Composition and Literature." *Handbook of Educational Research*. Ed. N. L. Gage. Chicago: Rand McNally, 1963. 966–1006.

Meyer, Charles F. "Functional Grammar and Discourse Studies." *Discourse Studies in Composition*. Ed. Ellen Barton and Gail Stygall. Cresskill, NJ: Hampton P, 2002. 71–89.

Murphy, James J., ed. *Quintilian on the Teaching of Speaking and Writing*. Carbondale, IL: SIUP, 1987.

Noguchi, Rei R. *Grammar and the Teaching of Writing: Limits and Possibilities*. Urbana, IL: NCTE, 1991.

Olson, Gary A. "Encountering the Other: Postcolonial Theory and Composition Scholarship." *Ethical Issues in College Writing*. Ed. Fredric G. Gale, Philip Sipiora, and James L. Kinneavy. New York: Peter Lang, 1999. 91–105.

Olson, Jon. "A Question of Power: Why Fredrick Douglass Stole Grammar." Hunter and Wallace 30–42.

Orwell, George. "Politics and the English Language." *Ten on Ten: Major Essayists on Recurring Themes*. Ed. Robert Atwan. Boston: Bedford, 1992. 309–20.

Ratcliffe, Krista. *Anglo-American Feminist Challenges to the Rhetorical Traditions: Virginia Woolf, Mary Daly, Adrienne Rich*. Carbondale, IL: SIUP, 1996.

Schell, Eileen E. *Gypsy Academics and Mother-Teachers: Gender, Contingent Labor, and Writing Instruction*. Portsmouth, NH: Boynton/Cook, 1998.

Severino, Carol, Juan C. Guerra, and Johnnella E. Butler, eds. *Writing in Multicultural Settings*. New York: MLA, 1997.

Shaughnessy, Mina P. *Errors and Expectations: A Guide for the Teacher of Basic Writing*. New York: Oxford UP, 1977.

Shor, Ira. *Empowering Education: Critical Teaching for Social Change*. Chicago: U of Chicago P, 1992.

Sledd, James. "Grammar for Social Awareness in Time of Class Warfare." *English Journal* 85.7 (1996): 59–63.

Sullivan, Patricia A., and Donna J. Qualley, eds. *Pedagogy in the Age of Politics: Writing and Reading (in) the Academy*. Urbana, IL: NCTE, 1994.

Sutton, Gary A. "Do We Need to Teach a Grammar Terminology?" *English Journal* 65.9 (1976): 37–40.

Tabbert, Russell. "Parsing the Question 'Why Teach Grammar?'" *English Journal* 73.8 (1984): 38–42.

Trimbur, John. "Literacy and the Discourse of Crisis." *The Politics of Writing Instruction: Postsecondary*. Ed. Richard Bullock and John Trimbur. Portsmouth, NH: Boynton/Cook, 1991. 277–95.

Weathers, Winston. "Teaching Style: A Possible Anatomy." *The Writing Teacher's Sourcebook*. 2nd ed. Ed. Gary Tate and Edward P. J. Corbett. New York: Oxford UP, 1988. 187–92.

Winchell, Donna A. "Teaching the Rhetoric of Grammar and Style." *Instructor's Manual and Answer Key to Accompany The Writer's Harbrace Handbook*. Ed. Robert K. Miller, Suzanne S. Webb, and Winifred B. Horner. New York: Harcourt College Publishers, 2001. 16–58.

Zemliansky, Pavel. "Mechanical Correctness." *Composition Forum* 10.2 (2000): 1–19.

The ESL Student in the Freshman Composition Class
By William G. Clark

Students for whom English is a second language are present in many freshman composition classes in both two- and four-year colleges. Sometimes they are sufficiently fluent in English to be able to perform well; sometimes they are not. Sometimes their instructors are familiar with ESL students and find them valuable additions to their classes; frequently they are not and do not. Many instructors have not had the experience which teaches them how to work with a class containing ESL students.

For those instructors who lack experience with ESL students, information about the process of acquiring a second language can make the difference between a pleasant, profitable class and an uncomfortable, unprofitable class. Obviously, I do not refer here to the problems of teaching beginning ESL students who know little English; those students belong with specialists in ESL instruction. The information I offer does apply, however, to ESL students with moderate competence in English — students, for example, who score 550 or above on the standardized Test of English as a Foreign Language (TOEFL).

Helping ESL students succeed in the conventional composition class requires not only the cooperation of the ESL students, but also the cooperation of English as a Native Language (ENL) students and the willingness of the instructor to take the steps necessary for success. The ESL student is usually quite willing to cooperate, the ENL student is usually ready to take a cue from the instructor, and the instructor can easily understand the pedagogical steps involved.

Assuming the cooperation of both ESL and ENL students, what the instructor should know can be divided into three categories:

1. The general process of second-language learning.
2. Factors which interfere with second-language learning.
3. Factors which facilitate second-language learning.

The Process of Second-Language Learning

Human beings learn language through the tacit internalization of patterns and principles that are acquired "through extensive exposure to and practical experience with the use of language in actual, natural contexts and situations" (Falk 440). Language learning follows the familiar process of generalizing a set of experiences into a principle and then applying the principle to new situations.

The unexpected feature of this generalizing is that the process works only when the mastery is by *tacit internalization.* That is, we cannot "teach" sets of rules and then expect students to consciously apply the rules. Students do not learn through examining the rules nor by memorizing them; such conscious activity is merely learning about language, not learning language. The process of "language acquisition is, by its very nature, an unconscious process" (440).

The crucial feature, and to most of us the deceptive feature, of language learning is that language acquisition comes about through tacit internalization of patterns. The learner's mind, like that of a child's learning her first language, fits together related features of the language and makes decisions about when to use which words and what forms and sequence of those words to use; but neither the child nor the second-language learner fits the features together and makes decisions about using them by conscious act: the mind performs these operations at a separate, unconscious level. In the process of learning, the learner will, at times, make conscious choices, but once the learning is complete, that happens infrequently.

Second-language learning often takes place without formal instruction. If the learner feels the need to acquire a second language and is in frequent contact with native speakers who can serve as models, the learner will begin to acquire skills in the second language. Indeed, given enough time, enough motivation, and enough contact with native speakers, the learner becomes fluent.

The ESL student taught by a specialist will learn more rapidly and acquire fluency sooner. Even though the specialist provides situations and activities which expedite the learning process, it is still the student who does the learning. "We must realize that the student must do the job for himself ... that [although] we can struggle with him in his task of learning the second language ... we can provide little more than encouragement and a certain, but not unimportant amount of help" (Wardhaugh 111).

For those of us who are not specialists in ESL, understanding language acquisition is of considerable importance. It tells us, for example, that we do our ESL students no favor by providing them with grammar drills or vocabulary exercises; such activities only take time away from useful activities.

Two other facts about second-language learning may also be helpful in working with ESL students:

1. When individuals are learning two languages simultaneously, they progress more rapidly in the language they use most. The significance of this fact is that the more ESL students practice English, the sooner they achieve fluency.

2. ESL students understand considerably more English than they can produce. A corollary here is that ESL students' writing and speaking are not valid measures of their understanding of English.

Our own experiences with foreign languages should remind us of the truth of the second statement; it is far easier for us to understand the written or spoken language than to speak or write it. When we listen or read, the hard work is done for us; someone else generates the vocabulary or chooses the correct form or assembles the words in the proper sequence. When we write and speak, we have to do that complicated work ourselves, and it is quite different from processing the communications which someone else has assembled. This fact reminds us that we must not judge ESL students' understanding of English by reading their writing and hearing their speech.

These two facts about second-language learning help us to understand what our ESL students do not need and to recognize that what we can see and hear of their use of English may be misleading.

Factors Which Interfere With Second-Language Learning

We also need to know those factors which interfere with ESL learning, for they tell us behaviors to avoid and behaviors over which we have no control.

Limited Motivation

Student motivation has considerable bearing on how much English students will learn and how well they will learn it. Some students are not interested in learning any more English than is absolutely essential to achieve their immediate goals. When motivation is limited, the students can spend hours in the classroom doing all that is required of them and still learn little.

John Schumann tells of an adult student with minimal motivation who studied seven months with a skilled ESL specialist on the use of negatives in English. At the end of the seven months, the man's knowledge of negatives in test situations improved significantly. However, his spontaneous use of negatives remained unaltered; he did not transfer the learning to his self-generated use of English. Evidently, he was not interested in mastering elements of English which were, to him, frills (267–68).

For students whose interest in English extends only to short-term goals that require no more than rudimentary control of English, the chances are slight of helping them write or speak appreciably better than they do at the outset. The chances that we can alter their motivation are equally slight. However, we should not be dissuaded from encouraging and otherwise seeking to motivate our ESL students, but we should also know why some of them won't respond to the motivation.

First, we should ensure a classroom atmosphere that is nonthreatening. We should be supportive and make certain that the student's limited progress is not the result of shyness or fear. And we must be content to help students with low motivation learn only enough English to achieve their short-term goals without disparaging their limited goals. Of course, we must accurately reflect in our evaluations the learning which does not take place. If we provide the appropriate setting, encouragement, and instruction, we've done what we can for the marginally motivated student.

Performance Inhibition

When we consider the difficulty that many capable native speakers of English experience when called upon to speak in public, we get some idea of the difficulty that some ESL students experience when faced with the need to communicate, formally or informally, with native speakers of English. Although many ESL students are reasonably fluent in English, their "shyness, perfectionism, and other factors ... mask knowledge of the second language by performance inhibition" (Erwin-Tripp 113). For these students, we must make a special effort to ease tension and to help them take the risk which performance in English poses for them. Once over the hurdle these particular ESL students will show far more fluency than in their previous communication.

Inaccurate Assessment of ESL Students' Fluency

Teachers who are misled by surface features of ESL students' language often conclude that the students are incapable of learning at the class level to which they have been assigned. Such misinterpretation can be devastating.

As instructors, we must be cautious in assessing the fluency of ESL students. It is particularly important that those of us not familiar with the writing and speaking of ESL students reserve judgment until the students have provided a detailed set of examples of their writing and speaking skills. Often our initial reaction to ESL communications is one of shock, but that shock frequently gives way in a short time to recognition of the students' comparatively fluent grasp of the basics of English grammar and syntax.

If that initial reaction does not change, we should seek advice from a more experienced composition instructor or an ESL instructor, and we should always bear in mind that the student's apparent lack of skill may be really our own lack of familiarity with the performance of ESL students.

To become familiar with that performance, we need to spend time consciously looking behind the variant spellings or the unusual syntax to find the basic elements of the communication. We should look for a limited controlling idea and for detailed and relevant support; we should look for organizational guidance which indicates awareness of audience and a desire to help the audience to follow the movement of the communication. As we become more familiar with the process of reading through the haze of the surface features, we will begin to see that many ESL students handle the important elements of communication with as much skill as the ENL students display.

Observe, for example, in the following journal entry of Chinese student Wen-Ling Tsai the skillful structure and movement of the explanation and the effective supporting detail. Observe, too, the enthusiastic tone and the light-hearted self-deprecation which easily come through the surface features. Then imagine the impact on this woman of a flood of revisions of her language and a paragraph or two of instructor comments on her grammar, syntax, and diction. Finally, guess what the next journal or theme would be like.

> From the first time I went to the supermarket, I crazily like all kinds of food storage containers. I like any shape of them, round, square, rectangular, cylinder, cube or rectangular solid, and any material of them: plastic, glass or acrylic.
>
> If I go to the supermarket, I will stand in front of the shelf of kitchen utensils for a while, or if I go to the shopping more, I will spend a lot of time on kitchenware store or a lot of time on the home center of department store. I look all the containers, touch their smooth surface and image what stuff can put inside. I like the picture on the stickers, too. That might be heaps of fresh, red strawberry put on a round, glass containers or green beans and corns on a square plastic containers, or varied small cookies on the yellow lip cylinder container. I like all of them and I think I can store my food like that way. They are beautiful, keep food fresh, and I just like them.
>
> At first my husband let me buy what I want, but after several times, he just allow me to watch and touch but not buy it. He will say, "We already have another square set." "But they are plastic" I might reply. However, we seldom buy food storage containers recently. Because we have only two persons in our house. We don't buy many food a week, and I cook adequate quantity every day; therefore we don't need many containers for store our food. Besides, we don't have plenty space to put more containers.
>
> But, stop to buy is one thing; I like it is another thing. I still spend much time on watching the containers, and touching them at the stores. Or if I have time at home, I will collect all the containers I have, examine how many I have, or how many shape, how many color I have.
>
> I can't explain my habitual inclination. Actually, in my country, we don't use container very often and we don't have various containers. I "think" the reasons are: we seldom store food because we go to the market everyday, we eat fresh meat and vegetable every meal, and if we need to store food, we have many bowls-this is totally the reasons, I guess. Bowls are our major dinner set; just like American's dishes, we have many kind and many size bowls; therefore, we can use bowls instead of using the real food storage containers. But the first time I saw varied containers here, I was

simply like it. I like their shapes and their lips. Specially, I like the sound when I seal the lip. That makes me feel I keep anything food fresh.

My husband said I am childish in loving this tiny things, but I don't care. I enjoy my hobby and I will keep it.

When we can move behind the unusual surface features to see the substance of the writing in terms of the controlling idea, the organization and organizational guidance, and the support, we can appreciate the real communication ability which the student displays and recognize the problems with mechanics and expression as interference rather than as the nature of the communication itself.

As we progress with our task of learning about ESL communications, we learn how to facilitate the learning of the ESL students. As we shift our attention from surface features to substantive features, we can in the process shift the attention of the ESL students from undue preoccupation with the surface features to a more rewarding preoccupation with the central communication elements. This is a desirable focus for the ESL students' attention because not only does it engage them in important learning, it moves them into an area where they can progress more rapidly and more productively.

Factors Which Facilitate Second-Language Learning

Sentence Combining

Naturally, ESL students need to continue the long battle to achieve a close approximation to native diction, grammar, and syntax, but such close approximation cannot come quickly; it must follow the route of being internalized in order to be mastered. A limited emphasis on linguistic skills and primary emphasis on rhetorical skills will often ensure steady progress in language learning and rapid improvement in other communication skills.

For instructors who wish to devote time to language learning that will benefit both ESL and ENL students, one helpful activity is the use of sentence-combining exercises twice each week for a semester. Doing these exercises once or twice will do the students little good, but doing 10 or 15 or more each Monday and Wednesday for 18 weeks does help many students. They pay attention to the language elements which they are called upon to manipulate, and they gradually make the various syntactic patterns a part of their internalized understanding of how to use English. Using sentence combining, both ESL and ENL students should improve the syntactic maturity of their writing by the end of the semester.

Freewriting

Another useful way to help students to improve their fluency in English is to require weekly freewriting journals of 400 or 500 words each. These journals are graded on quantity only and are not to be rewritten or carefully planned as coherent productions. The teacher's response to these journals is that of an interested reader who provides occasional marginal notes such as "I would have found that frightening" or "I remember coming home late one night when I was a child and finding my grandfather waiting up with a shotgun to save me from God knows what threat" or "That must have made you feel ten feet tall!"

Letting the students write without worrying about mechanics, grammar, vocabulary, or coherence frees them to experiment with English and to stretch their writing muscles a bit. It is useful practice for any student who has not been writing regularly.

A Period of Benign Neglect

Another technique which works well is for the instructor to refrain entirely from commenting on mechanical matters or expression during the first third (or even half) of the semester. The focus of the instructor's attention during that time is entirely on thesis, support, and organization, which should help all students make more than usual progress in those categories. A surprising number of ENL students will show improvement in mechanics and expression as well, probably just from exercising their composition muscles. The ESL students will show some of this improvement, too, and it will probably be about as much as they would have been able to make with thorough criticism of syntax, spelling, and other mechanical matters. (For the ESL student who solicits help with mechanics, circling or underlining some of the more noticeable departures from the American idiom will provide enough data for the student to begin practicing with.)

Motivation and Minimal Self-Consciousness

The two factors which do much to help ESL students in the composition class—motivation and lack of self-consciousness—are attributes which the students, in varying degrees, bring to class as potential assets. The potential will be realized only if the in-class experience permits it to be realized.

Strong motivation comes from the students' desire to learn English because they see a long-term need to be able to use it. Minimal self-consciousness is the ability to undergo the experience of learning without feeling painful emotional bruises from the process. This condition equates to being able to laugh at oneself or to being able to learn from making errors without being ashamed or troubled.

Obviously, we rarely find students who are so motivated that they never lose interest or students so free of self-consciousness that they can tolerate devastating criticism without pain or diminished learning ability. However, we will find many who can work in any circumstances which let them feel that they are making progress and are not threatened with failure or ridicule. The primary way in which instructors can facilitate the learning of the ESL students is to provide them with the supportive and encouraging atmosphere which will make the most of the students' potential.

When there is enough interaction among the students in a class to permit the ESL students to get to know the ENL students, both groups will be able to relax and to feel less pressure from the classroom situation and will be able to progress rapidly. The instructor's effort to create an unthreatening atmosphere for all the students provides them with the assurance that their learning is the goal of the course. They are then able to make the most of the opportunity to learn.

Grading

The troublesome issue of grading I leave to last because its role must be seen in the context of the ESL students' complex language-acquisition circumstance. Since our primary concern with students is to provide them with the knowledge, activities, and feedback which will do most to help them to learn, we must consider what impact our grading will have on their learning. If our conventional grading system (whatever it may be) interferes with their learning, we need to consider altering the system.

For the good of the ESL students, an alteration which places minimal emphasis on grading of expression and mechanics doubtless helps them to make more progress with their learning to communicate in English than would heavy emphasis on these features of composition.

For the good of the ENL students in the class, the same emphasis will probably lead to more progress with their learning to communicate. They, too, make changes in their expression and mechanics at a slower rate than changes in focus, organization, and support; a grading system which places less emphasis on expression and mechanics will show them, too, that they can make meaningful progress in their writing when they can spend less time worrying about matters which they can change only gradually.

For the good of both ESL and ENL students, limited emphasis on expression and mechanics means maintaining a low-key but consistent identification of problems in those areas. Students must continue to be aware of the need for some attention to their syntax, grammar, spelling, and diction. Limited emphasis on expression and mechanics also means that both comments about student communications and the grades which those communications receive should suggest that aspects other than expression and mechanics are important.

Naturally, such a change in grading needs to be explained carefully to the students. Once they understand that the system does not ask them to ignore syntax, diction, punctuation, and spelling, does not discard standards, does not proclaim "Anything goes!" they will be able to accept the opportunities the system offers them to improve the substance of their writing at a reasonably rapid rate and to improve the surface features of their writing at the slower rate which is best for that kind of learning.

Summing Up

Helping the ESL students in the composition class entails, first, understanding the nature of the process by which they acquire their new language. The key knowledge is that the acquisition is by internalization of the rules of the new language; the process is slow and cannot be significantly speeded up, except by the concentrated efforts of specialists. Becoming fluent in the new language requires many years, and we cannot hope to assist ESL students with very many linguistic matters in the short time we have. What we can do is to provide frequent writing assignments and situations that require the use of either oral or written English. The combination will give students opportunity to improve both their rhetorical and their linguistic skills.

A second important fact about working with ESL students is that we should not let the surface features of ESL students' writing and speaking mislead us into believing that their control of English is much weaker than it really is. If we do, we are inclined to misjudge the quality of ESL performance. We should not work with surface features first, but with rhetorical features.

A third important fact is that the ESL students will be able to perform at their best when they feel secure. Improving both their writing and speaking skills depends on a comfortable learning environment; such an environment gives free rein to their motivation and to their willingness to take the chance of making mistakes in order to learn.

Works Cited

Erwin-Tripp, Susan M. "Is Second Language Learning Like the First?" *TESOL Quarterly* 8 (1974):111–27.

Falk, Julia S. "Language Acquisition and the Teaching and Learning of English." *College English 41* (1979): 436–47.

Schumann, John. "Second-Language Acquisition: The Pidginization Process." *Second Language Acquisition.* Ed. Evelyn Hatch. Rowley, MA: Newbury, 1978. 256–71.

Wardhaugh, Ronald. "Current Problems and Classroom Practices." *TESOL Quarterly* 3 (1969): 105–14.

The Best of Both Worlds: Teaching Basic Writers in Class and Online

By Linda Stine

LINCOLN UNIVERSITY – PENNSYLVANIA

Computers and Basic Writers: The Issue

In a 1994 ERIC Clearinghouse summary on computer-assisted writing instruction, Marjorie Simic noted, "Writing researchers have long advised that the key to fluent writing is to write as much as possible. The key to exact writing is to revise repeatedly" ("Revising," par. 1). Basic writers, so much in need of increased fluency and exactness, have from the onset seemed ideal candidates for a writing course featuring word processing, precisely because of the computer's promise in these two areas. It is now the rare developmental course that does not, at least minimally, incorporate computer use into its curriculum. In a remarkably short time, the computer has evolved from being a tool with potential to improve student writing to being the tool with which people write, and if Peter Elbow is correct that "the best test of a writing course is whether it makes students more likely to use writing in their lives" (136), then most writing teachers today would have to agree that it is hard to justify a basic writing course that does not explore and exploit the advantages of word processing.

Agreement is harder to find, however, on the question of whether *online* instruction is equally justifiable for basic writers. The following article describes a hybrid option, in which students meet on campus every other week and work online during the off weeks, as one possible means of minimizing problems encountered in fully online writing classes while still allowing students to gain access to learning experiences unique to online instruction. This particular hybrid is, to be sure, only one of many possible variations. Richard Straub, considering how faculty can best comment on student papers, once acknowledged that "different teachers, in different settings, with different students, different kinds of writing, different course goals, and alas! with different time constraints may do different things with their comments, and do them well" (2). The same applies to teaching with technology: one size does not fit all. Nevertheless, the more options we consider, the more likely we are to find the match that best fits our students' needs, our institutional resources, and our own individual teaching strengths. And, if we are lucky, that match may turn out to involve neither expensive equipment nor extensive technology skills on the part of teachers and students. In "From Pencils to Pixels," Denis Baron reminds us, "Researchers tend to look at the cutting edge when they examine how technology affects literacy. But technology has a trailing edge. . ." (32). With so many overworked and under-supported basic writing teachers feeling fortunate if they can grab hold of even the trailing edge of technology, it is worth noting that a hybrid course like the one described below can double the number of students who can use a school's scarce computer laboratories and, at the same time, halve these students' commuting costs.

Basic Writers Online: The Problems

A number of arguments can be made to explain why developmental students and online learning might not, in general, make a good match. One group of arguments raises societal issues. There is, for instance, the obvious problem of accessibility.

As Charles Moran has stated, "The issue of access is easily and quickly framed: in America wealth is unequally distributed; money buys technology; therefore technology is inequitably distributed" (207). A 2000 report from the United States Commerce Department on Americans' access to technology tools, *Falling through the Net: Toward Digital Inclusion*, concludes that while people of all ethnic groups and income and educational levels are making gains, noticeable divides still exist between those with different levels of income and education, different racial and ethnic groups, old and young, single and dual-parent families, and those with and without disabilities. Basic writing students, typically older, poorer, less apt to come from stable, highly educated families, and more apt to have learning disabilities, are still less likely than the average student to have easy access to the kind of technology that distance learning requires, both in and out of the classroom. Are we justified in requiring basic writing students to work online, given the hardships that may cause for some?

Also troubling is the homogeneous culture into which our disparate students are asked to fit. As Richard and Cynthia Selfe have warned, "Students who want to use computers are continually confronted with . . . narratives which foreground a value on middle-class, corporate culture: capitalism and the commodification of information; Standard English; and rationalistic ways of representing knowledge" (494). They encourage teachers to recognize, and help their students understand, that the computer interface is "an interested and partial map of our culture and . . . a linguistic contact zone that reveals power differentials" (495). How should our pedagogy reflect this concern? Is it enough just to remind students of the limitations of grammar and spell checkers or do what we can to make sure that the physical layout of our classrooms does not reinforce a hierarchical structure? Or should we, who teach those students most likely to be marginalized, also make technology itself—its potential for liberation as well as oppression—the subject of more discussions and essays? How actively should we be working in our basic writing courses to raise student consciousness about the power of symbols and the politics of the technological contact zone?

A third set of worries for teachers of basic writers is related to technological issues. Distance education requires students to learn writing while often at the same time learning the relatively advanced computer skills required to produce writing online (for a discussion of this problem, see "Issues of Attitude and Access: A Case Study of Basic Writers in a Computer Classroom" by Catherine Matthews Pavia in this issue). Most of the adult students I encounter know how to use their computer for a few clearly defined tasks but have not developed a broad range of technology skills. Stuart Selber argues in a recent *CCC* article that students must be able to *control* a computer—that is, possess what he calls functional literacy, not just computer literacy—in order to work with it effectively (470-503). If students lack this type of functional literacy, how much does it interfere with an acquisition of writing proficiency? A related problem, which Lauren Yena and Zach Waggoner term "muting," occurs as a result of either an *actual* lack of technological literacy on the student's part or the anxiety that he or she experiences about a *perceived* lack of computer expertise ("Student Muting"). Will efforts to offset this problem double the responsibilities of the teacher, who must provide directions not only for what students are expected to say but also for how to navigate through the technology comfortably enough so that they are able to say it? Another technology-related problem, which applies whether students are writing online or off, is the tendency for developmental writers to put too much faith in the computer's authority. Might an online class tempt students even more to obey without question the dictates of those red and green "squiggly lines" produced by the computer's spelling or grammar checker (Whithaus) or to accept the largesse of their browser's search engines blindly, without the type of useful reflection that leads to linguistic and cognitive growth?

Another set of questions focuses on pedagogical issues. Chris Anson writes of "our basic beliefs about the nature of classroom instruction, in all its communal richness and face-to-face complexity" (263). Does the Internet—though undoubtedly rich and undoubtedly complex—provide such an atmosphere? And what might be the effect of the reduced cues environment in which distance learning functions? Haythornthwaite, Kazmer, Robins, and Shoemaker have characterized this environment as "text without voice, voice without body language, class attendance without seating arrangements." They point out that the very same environment that reduces the fear of *negative* feedback—when writers type something silly or inappropriate online, they cannot see the readers rolling their eyes, so they feel free to keep typing—also reduces *positive* feedback. In such a setting, individuals do not know if they are saying the "right" thing. How much might this add to the writing anxiety basic writing students struggle with in the best of situations?

Additional pedagogical issues of concern grow out of changes that the Internet and widespread computer use are bringing about in composing and reading processes. Leslie C. Perelman, director of the writing-across-the-curriculum program at MIT, describes the difference in the way people compose today by explaining that writers normally think out the entire sentence before they start writing it on paper; otherwise, things get too messy because everything is crossed out. "But on a computer," Perelman explains, "people just start a sentence and then go back and move things around. The computer screen is elastic and therefore the composing process has become very elastic" (qtd. in Leibowitz, A67–68). While such elasticity could prove liberating for basic writers, could it not just as easily reinforce bad habits for students who often lack a sense of the shape or boundary of a sentence or are not sure where they are going with an idea when they start?

A related question can be asked about online reading. According to James Sosnoski (161–78) good hyper-readers possess the following "positive" skills:

- Filtering (selecting out only details of the text that they want to read)
- Skimming (reading less text)
- Pecking (not reading in linear sequence)
- Imposing (constructing meaning by one's self more than from the intent of author)
- Filming (paying more attention to graphical than verbal elements to get meaning)
- Trespassing (plagiarizing code, cutting and pasting and reassembling)
- De-authorization (following links, losing sight of the author)
- Fragmenting (preferring fragmented texts because such texts are easier to reassemble)

Basic writing teachers, who struggle continually with their students' tendency to read selectively and thus miss main arguments, read only parts of a text and not get the underlying meaning, read with a limited range of internalized schema that would help them gather meaning, find only those meanings they want rather than ones that the author presented, and misunderstand the boundary between paraphrasing and plagiarizing, might well question whether requiring basic readers to do much or all of their reading online could inadvertently reinforce poor print reading habits. The hypertext reading "skills" Sosnoski applauds seem remarkably like many reading weaknesses we try to help our students overcome. Similar misgivings emerge because of differences between the writing conventions appropriate to e-mail, chats, and online discussion postings and those conventions that teachers encourage in the classroom. The different rhetorical situations call for different styles; the writing displayed in a chatroom would not be acceptable in an academic writing assignment. Can we be sure that any increased fluency and confidence students gain by participating in a variety of online writing tasks will prevail over the "bad" habits such online writing might foster?

Yet another set of reasons that developmental writers sometimes fare poorly in online courses involves student-related issues. Online courses require self-direction, but basic writers, while often highly motivated, frequently have not developed the structured study habits and time management essential to success in distance education. When family, work, and other personal problems interfere, students can easily—and invisibly—fade away. Another worry is the possibility of overloading, with time spent on developing necessary technology skills getting in the way of a focus on writing skills. K. Patricia Cross has described what she calls the Chain of Response model of learning. One tenet of this model is that higher order needs for achievement and self-actualization cannot be realized until lower order needs for security and safety are met. If students do not feel safe online, secure in their technical abilities, will they be able to move on to the next writing challenge? An additional student-related problem arises because distance learning, unlike the face-to-face classroom, requires a basic writer to function in what is predominantly a text-based environment, even allowing for the multimedia options that the Internet enables. Will that demand play to the weakness rather than the strength of many developmental students? Furthermore, as Collison, Elbaum, Haavind, and Tinker warn, "Participants in net courses, even those who don't consider themselves new to the digital world, seem to lose their usual set of problem-solving strategies in the new environment. . . . [E]ven when instructions are provided, some participants still need help interpreting the directions to the discussion area or a particular thread" (52). No matter how many hours teachers spend creating detailed step-by-step directions—in words and pictures—to show students how to log on and respond to an online discussion list from home or where to post an essay draft for online review, some students will still call in a panic because the directions "aren't working" and they cannot complete their assignment.

Finally, having to anticipate all the potential problems described above and address those that may materialize later adds to the demands placed on faculty members who must find the time to create, maintain, and teach an online class. In one of the modules of Teaching Composition, a faculty listserv run by McGraw-Hill, J. Paul Johnson concludes that online writing courses work "only for faculty with expertise and experience." How do we gain this needed expertise and experience when faculty time and institutional budgets are so limited? Teaching online requires more up-front planning, more detailed course design, and often as many, if not more, contact hours with students than traditional classroom-based courses require. Furthermore, teachers have to keep up with the pace of technological change. In a recent *Computers and Composition Online* article, Evan Davis and Sarah Hardy likened faculty using technology to "travelers on sightseeing boats, hugging the coast while priding [themselves] for venturing into the ocean." Writing teachers in general, basic writing teachers in particular, rarely have the time and institutional support to explore the depths of the ocean of technology. Thus, the result Kristine Blair and Elizabeth Monske note: "In the rush to meet institutional pressures and curricular demands to create effective distance learning environments, as teachers we may be the ones who benefit *least* within these new virtual communities" (449).

Basic writing instructors must, at the least, carefully consider how they will address problematic issues accompanying online instruction, both in their pedagogy and with their students, before jumping on the technology bandwagon.

Basic Writers Online: The Potential

All these legitimate cautions and concerns notwithstanding, however, many features of online learning still seem made to order for basic writing students. Advantages of Web-enhanced courses fall into ten general categories. First comes what I think of as the "Can You Hear Me Now?" argument. Unlike class discussions, in which timid voices may go unheard, online learning—at least when using asynchronous features such as discussion lists—greatly extends possible reflection time: it lets students participate at their rate of speed and skill, think through a question, and polish up a response as long as needed before posting it.

Then there is the "Ken Macrorie" argument. In *Twenty Teachers*, Macrorie's book profiling the kind of teachers who enable students to learn, a basic assumption is that students learn by doing something worth doing. Rightly or wrongly, the Internet is considered "worth doing." Even something as mundane as practicing subject/verb agreement—should you want your students to do that—gains authority simply by being on the Web. Paradoxically, writing done virtually seems more "real."

A third consideration is expressed in the "Only Game in Town" argument. The vast majority of adult basic writers have no option other than online learning if they want to carve a few precious hours out of their busy week to go to school. Many single parents with jobs and families simply cannot get away to attend class, even when classes meet on evenings and weekends. They are also unlikely to be able to spend extended periods of time conducting library research or meeting face to face with other students for group projects, so even if they are able to make it to campus, their participation and, thus, their learning opportunities, are limited.

Related to this issue is the "Time Management" argument. When teaching online, faculty can provide their overworked adult students with a wealth of resources just a mouse click away rather than requiring a long ride to a library or a campus. Using software like *CommonSpace* or Bedford St. Martin's *Comment*, for instance, teachers can link a problematic phrase in a student draft to a rule and examples in an embedded handbook or enable online peer review. They can provide a list of useful URLs through which students can access the riches of all the OWLs (Online Writing Labs) on the Web, or download helpful tools like *ReadPlease*, a simple and free voice recognition program that helps with proofreading by reading students' essays back to them.

A fifth set of reasons focuses on the "Academic Skill-Building" argument. Davis and Hardy, describing their experience teaching with Blackboard course management software, suggest that such software is useful because "students need the skills that it foregrounds: organizing and tracking documents, participating in a community discussion, sharing work with peers, claiming a voice through writing." Basic writers, it can reasonably be argued, need precisely these skills and thus should be exposed, if at all possible, to a learning environment that fosters them.

Less concrete but no less important is the "Virginia Woolf" argument. Paul Puccio, pointing out that "the setting in which we meet with our students is a factor in the composition of student-teacher relationships," compares his feelings about his computer classroom at the University of Massachusetts with Virginia Woolf's desire for a room of her own. His thesis is that teaching writing in a room set up to teach writing, with all the modern amenities, has a positive effect on his students' intellectual work as well as on their sense of community. "Schools," claims Puccio, quoting nineteenth-century educator F. W. Sanderson, "should be miniature copies of the world we should love to have." I would argue for extending this analogy to the virtual classroom and making even disadvantaged students welcomed guests online, with full run of the house.

Once students have a room of their own, of course, they tend to invite company over. That leads to the "Howard Dean" argument. A February 22, 2004, *New York Times* article about Howard Dean's presidential campaign strategy and the social impact of the Internet quoted Cass Sunstein, author of *Republic.com*, as saying, "If you get like-minded people in constant touch with each other, then they get more energized and more committed, and more outraged and more extreme" ("So What Was *That* All About?" section 4, 3). Though not necessarily wanting outrage and extremism, teachers of basic writers do continually look for ways to energize students and keep them committed to the learning process. Web-based communication has the potential to create some Deaniac-type energy otherwise difficult to engender among socially and geographically isolated basic writing students.

This, in turn, leads to the "John Dewey" argument. Beatrice Quarshy Smith, in a thought-provoking article about what she calls the colonial pattern that permeates our use of technology, points out the fact that her community college students by and large have inadequate access not only to the technologies but also to the literacies of power. Arguing for a *transactional* conception of technologies, Smith writes of John Dewey and Arthur Bentley, "For them knowing was a process of learning though reflection on experience and through the exchange of ideas with others" (5). Developmental writers typically have such sadly limited time and opportunity to participate in person in that sort of reflective conversation that the opportunity the Internet opens for virtual idea exchange, be it through chatrooms, e-mail, blogs, listservs, or simply Googling a concept, is in itself a powerful argument for moving classes online.

For teachers of adult students, the "Nike" argument holds special merit. The most effective learning occurs, experts agree, when students follow Nike's advice and "just do it." Active learning, important for students of all ages, is essential to adults. Arthur Wilson contends that . . . adults no longer learn from experience, they learn in it as they act in situations and are acted upon by situations" (75). Online courses, at least those that are well designed, force students to play an active role in the learning experience—posing questions, voicing opinions, engaging in discussions, spending as much time as necessary on weak areas, and self-testing their knowledge when and as appropriate.

Finally, and perhaps most generally persuasive, is what might be termed the "Can We Talk?" argument. As Sharan Merriam points out, "Critical reflection and awareness of why we attach the meanings we do to reality . . . may be the most significant distinguishing characteristic of adult learning" (9). The "persistence" of online communication enables and encourages this critical reflection. Thomas Erickson, from IBM's T. J. Watson Research Center, describes "persistence" in the context of online communication as follows:

Persistence expands conversation beyond those within earshot, rendering it accessible to those in other places and at later times. Thus, digital conversation may be synchronous or asynchronous, and its audience intimate or vast. Its persistence means that it may be far more structured, or far more amorphous, than an oral exchange, and that it may have the formality of published text or the informality of chat. The persistence of such conversations also opens the door to a variety of new uses and practices: persistent conversations may be searched, browsed, replayed, annotated, visualized, restructured, and recontextualized, with what are likely to be profound impacts on personal, social, and institutional practices. (par. 3)

Gaining access to the "persistence" of the communication on the Internet—talk going on 24 hours a day, around the world, accessible at least as long as the web site lasts—can be profoundly important in helping basic writers view themselves as writers and participate in the sort of critical reflection Erickson describes.

We need to help our students become part of that persistent conversation, as skilled listeners and as persuasive speakers, if we are indeed going to help them find, and value, their own voices. Last semester, one of my students who works for campus security at a neighboring university, whose essays generally consisted of short, underdeveloped paragraphs, wrote a lengthy, thoughtful, fully developed response to an online discussion topic. Answering my e-mail complimenting her on both the writing and the content, she replied:

> Message no. 713: Thanks, Professor. This is the first time, in a long time, that I get to express my opinions without being accused of being insubordinate. Having a good old time!

Although I try to make all course work relevant, assigning essays that ask my adult students to explore issues they know and care about in their work and personal lives, this student did not feel comfortable expressing ideas and defending her opinions until she left the classroom environment, where she had defined herself, narrowly, as a student, and moved online, where she was free to redefine herself as a writer.

The Best of Both Worlds: Teaching in a Hybrid Environment

Instructors' assessment of the relative pros and cons of an online basic writing class will differ, of course, depending on their own personal and institutional conditions. The students I teach at Lincoln University in Pennsylvania are predominantly African American (Lincoln is a historically black university), range in age from about 25 to 64, and must be employed full time in a human service agency as a condition for admission. The Pre-master's Program, as this developmental writing course is informally called (the official name is the Pre-graduate Semester in Writing and Critical Thinking Skills) was created to help students improve their basic academic skills so as to be eligible to enter Lincoln's non-traditional Master of Human Services (MHS) Program, a graduate program in which applicants may qualify for admission based on years of work experience in the human service field without having first earned a bachelor's degree. Most applicants, employed in a field in which talking and listening skills learned from life experience are more important than academic writing proficiency, come to the MHS Program with little or no college training; they tend to be uncomfortable communicating in Standard Written English and inexperienced at meeting the demands of academic writing. Depending on their score on the writing portion of the entrance exam, students may be assigned to the Pre-master's Program before entering the MHS Program for a 15-week semester, an accelerated 8-week semester, or a "stretch version," which extends the one semester's work over two semesters. It is this last option, the two-semester program, which we offer in the hybrid form described in this article.[1]

Students in this program are all commuters, some traveling considerably more than 100 miles to attend once-a-week classes, which are held either in the evening or on Saturdays. These students fit neatly into Mina Shaughnessy's description of basic writers as students who tend to produce "small numbers of words with large numbers of errors . . . restricted as writers but not necessarily as speakers, to a very narrow range of syntactic, semantic and rhetorical options, which forces them into a rudimentary style of discourse that belies their real maturity or a dense and tangled prose with which neither they nor their readers can cope" (179). Hoping to widen the range of options for our adult students as much as possible in as short a time as possible, we chose to design the writing course around computer-mediated teaching and learning. The setting in which classes are taught has evolved steadily since its 1987 beginnings in a basement room equipped with 15 Apple IIs, moving first to faster, standalone Windows-based PCs, then to a networked lab, next to a networked lab with Internet access, and finally to a networked lab enhanced with WebCT course management software. In 2002, after weighing the advantages and disadvantages of distance education, we decided to take the next step and add a distance component to the writing program. Students enrolled in the second semester of the two-semester "stretch version" of our basic writing course[2] now have the option of meeting in the campus writing lab only every other week, working from home using WebCT on the off weeks. The class is still evolving, but in general in-class meetings are used to introduce grammar and writing issues and describe assignments; in these sessions students also work in groups for idea generation and take all quizzes and exams. During the online weeks, students practice the grammar and composition issues discussed the previous week, respond to discussion topics, write and revise essays, and participate in online peer review. We initially saw the hybrid version of the course simply as an interim step towards a totally online program, but our experiences with both the difficulties and the successes of online learning over the past two years have led us to believe that it is the hybrid experience itself that offers our particular students the best of both pedagogical worlds.

It has been fifteen years since the "Seven Principles for Good Practice in Undergraduate Education" were first published in the *AAHE Bulletin* as a model for best teaching practices (Chickering and Ehrmann). Although articulated well before the Internet had begun to change the way learning and teaching took place, these seven principles still provide a concise overview of effective pedagogy. In the final section of this article, with hopes of stimulating further conversation on models that other instructors have found useful and encouraging more research about the ways technology could or should advance the basic writing curriculum, I group the "value added" aspects that I have begun to experience from my hybrid writing class around these seven principles, describing how a hybrid approach has offered us a means of lessening the negative effects of many of the problems described in the first part of this article while still allowing students to benefit from the advantages listed in the second.

Good Practice Encourages Student/Faculty Contact

The opportunity for unlimited office hours via e-mail or chatrooms is a clear advantage in online courses, which frequently cater to commuting or geographically distant students. Students get used to sending off an e-mail or setting up an online chatroom meeting when a problem arises rather than letting it go unquestioned. Teachers can provide the needed information promptly, preventing student frustration and lessening the chance for a late or incorrect assignment. A study by Robert Woods and Samuel Ebersole has found instructor immediacy in feedback to be "the strongest predictor of learning—both affective and cognitive learning—among students."

The benefit that comes from having my online students in my physical classroom as well, on alternate weeks, is that I can follow up one-mails, deal with new or remaining problems, and give the students a chance to explore their issues in more depth. E-mailed requests and personal conversations seem to be used for different purposes, with e-mails being more task-oriented (asking about assignments, due dates, technical problems, etc.) or else reserved for the kinds of problems students are embarrassed to bring up in person. Face-to-face discussions typically involve working through academic problems thoroughly, as well as following up e-mailed comments on life events as needed. An e-mail can give an answer; a face-to-face meeting can show how the answer was obtained. Students are not forced to rely solely on text-based communication for their questions and answers.

Good Practice Encourages Cooperation Among Students

Online access to e-mail, discussion lists and chatrooms clearly expands collaborative opportunities exponentially. For one thing, despite the potential harm to our collective egos, writing teachers in this Internet age are, as Gail Hawisher and Cynthia Selfe point out, experiencing Margaret Mead's concept of "prefigurative cultures," that is, cultures in which the adults are trying to prepare children for experiences the adults themselves have never had. In such a world, students have no alternative but to bond with and learn important lessons from each other (4). This benefits both the teacher and the learner.

What a hybrid class adds is the chance to strengthen the personal ties so important to effective collaboration. Caroline Haythornthwaite, in a paper presented at the Hawai'i International Conference on System Sciences, notes that, because of the "reduced cues" environment, online communication is less appropriate or useful for emotionally laden exchanges, for the delivery of complex information, and for creating a sense of "being there." This presents a problem for classes conducted entirely online, since obviously, these factors are essential to an educational setting. She found, however, that strongly tied pairs, with their higher motivation, eagerness to communicate, and desire to include more intimate and varied communications, manage to modify this "lean" environment to support their needs, while weakly tied communicators do not. Maintaining connectivity among both the strongly and weakly tied members of a group, Haythornthwaite argues, requires a means of communication that reaches all group members, yet requires little effort or extra work from them. A schedule that allows students to meet face to face in class every other week satisfies that criterion. If students do nothing more than show up in class, the weak ties required for basic connectivity after they leave the classroom are established. At the same time, the personal bonds which classroom interactions create should encourage the development of stronger ties and therefore lead to more proactive communication outside of class, resulting in less chance of muting and, ideally, better participation and retention of students.

Good Practice Encourages Active Learning

Stronger interpersonal ties lead communicators to seek out the means and opportunities for exchanges that support their relationships. This results in a more active learning experience. In online discussion group assignments, for instance, students can satisfy their desire for interaction while at the same time applying the principle of "write to learn/learn to write" (Mayher, Lester, and Pradl).

I had initially planned for discussion to take place solely online until student evaluations after each of the first two semesters consistently requested more time afterwards to explore the issues in the classroom. When students discuss a topic online one week and carry that discussion over into the face-to-face class the next, the best features of both activities apply. Online, the students have time for thoughtful, reflective response; in class, the follow-up discussion allows for the serendipity that perhaps only occurs in the rapid give and take of face-to-face conversation. Additionally, any meaning missed because of the "reduced cues" environment online can be regained in the oral classroom setting.

Good Practice Gives Prompt Feedback

In addition to getting prompter teacher responses, students can take quizzes or do practice exercises online and get immediate feedback. Course management tools like WebCT and Blackboard allow teachers to post their own practice quizzes, adding with relative ease personalized explanations for the correct options as well as explanations of what makes the wrong choices incorrect. I have found that students will work much longer at online exercises than they do on the same exercises in their workbooks, The tasks are more visual and more fun. Working online also strengthens students' on-screen proofreading skills and can be done at the point of need, with slower students being required to do more tasks or allowed a longer time to finish an assigned task.

When a face-to-face meeting follows an online experience, students get the added benefit of going over things together after the fact and hearing others' questions, thus reinforcing what they had learned on their own. Students take charge of their own learning needs, noting the places where they require additional instruction and profiting from the realization that they can sometimes answer questions raised by others.

Good Practice Promotes Time on Task

Course management software like Blackboard or WebCT has several features that enable teachers to model ways to structure time effectively. The calendar tool can remind students each week what is due when. The content module feature allows all the materials needed to write a given essay—preliminary reading, planning tools, essay directions, peer review questions—to be assembled in one place, available wherever the student has access to the Internet, eliminating the "I lost the reading assignment" or "I didn't have the essay directions" excuse. Nevertheless, those features and all others work only insofar as a student is motivated to use them; that is where the face-to-face class comes in, students know that they will have to face their instructor's wrath in person if they are not prepared while enjoying positive reinforcement when they are. They can drift away in the anonymity of cyberspace for no more than a week.

Good Practice Communicates High Expectations

Because the convenience of the Web, students can reasonably be expected to read more, write more, and do more group projects. Even students with limited time can do research through online academic data bases. The "Dean effect"—the motivation engendered by persistent conversation—can also be counted on to improve performance. Moreover, as Alvan Bregman and Caroline Haythornthwaite explain, "When we approach persistent conversation, we are faced with communication that inherits genre from both speech and literary practices. The learning environment inherits the speech genres of the traditional classroom, such as how to participate in class, communicate with an instructor, or carry on a discussion with fellow students, as well as the literary practices of academia, such as how to write a term paper, complete a homework assignment, or present a written argument."

When students have the opportunity to discuss both online and face to face, to submit an assignment in print form or as an online posting, to argue a point in person or via e-mail, many more of the possible communication modes are used, practiced, reinforced, and made visible. This can help to make up for any actual or perceived lack of "richness" in the online environment, and enables us in a sense to teach the students a double lesson: how to function effectively as members of two different and equally important academic discourse communities, the virtual and the actual classroom.

Good Practice Respects Diverse Talents and Ways of Learning

One student told me toward the end of last semester that she really likes and uses all the online resources available to her via WebCT. She can do her homework faithfully, do all assigned practice exercises, view explanations in the PowerPoints I have posted, and study the reading selections. But it is not until she comes to class and participates in a discussion reviewing the concepts that it all comes together for her. For many students, directions, demonstrations, and explanations—at least at some point in the learning process, whether as preview or review—need to take a form other than print. Even Murray Goldberg, the "father" of WebCT, acknowledged in a 2001 column for the *Online Teaching and Learning Newsletter* that variety provides the spice of academic life: "We all know by research or intuition that some people simply learn better when they can see a person's face and converse in real time with a peer or instructor. My own research shows that students perform best when they have access to lectures in addition to a web-based course as opposed to the web-based course alone."

When given the opportunity to learn both online and in class, students, whatever their preferred learning style, are affirmed and stretched. They also find skills other than writing—graphical, technological, organizational, group-building—being evaluated and valued, so more opportunities exist to acknowledge strengths instead of simply identifying weaknesses.

Conclusion

It has been my experience that adult basic writers arrive in class with a curious and difficult-to-deal-with mixture of dependence and independence. A number of years ago we tested our students—slightly more than 150 at that time—on the

Grasha-Riechmann Student Learning Style Scales, an instrument developed in the 1970s that categorized student preferences with respect to classroom interactions with peers and teachers along six dimensions: cooperation/competition, participation/avoidance, and independence/dependence. We were not surprised to see how our students fit clearly into the expected profile of adult learners: more *cooperative* than *competitive* and much more *participant* than *avoidant*. What did at first surprise us was that they strayed from the adult norm by emerging as more *dependent* than *independent* in their learning preferences. Further research showed us that this conflict was not unusual. Robert Sommer, for instance, points out that adults returning to school "may regress to the conditioning of early education and past roles of dependence and submission to the authority of teachers and institutions" (9). We realized that a vacillation between independent and dependent learning preferences was to be expected from our student population, whose lack of traditional academic experience created a sense of uncertainty that was at war with their adult sense of independence. Given this ongoing conflict, the current structure of this basic writing course, with one week online and one week face to face in a classroom, seems to offer our students the best of both worlds: the infinite freedom of the Internet enhanced and made manageable by regular classroom interactions.

Acknowledgment

Portions of this article were first presented at the March 2004 Conference on College Composition and Communication held in San Antonio, Texas.

Notes

1. Anyone interested in more specific information about either Lincoln University's Master of Human Services Program or the Pre-master's Program is invited to visit our website at http://www.lincoln.edu/mhs or contact me directly at stine@lu.lincoln.edu.

2. We chose to offer only the second semester in hybrid form, wanting to be sure that all students had a semester of WebCT use in a Web-enhanced face-to-face class so that they could become comfortable with the software. We hoped in this way to prevent technological concerns from distracting from or impeding writing instruction when students moved out of the familiar classroom setting.

Works Cited

Anson, Chris. "Distant Voices: Teaching and Writing in a Culture of Technology." *College English* 61 (1999): 261–80.

Baron, Denis. "From Pencils to Pixels: The Stages of Literacy Technologies." *Passions, Pedagogies, and 21ˢᵗ Century Technologies*. Ed. Gail E. Hawisher and Cynthia L. Selfe, Urbana, IL: NCTE, 1999. 15–34.

Blair, Kristine L., and Elizabeth A. Monske. "Cui Bono?: Revisiting the Promises and Perils of Online Learning." *Computers and Composition* 20 (2003): 441–53.

Bregman, Alvan, and Caroline Haythornthwaite. "Radicals of Presentation in Persistent Conversation." *Proceedings of the Jan. 3–6, 2001 Hawai'i*

International Conference On System Sciences. 1 Feb. 2004 <csdl. computer.org/comp/proceedings/hicss/2001/0981/04/09814032.pdf>.

Chickering, Arthur W., and Stephen C. Ehrmann. "Implementing the Seven Principles: Technology as Lever." *AAHE Bulletin* (October 1996): 3–6.

Collison, George, Bonnie Elbaum, Sarah Haavind, and Robert Tinker. *Facilitating Online Learning: Effective Strategies for Moderators.* Madison, WI: Atwood, 2000.

Cross, K. Patricia. *Adults as Learners: Increasing Participation and Facilitating Learning.* San Francisco: Jossey-Bass, 1981.

Davis, Evan, and Sarah Hardy. "Teaching Writing in the Space of Blackboard." *Computers & Composition Online* (Spring 2003). 15 Feb. 2004 <http://www.bgsu.edu/cconline/theory.htm>

Elbow, Peter. "Reflections on Academic Discourse: How It Relates to Freshmen and Colleagues." *College English* 53 (1991): 135–55.

Erickson, Thomas. "Editor's Introduction" *Journal of Computer-Mediated Communication* 4.4 (1999). 4 Mar. 2004 <http://www.ascusc.org/jcmc/vol4/issue4/>.

Goldberg, Murray. "Synchronous vs. Asynchronous: Some Thoughts." *Online Teaching and Learning.* 11 Sept. 2000. 14 Feb. 2004 <http://www.webct.com/service/viewcontentfrarme?contentID=2339346>.

Hawisher, Gail E., and Cynthia L. Selfe. "The Passions That Mark Us: Teaching, Texts, and Technologies." *Passions, Pedagogies, and 21st Century Technologies.* Ed. Gail E. Hawisher and Cynthia L. Selfe. Urbana, IL: NCTE, 1999. 1–14.

———, eds. *Passions, Pedagogies, and 21st Century Technologies.* Urbana, IL: NCTE, 1999.

Haythornthwaite, Caroline. "Tie Strength and the Impact of New Media." *Proceedings of the Jan. 3–6, 2001, Hawai'i International conference on System Sciences.* 1 Feb. 2004 <http://alexia.lis.uiuc.edu/~haythorn/HICSSO1_tiestrength.html>.

———, Michelle M. Kazmer, Jennifer Robins, and Susan Shoemaker. "Community Development Among Distance Learners: Temporal and Technological Dimensions." *Journal of Computer-Mediated Communication* 6.1 (2000). 12 Feb. 2004 <http://www.ascusc.org/jcmc/vol6/issue1/haythornthwaite.html>.

Johnson, J. Paul. "What Happens When Teaching Writing Online?" 2003. 15 Feb. 2004 <http:www.mhhe.com/socscience/english/tc/johnson/JPJohnsonModule.htm>.

Leibowitz, Wendy. "Technology Transforms Writing and the Teaching of Writing." *Chronicle of Higher Education* (26 Nov.1999): A67–68.

Macrorie, Ken. *Twenty Teachers.* New York: Oxford UP, 1984.

Mayher, John S., Nancy Lester, and Gordon Pradl. *Learning to Write/Writing to Learn.* Portsmouth, NH: Boynton/Cook, 1983.

Merriam, Sharan, ed. *An Update on Adult Learning Theory.* San Francisco: Jossey-Bass, 1993.

Moran, Charles. "Access: The 'A' Word in Technology Studies." *Passions, Pedagogies, and 21st Century Technologies.* Ed. Gail E. Hawisher and Cynthia L. Selfe. Urbana, IL: NCTE, 1999. 205–21.

Puccio, Paul M. "The Computer-networked Writing Lab: One Instructor's View." ERIC Clearinghouse on Reading, English, and Communication Digest #80. EDO-CS-93-03. Apr. 1993. 14 Mar. 2004 <http://www.indiana.edu/~reading/ieo/digests/d80.html>.

Selber, Stuart. "Reimagining the Functional Side of Computer Literacy." *College Composition and Communication*, 55 (2004): 470–504.

Selfe, Cynthia, and Richard Selfe. "The Politics of the Interface: Power and Its Exercise in Electronic Contact Zones." *College Composition and Communication* 45 (1994): 480–504.

Shaughnessy, Mina. "Basic Writing." *Teaching Composition: 10 Bibliographical Essays*. Ed. Gary Tate. Fort Worth, TX: Texas Christian UP, 1976. 177–206.

Simic, Marjorie. "Computer-Assisted Writing Instruction." ERIC Clearinghouse on Reading, English, and Communication Digest #97. EDO-CS-94-10. Jun. 1994. 20 Feb. 2004 <http://www.indiana.edu/~reading/ieo/digests/d97.html>.

Smith, Beatrice Quarshy. "Teaching with Technologies: A Reflexive Auto-ethnographic Portrait." *Computers and Composition*, 21.1 (2004): 49–62.

"So What Was *That* All About?" *New York Times* 22 Feb. 2004: section 4, 3.

Sommer, Robert F. *Teaching Writing to Adults: Strategies and Concepts for Improving Learner Performance*. San Francisco: Jossey-Bass, 1989.

Sosnoski, James. "Hyper-readers and Their Reading Engines." *Passions, Pedagogies, and 21st Century Technologies*. Ed. Gail E. Hawisher and Cynthia L. Selfe. Urbana, IL: NCTE, 1999. 161–78.

Straub, Richard. *A Sourcebook for Responding to Student Writing*. Cresskill, NJ: Hampton, 1999.

United States. Department of Commerce. *Falling through the Net: Toward Digital Inclusion*. Oct. 2000. 13 Aug. 2004 <http://www.ntia.doc.gov/ntiahome/fttn00/Front00.htm#Mineta>.

Whithaus, Carl. "Think Different/Think Differently: A Tale of Green Squiggly Lines, or Evaluating Student Writing in Computer-mediated Environments." *Kairos* 7 (2002). Mar. 1 2004 <http://wac.colostate.edu/aw/articles/whithaus2002/>.

Wilson, Arthur. "The Promise of Situated Cognition." *An Update on Adult Learning Theory*. Ed. Sharan Merriam. San Francisco: Jossey-Bass, 1993. 71–81.

Woods, Robert, and Samuel Ebersole. "Becoming a 'Communal Architect' in the Online Classroom: Integrating Cognitive and Affective Learning for Maximum Effect in Web-based Learning" *Online Journal of Distance Learning Administration*, VI (2003). 20 Feb. 2004 <http://www.westga.edu/%7Edistance/ojdla/spring61/spring61.htm>.

Yena, Lauren, and Zach Waggoner. "One Size Fits All?: Student Perspectives on Face-to-Face and Online Writing Pedagogies." *Computers & Composition Online*, Fall (2003). 30 Jan. 2004 <http://www.bgsu.edu/cconline/virtualc.htm>.

It Wasn't Me, Was It?" Plagiarism and the Web

By Danielle DeVoss and Annette C. Rosati

MICHIGAN STATE UNIVERSITY—EAST LANSING, MI
CLARION UNIVERSITY OF PENNSYLVANIA—CLARION, PA

Issues of plagiarism are complex, and made all the more complicated by students' increasing use of the World Wide Web as a research space. In this article, we describe several situations we faced as teachers in writing-intensive classrooms — experiences common to most teachers of writing. We share these examples to explore how issues related to plagiarism and its effects are both reproduced *and* change in new research spaces. We also share these stories to discuss how we can best handle plagiarism in first-year writing classrooms and how we can best equip students with the tools necessary to do appropriate research—both online and offline.

Sharing Our Stories

It Wasn't Me, Was It?

Having experienced plagiarism in her classes, Annette has adopted a twofold approach to avoiding it: First, early in a class, she engages students in discussions of plagiarism, talking with them about what plagiarism is, why it's wrong, and how they can avoid it. Secondly, she designs assignments that deter students from plagiarizing by encouraging original ideas, a focus on process, and multiple drafts.

In a recent introduction-to-literature course she taught, students read *King Lear*. After reading the first papers that students in her class submitted, out of curiosity, she went to an online paper mill just to see what sort of papers were available on the topic of *King Lear*. As she skimmed the papers available for download, she realized that several seemed quite familiar. Without intentionally looking for any one student's paper, she inadvertently found that three students in her class had plagiarized—had downloaded papers from the Web and turned them in as their own. In class the next day, she castigated the act and invited all of the students to visit her during her office hours, but noted that if the three people who plagiarized (she didn't point them out publicly) didn't come to speak with her, they would fail the class.

At her office hours the following week, a student shuffled in. She was surprised to see him, as he wasn't one of the plagiarists. He was nervous and asked, "It wasn't me, was it?" Annette asked why he felt he had plagiarized, and he admitted that he used a Cliff's Notes version of *King Lear* to better understand the text and write his paper. Annette explained why this wasn't plagiarism and sent him on his way. The same story played out with three more students, all worried that they had plagiarized. Finally, when Annette looked in the hallway, she was shocked to see a line of students still waiting to see her. A total of 14 students visited her office. The three plagiarists were among the fourteen, but the remaining eleven students weren't sure if they had plagiarized or not.

Dànielle DeVoss and Annette C. Rosati. "'It Wasn't Me, Was It?' Plagiarism and the Web." *Computers and Composition* 19.2 (2002):191–203. Reprinted with permission of Elsevier.

You Have to Do All That?

Dànielle always arranges for a library tour with students in her first-year composition courses. Last fall, one of the students in her course didn't show up for the tour. He was an older student, with a bit more academic experience, and she was willing to give him the benefit of the doubt. When she looked over the first draft of his paper, however, it was evident he would have benefited from the tour. All of his sources were web sites, and a few of them were really shaky—not credible at all.

Dànielle met with the student at the library and she provided a quick run through of their services, then together they headed to a computer to search the library databases for material. They did a search on a service called Infoseek and he found a couple of articles he wanted. Dànielle explained the steps to receive them: You copy or print the author's name, title, magazine name, volume, and issue. Then you go to the library holdings area of the library web site. You look to see if the library carries the magazine, and, if so, you copy the library code you need to find the magazine on the stacks. Then you go look up the volume you're looking for, find the article, and photocopy it. He balked. He stared at Dànielle, mouth open, and asked, "You mean I have to do ALL THAT?" Research, to him, was going to Y! (a commonly used search engine on the Web), doing a simple search, and using the first 10 or 20 hits.

No...I Didn't Write the Paper

The first paper that an international student submitted in a first-year composition course Dànielle recently taught was engaging and smart—he was a good writer and had incredibly interesting ideas. The paper had quite a few of the problems typical of students who learn and speak English as a second language, and, during Dànielle's office hours, they walked through these and talked about them, about American style conventions, and about how he could read for and identify these differences. The second paper he turned in was flawless but flat— it was lacking the spark of imagination in the first paper. Dànielle knew right away that he hadn't written the paper. She asked him to stop by her office to talk about the paper, and she asked him about the research he had done preparing for the paper and also asked to see his earlier drafts of the paper.

During their meeting, the student was clearly uncomfortable, and his answers were short. Finally, she asked if he had plagiarized the paper. He said, "No." She asked if he wrote the paper himself. He said, "Yes." She paused for a moment, while he stared at the floor, and asked again if he had written the paper. He said "No ... I didn't write the paper." He admitted that he had found it on the Internet and decided to turn it in. This was a tough moment—he had wanted to please Dànielle, he was shy about his writing, and he knew he had done something wrong. They talked about typical writing practices taught in schools in his country, and he explained that it was more acceptable in his country to quote extensively from other sources and that giving credit wasn't as formal as in American schools. But he did admit that he understood that — both in his home country and the United States—it was unacceptable for students to copy another person's paper in its entirety and turn it in as their own.

What These Stories Tell Us

These stories remind us that issues of research and issues of plagiarism are complex and often interconnected. Stories about papers stored in the basements of fraternity houses and available for students to plagiarize have circulated among composition teachers for quite some time, but the virtual space of the Web and the download and cutting-and-pasting techniques available pose new questions related to issues of plagiarism, questions that we, as composition instructors, must address to be best equipped to better understand plagiarism, deter students from plagiarism, and encourage students to be thoughtful and critical researchers.

Two beliefs scaffold this article: First, we are witnessing students adapting their literacy, research, reading, and writing skills and processes to the virtual space—and complexity—of the World Wide Web. Second, first-year composition teachers have a key role in helping students adapt to this space, and encouraging students' critical research and writing skills in this space. Although students enter our classrooms well versed in writing-related values and ideas relayed to them in their past school experiences, often this instruction does not address—or does not go far enough in addressing—issues of online research and writing. First-year composition seems, to us, to be the ideal place to initiate discussions related to such issues; first-year composition courses tackle (among many other functions) the task of acculturating students into academic writing. Because academic writing now relies so heavily on the reading, writing, and research accessed via virtual spaces, it is necessary for first-year composition courses to address research and writing in electronic realms and to help students develop techniques that will aid them to best use these systems. From this perspective, we address the intersections of online research and plagiarism, discuss how we can best handle plagiarism in our first-year classrooms, and how we can best equip students with the tools necessary to do appropriate research—both online and offline.

Why Plagiarism? Disciplinary Functions and Rethinking Plagiarism

A.E. Malloch (1976) asked a question in 1976 that is still relevant today: "Why plagiarism?" (p. 165). Why do we penalize and punish, discipline and drill where plagiarism is concerned, especially when, as Malloch noted, there are other worthy vices in academia (for example, laziness, carelessness)? Malloch argued that part of the reason we punish plagiarism is that, frankly, plagiarism makes us look—and feel—bad. We preach process, we teach approaches, and we scour student work, commenting, suggesting, and exclaiming—to find that some of the students in our classes have downloaded their papers from the Internet.

It is not surprising that plagiarism is still a common subject of discussion and research as plagiarism is a fairly contemporary notion—individualistic authorship is a relatively new idea. Prior to our Modernist notions of author and authorship, most work was collaborative in a larger sense (Barthes, 1985; Foucault, 1984; Howard, 1995). Roland Barthes and Michel Foucault both noted that the author figure came into being as we know it today when the value of the individual became prestigious and our notions of subjectivity shifted.

Many of us are well read in contemporary composition theory and have adopted a process approach—and even an approach that both addresses and somewhat dismisses the romantic, modernist notion of Author (writing in isolation, suffering, the tortured artist at *his* craft)—most of us at the same time still focus on a polished, final product by an author whose name appears (alone) at the top of the first page. And our institutions hold these same values.

Most academic institutions offer definitions of academic honesty for students and recommended actions for teachers to deal with situations of academic dishonesty. Embedded within these policies are language and attitudes toward plagiarism typical of the rhetoric of crime and punishment regarding plagiarism.

Generally, instructors are expected to report, in writing, all students who break or even bend policy. Reported students face punishment ranging from failing a class, being put on academic probation, and/or facing suspension or expulsion from the university. Malloch (1976) compellingly argued, however, that policies such as these have little or no impact until and unless we convince students that their written work is valuable *and* valued — a small, but potent gesture (Selfe, 1999) toward encouraging students' writing, thinking, and development.

Although institutional policies are broad and totalizing, alternative approaches to understanding plagiarism have been proposed. Rebecca Moore Howard (1993), for example, noted that most policies define plagiarism only in negative terms. Howard suggested that students engaging in the sort of work often attacked as plagiarism are often engaging in a positive activity she called *patchwriting*, which allows students a place to borrow from text, manipulate it, and work through new concepts by piecing their writing with the original work. Malloch (1976) characterized plagiarism as *kidnapping*, rather than theft, and referred to this type of borrowing, weaving writing as *impersonation*—writing as experimentation, as mimic. This sort of writing — clearly a *stage* in writing development— allows students to test new approaches, process new ideas, and learn new writing strategies. These patchwriters, rather than "being unethical plagiarists, often strive to observe proper academic conventions" (Howard, 1993; p. 236).

Why Students Plagiarize

Equally as interesting as how teachers and their institutions define plagiarism is *why* students plagiarize. Reasons for plagiarizing are as diverse and complex as definitions of plagiarism. Students may plagiarize because they feel that assembling sources, citations, and quotes is the primary goal of writing a paper—and that their original ideas are secondary (Whitaker, 1993). Students may stumble toward plagiarism when they fail to cite properly because they don't entirely understand the point or argument of a primary work, or in a struggle to define what "common knowledge" means, they struggle to identify which information merits a citation (Whitaker, 1993). Plagiarism might emerge because students have a poor understanding of an assignment or of the rhetorical aspects of an assignment—that is, a weak understanding of situation, audience, and their purpose in completing an assignment (1990). Students may plagiarize because they feel pressured to privilege a project or paper for another course or to free up time to put in more hours at work. Students may plagiarize to get the work done; as Augustus Kolich (1983) noted, "the stolen essay serves a practical purpose; it is a finished product that fits into a specific slot and that completes an assignment" (p. 146). Finally, students may plagiarize because of the often-appearing-unconscious cultural principles of written work. Cultures vary in how writing, authorship, identity, individualism, ownership rights, and personal relationships are perceived, and these variances in values and approaches to text affect student writing (Fox, 1994).

Although we regularly tell students that plagiarism is wrong, a variety of factors and temptations beyond those listed above complicate this generic warning. American academic writing is full of often conflicting complications, the most obvious of which is expecting students to come up with and develop an original idea, while requiring them to find plenty of material to back up their supposedly new and original idea or perspective on a subject. Those of us indoctrinated into academic writing traverse this complication quite easily—that is, we can explain new ideas and complement them with existing research and theory—but it should still be clear to most of us that this complication poses a challenge to students in our classes.

Further complicating students' negotiations of both comfortable and new ideas is the fact that although many seasoned academic writers can often negotiate the original ideas/supporting work paradox a bit more easily, this seemingly contradictory task leaves many high school and college-level composition students in an intellectual lurch. Common questions may include: Where does one person's work leave off and another's begin? What can be considered "common knowledge?" Does *everything* have to be cited? Is it cheating or plagiarizing to use resources like Web sites offering summaries or Cliff's Notes, as the nervous students in Annette's class did?

We can tell students that plagiarism is an academic crime, but we often assume they understand what that means and that they hold academic honesty policies in as high esteem as we do. Asking a student to create original ideas encourages plagiarism in the sense that students often feel the need to consult sources for help. How many new insights are readily available for readers of *King Lear*, for example? We ask students not just for their insights, but for their original ideas, ideas that must also — in some instances—be "correct." For example, it would not be correct for a student to write an essay describing how King Lear loved Goneril more than he loved Cordelia. Such ideas are certainly original, but not correct within acceptable, intellectual, shared discourse *on Lear*. This need to be correct motivated the students in Annette's class to seek additional sources for originality. They searched to meet the demand imposed upon them—to conjure up their own perspectives on *King Lear*. In other classes, however, the line defining what is "correct" is quite blurry. Courses that focus with a broad cultural lens or ask students to consider social issues, for example, may have a body of related work suggesting "correct" stances, but many of us may, in fact, discourage students from a final, fixed belief about an issue. Students often have classes that encourage them to learn a fixed, correct approach to an idea or theory, *and* classes that encourage them to retain a broad, critical, "gray-area" approach to a subject.

Online plagiarism is just as, if not more, complicated as any other form of plagiarism, and these same—and different—complications apply to research and writing in online realms. Students may plagiarize from online research spaces because it's easy to do so; cutting and pasting is a common virtual text manipulation trick. Students may plagiarize from online research spaces because there is no review, publication, and catalogue process for most Web pages, and, on top of that, authors aren't always privileged the way they are in print texts. Students may plagiarize from virtual realms because they lack sophistication in searching and evaluating sources within this realm and, frustrated, resort to stealing texts. Students may plagiarize from web pages because they are refocusing their literacy, research, and writing skills to online spaces, and they are adapting to the rhetorically and technologically complicated demands of the Web.

One of these complicated demands is the evolving idea of what a *text* is. What we consider to be texts have shifted due to online realms (see, for example, Bolter; Joyce; Landow and Lanham). Texts now include sound and integrate visuals in ways that allow for more complex and fragmented presentations of connections, topics, and representations within richly layered systems. Thus, the tools that we and the students in our classes need to write, read, and understand new variations of composing have also changed. One such tool is understanding the complicated interfaces of machines—what is seen on the screen. The virtual–visual interface of the operating system (for example, 95, *Macintosh* O/S 8.5) is sophisticated and complex. The other software installed on the machine presents an equally complex literacy challenge, with sophisticated error messages, complex toolbars, elaborate menu bars, and incredibly detailed and embedded help features. Users have to negotiate both a textual ("File," "Edit," and so on.) and a graphical (icons that represent "open file" or "paintbrush") interface.

Through these interfaces and with this software, students go online, and face yet another layer of complexity. On the Web, students must learn to navigate complex and layered hypertexts, texts that often have embedded and complex graphical content, audio, and rich visual textures. For students who have typically been asked to negotiate traditional texts, navigating and interacting within these new realms is a strange and often quite difficult, frustrating task.

Addressing Plagiarism in Changing Research Spaces

Finding a Foothold

A variety of scholars have offered grounded, practical approaches to addressing issues of plagiarism, ranging from the suggestion that writing teachers develop a stronger understanding of students' approaches to tasks and the invitation that we trust students' understandings of responsibility and authorship (Kolich, 1983). Likewise, we should share with students definitions of academic honesty and cases of plagiarism to enable students to read, analyze, and understand institutional approaches to academic dishonesty (Hawley, 1984; Whitaker, 1993; Wilhoit, 1994). In our classrooms and curricula, building strong rhetorical purpose into our assignments allows students to have a much more clear focus when they begin their work, and as they work through a writing activity (Kantz, 1990). Focusing on microtasks and task management is another approach to encouraging students to better understand and manage a complex assignment and to deter them from plagiarism (Kantz, 1990; Kloss, 1996).

All of these suggestions are helpful for dealing with issues of plagiarism and provide a crucial foundation for better understanding plagiarism, online or offline. None of them, however, directly addresses issues of Internet plagiarism. In the rest of this article, we explore available remedies for us and for the students in our classrooms as we attempt to bolster our approaches to reading, writing, and research in new realms.

Negotiating Online Spaces

The Web offers a current, vast, and rapidly expanding research and information-delivery system. The Web, however, exacerbates existing problems that we don't often enough address in writing-intensive classrooms, including the issue of plagiarism. In a realm where anyone with a computer, Internet access, and a basic knowledge of HTML and web publishing can be an electronically published "expert," information changes shape, as do our approaches to it. Information is also much easier to plagiarize from the Web. We might even go so far as to say that cutting and pasting is almost natural in this realm, as the Web is typically accessed through an interface where cutting and pasting are basic and often-used techniques.

There are few checks and balances in the electronic realm—no librarians, no one thoroughly checking the validity of information posted, and no one checking the validity of source material. In addition, savvy students are copying or downloading entire papers and industrious web designers are copying not only code, but also content from web sites. In this realm, it's almost surprising to imagine students *not* being tempted to follow suit.

Of course, most students buying a paper from a paper mill (online or physical) or borrowing a paper from the filing cabinet in the basement of their fraternity or sorority house probably know that they are doing something wrong. And, we would probably not rely on postmodern theories of authorship and shifting subjectivity to excuse their behavior. However, the vast majority of students who plagiarize might not even realize that they are plagiarizing, and others may even harbor a somewhat constant fear that they are possibly plagiarizing. We want to believe that many students aren't necessarily evil or unthinking, but instead they're learning to negotiate and do research in new spaces, in spaces that can offer fresh and exciting research possibilities, but also offer technical tricks like cutting and pasting and rhetorical complications like "eye candy," distracting gimmicks, and advertisements.

Recommendations for Research and Writing in Online Spaces

Although a variety of articles in the popular press have addressed online plagiarism (see, e.g., Chidley, 1997; Hickman, 1998; Innerst, 1998; Jones, 1997; Kleiner & Lord, 1999; Mooney, 1999; Plotz, 1999; Sanchez, 1998; Witherspoon, 1995), few scholarly resources offer specific advice to teachers of writing. Vicki Tolar Burton and Scott Chadwick (2000) analyzed the Internet-oriented advice offered in a variety of handbooks for composition students and concluded that most handbooks that supposedly offer advice related to Internet research are merely supplemented by Internet source citation styles. Burton and Chadwick argued that even among the burgeoning supply of Internet how-to guides marketed for writing students, a number of authors who minutely document every move involved in an Internet search tend to gloss over the critical thinking processes involved in evaluating research sources on the Internet and assume students will intuitively know how to assess the sources they find (p. 312). Burton and Chadwick provide an excellent analysis of Internet research, but, like many other authors addressing issues of Internet research, do not discuss issues of plagiarism.

Here we offer two approaches that apply to both offline and online research and writing—supplements crucial to our first-year composition classes if we are to successfully integrate web work into our curricula, a choice not up to us to make as more and more students rely on the Web as a research space and as more and more institutions adopt web-based teaching interfaces (like WCT, B, and D Online).

Intellectual Property as a Lens

Karla Kitalong (1998) shared a cut-and-paste story, noting the ease with which one of students admitted to plagiarizing the design of a web page. The student—after the original web author contacted the student and his professor—admitted "I really didn't think I had done anything wrong," but later admitted to being "hasty and impulsive" (p. 254). The question Kitalong asked is the same we are still faced with: Did this student plagiarize? How does electronic publishing complicate our print-based assumptions about what plagiarism is and isn't? What is common practice on the Web? How do we separate code from design in online space? Design from content?

The student whose site was plagiarized in the instance Kitalong (1998) shared added a warning on his site after the incident. In doing so, he accepted some responsibility in deterring anyone from plagiarizing his online work. This is also a possible remedy to plagiarism, but a warning on one site might mean that an absence of a warning on another site is an invitation to plagiarize. Calling attention to copyright and authorship issues generally and on web sites specifically serves as one activity composition teachers can use for leverage in discussing issues of plagiarism.

At Michigan Technological University, the majority of students are engineers and are highly industry oriented (in fact, more and more majors at the university are requiring earlier co-operative experience, internships, and industry-led courses). A useful tactic to "sell" the notion of plagiarism to students is to introduce the topic of plagiarism embedded within a discussion of intellectual property. Students understand plagiarism as relating to school work, which often comes secondary to their industry focus. Intellectual property, however, allows for a broader discussion of ethics and responsibility. (Clearly, however, plagiarism as school related and intellectual property as industry related is a false dichotomy; in everyday academic work students come into contact with a variety of copyrighted works in their everyday academic work, such as textbooks, lab materials, equipment, and so on.)

The primary reason that we suggest focusing on issues of plagiarism through the lens of intellectual property is we sometimes find ourselves having to convince students why plagiarism is wrong. It is, as we argued earlier, not enough for us to just say, "Don't do it"; it is important to tell students why plagiarism is important and *why* and *how* it should be avoided. It's one thing to tell students that it is wrong to steal a few sentences of someone's work, but it's another thing entirely to demonstrate the importance of respecting another's work by using a "real-world" legal example of an intellectual property issue. An example Dànielle has used with her classes is the Vanilla Ice "Ice Ice, Baby" case. In the early 1990s, the wrapper of Vanilla Ice sampled an identifiable riff from an earlier Queen/David Bowie collaboration. Vanilla Ice did so without the explicit permission of the original artist, and a lawsuit ensued. Eventually, the case was dropped, but only after Vanilla Ice's label had invested tens (if not hundreds) of thousands of dollars in their legal defense. Likewise, another band — The Verve — slightly altered and reproduced a copy of a Rolling Stones' song ("Bittersweet Symphony") without the permission of the Rolling Stones or their corporate representation. The further reproduction and distribution of the album, after an initial run, was halted by the legal team representing the Rolling Stones, providing a grand set-back to The Verve and costing their recording company a good deal of money. And Napster is, obviously, an excellent example of intellectual property changing shape online, and a great topic to use to encourage discussion of the ownership of texts, ideas, and recordings.

Examples like these—embedded in a larger discussion of issues of copyright, fair use, and plagiarism—help solidify the importance of respecting the work of others. These discussions are particularly rich when focused on the shifting legal and ethical landscape of the Web and what intellectual property means in virtual space.

Encouraging Critical Online Research

Believing that issues of research and plagiarism are often closely connected and believing that first-year writing instructors should support students as they negotiate new research spaces, we also suggest equipping students with the skills to be critical thinkers and critical researchers in all of the realms in which they do research, especially within online spaces. The first step is to help them be effective searchers of the Web and evaluators of the information they find. Doing on-line research, for many students, means connecting to the search engine they're used to; doing a basic, unnarrowed search; and then looking at the first hits that come up and using the material from those sites.

Madeleine Sorapure, Pamela Inglesby, and George Yatchisin (1998) also argued that the assessment and evaluation of online sources be taught in composition courses. These authors pointed out three of the challenges the Web poses: First, no universal cataloging or categorizing takes place on the Web (although at this point in time, search engines have become more and more sophisticated, changing at a fast pace in the years since the 1998 article by Sorapure, Inglesby, and Yatchisin.) Second, the Web is rhetorically complex—web sites sell products, offer information, give data and statistics, and so on. And, finally, the design of web sites doesn't often reflect their purpose, and the interface of the Web is incredibly rich with text, images, animated images, video clips, and audio files. Discerning how the multimedia pieces of a web site come together to serve a specific purpose can be a daunting task. Sorapure, Inglesby, and Yatchisin draw upon resources offered by university library sites and by web design and publication sites for guidance on evaluation.

To scaffold the activities listed below, we also adopted a web-page evaluation approach and generated the following categories of questions:

author/credibility (for example, "What is the authority or expertise of the author of the page?" "With what organization or larger site is the web page connected/affiliated?")

reliability of information (for example, "Who do you think is the expected audience?" "What is the primary purpose of the page?" "Does the information support or contradict what you know or what you already have learned from another source?")

interface design (for example, "Is the site conceptually exciting? Does it do more than can be done with print?" "Do the graphics serve a rhetorical purpose, or are they decorative?")

navigation (for example, "Can you find your way around the page to find the information you want?" "Do all of the links work?").

Clearly, most of these are questions we should encourage students to ask of all media and all texts, not just those gathered within online realms. However, although we—and the students in our classrooms—may be comfortable evaluating the credibility of paper texts, evaluating the credibility of online texts is a task that often feels foreign, mainly because of the lack of clear catalogue processes and the complicated nature of online, multimedia texts.

There are a variety of practical, critical, writing-rich ways to engage students in web-based research and evaluation. A few suggestions include:

- Have students write a short self-reflective paper analyzing their research methods and how they approach different types of sources.

- Have students bring to class a print source and a web source and analyze and critique each, then practice summarizing, paraphrasing, and quoting from each.

- Have students create a handout for the class to use including recommendations for citing web sources in their papers.

- Have students search for information on evaluating sites on the Web. Have groups of students evaluate the information on evaluation, then have students present their findings and collaboratively create guidelines for evaluating online sources handout for the class.

- Have students choose a web page to revamp, drawing upon the evaluation criteria (how would they improve this page? What is this page missing? What new information is needed to make the page more effective?).

- Have students perform the same search—using the same key words and search criteria—on several different search engines and write a paper explaining the differences (and, if applicable, similarities) in the results and why they think such differences exist.

- Have students do a Web versus the library search—provide the students with five questions. Have half the students look up the answers in the library, and have half look up the answers on the Web. Then have them switch roles. Ask students to write a paper evaluating the strengths and limitations of each research space.

- Have students research and come up with their own definitions for and examples of plagiarism. Have students present their findings and collaboratively create a plagiarism guidelines handout for the class.

- Have students research the different approaches or guidelines different institutions or colleges suggest and enforce about plagiarism and intellectual property.

- Have students research the process for getting something copyrighted or trademarked and also research what copyright or trademark protection allows. Require that students include examples and, if possible, legal cases.

- Have students find something with a trademark or copyright symbol on it and research what the symbol means (using the object itself, information on intellectual property, the company's web page, and so on) and also research what the symbol allows or protects.

Each of these activities offers several rhetorically smart possibilities: Students hone their research skills; students write documents for a real audience (the other students in the class); students work collaboratively and engage in discussions about what plagiarism is and what it means; and students explore plagiarism and intellectual property issues, hopefully leading to a stronger realization that the rules of academia aren't entirely divorced from the "real-world" issues of industry.

Conclusion

To make the Web a better research space—a space where students will be doing critical, thoughtful, thorough research instead of searching for papers to plagiarize—we must engage students in tasks appropriate to the complexity of online space. At the same time, we should engage students in a complex understanding of what plagiarism is and why it's penalized in our institutions. We also have to reconcile our understanding of plagiarism, the author function, and what a text actually is and what purpose a textual product serves, especially in light of online text. This approach should enable students in our classes to be thoughtful online researchers and careful, critical writers.

Rather than approach plagiarism as an affront to our values and authority as teachers, issues of plagiarism can provide a scaffolding for discussions relating to appropriate research, good writing, similarities and differences in research spaces, intellectual property rights, and the pitfalls and potentials of electronic media. With broader and more intense information dispersion, teachers will have to help prepare students to do research in online spaces. This is incredibly exciting work because many of us are on the verge of a turning point in our teaching: We're currently moving from a more how-to approach (how to get on the Web, how to use a search engine, and so on) to a rhetorically savvy, complex, and critical approach to Internet research. This is also important work because of the function first-year writing serves.

Admittedly, most first-year writing courses and curricula are already packed, perhaps overloaded—a testament to the importance of first-year writing. But as we work toward acculturating students into the processes and function of academic writing *and* engaging them in appropriate academic processes, we must make room for addressing new research and writing spaces. This does not mean we have to entirely shift our focus or replace much of our curricula. What this means is that we need to shift and adapt our curricula to include new research spaces and the promises and perils they pose. This sort of approach is what we need to further develop if we are going to better understand the temptations students face in online realms, and the complications they face in adapting their literacy, research, and writing skills and processes to the virtual space—and complexity—of the Web.

References

Barthes, Roland. (1985). The death of the author. In *Image/music/text* (Trans. Stephen Heath) (pp. 142–148). New York: Hill and Wang.

Bolter, Jay David. (1991). *Writing space: The computer, hypertext, and the history of writing*. Hillsdale, NJ: Lawrence Erlbaum.

Burton, Vicki Tolar and Chadwick, Scott. Investigating the practices of student researchers: Patterns of use and criteria for use of Internet and library sources. *Computers and Composition* 17 (2000), pp. 309–328.

Chidley, Joe. (1997, November 24). Tales out of school: Cheating has long been a great temptation, and the Internet makes it easier than ever. *Maclean's*, pp. 76–80.

Drum, Alice. Responding to plagiarism. *College Composition and Communication* 37 (1986), pp. 241–243.

Foucault, Michel. (1984). What is an author? In Paul Rabinow (Ed.), *The Foucault reader* (pp. 101–120). New York: Pantheon Books.

Fox, Helen. (1994). *Listening to the world: Cultural issues in academic writing*. Urbana, IL: National Council of Teachers of English.

Hawley, Christopher S. The thieves of academe: Plagiarism in the university system. *Improving College and University Teaching* 32 (1984), pp. 35–39.

Hickman, John N. (1998, March 23). Cybercheats: Term-paper shopping online. *The New Republic*, pp. 14–16.

Howard, Rebecca. A plagiarism pentimento. *Journal of Teaching Writing* 11 (1993), pp. 233–245.

Howard, Rebecca. Plagiarisms, authorships, and the academic death penalty. *College English* 57 (1995), pp. 788–806.

Innerst, Carol. (1998, March 9). Students are pulling off the big cheat. *Insight on the News*, p. 41.

Jones, Patrice M. (1997, December 8). Internet term papers write new chapter on plagiarism. *Chicago Tribune*, p. 1.

Joyce, Michael. (1995). *Of two minds: Hypertext pedagogy and poetics*. Ann Arbor: University of Michigan Press.

Kantz, Margaret. Helping students use textual sources persuasively. *College English* 52 (1990), pp. 74–91.

Kitalong, Karla. A web of symbolic violence. *Computers and Composition* 15 (1998), pp. 253–264.

Kleiner, Carolyn, & Lord, Mary. (1999, November 22). The cheating game. *U.S. News and World Report*, pp. 54–66.

Kloss, Robert J. Writing things down vs. writing things up. *College Teaching* 44 (1996, Winter), pp. 3–7.

Kolich, Augustus M. Plagiarism: The worm of reason. *College English* 45 (1983), pp. 141–148.

Landow, George P. (1992). *Hypertext: The convergence of contemporary critical theory and technology*. Baltimore: Johns Hopkins University Press.

Lanham, Richard A. (1993). *The electronic word: Democracy, technology, and the arts*. Chicago: University of Chicago Press.

Malloch, A.E. A dialogue on plagiarism. *College English* 38 (1976), pp. 65–74.

Mooney, John. (1999, February 11). Universities battling sale of term papers. *Sun News*, p. 6A.

Plotz, David. (1999, October 14). New frontiers in cheating. *Rolling Stone*, p. 107.

Sanchez, Roberto. (1998, December 21). College, cheaters, computers coincide. *The Seattle Times*, p. B1.

Sorapure, Madeleine; Inglesby, Pamela; Yatchisin, George. Web literacy: Challenges and opportunities for research in a new medium. *Computers and Composition* 15 (1998), pp. 409–424.

Whitaker, Elaine E. A pedagogy to address plagiarism. *College Composition and Communication* 44 (1993), pp. 509–514.

Wilhoit, Stephen. Helping students avoid plagiarism. *College Teaching* 42 (1994), pp. 161-164.

Witherspoon, Abigail. (1995, June). This pen for hire: On grinding out papers for college students. *Harper's Magazine*, pp. 49–58.

PART

4

Handouts and
Transparency Masters

Invention Strategies/Prewriting Techniques

Freewriting   Write without stopping and without worrying about punctuation and grammar.

Focused Freewriting   Write on a specific topic without stopping.

Clustering
(also known   Begin with a topic in the center of the page; write as down every idea that occurs to you; group related thoughts and images by connecting
Bubbling or **Mapping)**   them with lines. Strive to fill the page quickly.

Listing   Make a list down a fresh page of all ideas that occur to you without worrying about creating complete sentences.

Doodling   Draw and jot down words to free creativity. This method is often helpful for visual learners.

Taping   Record associative ideas on a topic on a hand-held tape recorder (voice activated is useful) and then play back the tape. Auditory learners often find this an effective method of generating ideas.

Reasons for Using Invention Strategies/Prewriting Techniques

Prewriting and Invention Strategies

- break writer's block

- help find what interests you within an assigned topic

- help uncover unverbalized opinions and ideas

- lead to the creation of a topic sentence or thesis statement

- generate supporting details

- connect ideas into groups, which may eventually become paragraphs

- tap into creativity

- encourage an attention to detail that is normally filtered out

An Example of Freewriting (Definition Paragraph)

Good actions. that may need to be defined. For example, are apologies good action? giving gifts? Taking care of animals? Doing things that make others feel good? Or is it only when you are helping others who are in need? I've never even questioned this before. I'm stuck. Wahere was I? It seems to me that many actions that we do which we name "good" are just cultural expectations that we are tring to satisfy .... Christmas gifts, tithing, volunteer work. It seems that it must have something to do with the spirit or quality of heart in which something is don. Am I rigtht about that? The mindfulness, selflessness. And then if one starts to regret the selfless action because it is not appresiated, does it become the opposite of a good action? Telling the truth when it will have repercussions on oneself. Giving when it will cause personal sacrifices. Giving time to others rather than to one's own pursuits. But if one is only doing these things to be thought of as a good person . . . !!!! Doesn't that negate the good action? Each day lived to the fullest is a good action, i think. A person for who good actions are integral in their lives may have trouble remembering their good actions because it is a way of live for them. And they don't expect a reward. If you are paid for doing something good, is it still a good action? not doing a bad action that someone wants to do might be considered a good action.

Paragraph Drawn from Freewriting

Many people I talk to refer to "good actions" or "good works" with suggestion that we have a simple, common definition. However, I realized that attempting a definition of "good actions" can be very slippery indeed. First, we need to realize that many of the things we may do which make us feel good about ourselves are not necessarily good actions. We actually do them because of cultural expectations. Some examples of these actions might be giving gifts for birthdays or holidays, giving blood, giving money in the offering plate each Sunday, and coaching a Little League team. Second, if one is doing a good action in order to be thought of as a good person by one's friends, family, or community, then the action in itself may not be purely good. One example from my experience is the time I gave a dollar to a homeless man, which made me a hero with my friends. The truth is, I had five dollars in my pocket. I could have given the homeless man all of my money, but I didn't think he deserved it. Third, if one ends up regretting a good action because it wasn't appreciated properly, one's good action becomes tainted. I once gave my jacket to a classmate who was cold, and she told her friends that my jacket had a bad smell. I was angry that she didn't appreciate my selflessness and talked badly about her for a year after that. The conclusion that I have come to is that good actions must be deeds which help others, which are a personal sacrifice, and which are done without desire for reward or thanks.

The Elements of Good Writing 1

Subject   What am I writing about? What aspect of my subject interests me most?

Purpose   Why am I writing? What do I wish to prove or disprove? Am I explaining a concept, defining an idea, classifying information, comparing two topics to find similarities or differences, showing how to do a project, describing an event, narrating a story, or showing the causes or effects of a course of action?

Audience   Whom am I writing to? Who most needs to receive the information I have to offer? What is the best approach for reaching these readers?

Voice   What attitude do I have toward my subject matter? What attitude do I have toward my audience? How can my word choice best reflect these attitudes?

Unity   What is my *thesis*? What is the topic sentence of each paragraph? Do the topic sentences relate to the thesis? Do the sentences in each paragraph clearly expand the topic sentences?

Coherence   How have I *organized* my information? Is the progression of my thoughts logical and clear? Have I provided enough transitional words and phrases to help readers understand the relationship of each idea to the others?

The Elements of Good Writing 2

Writers should pay attention to six important basic areas if they are going to communicate well: subject, audience, purpose, voice, unity, and coherence.

Subject
Also called the *topic* or *central theme*, your *subject* is what you are writing about. Writers often narrow their subject to some aspect that is of special interest.

Audience
From the same root word as *audio* (audire, to hear), *audience* means literally "people who hear." Who needs to hear the message you are writing about? Who would benefit the most? An audience for a piece of writing could be your family (a note on the refrigerator), your best friend (a letter), your boss (a memo or email), or a group of people–older students who work, third graders, people your age, people who ride motorcycles. The list is endless. The point is you define whom you want to reach. Once you know your audience, you can tailor your language and approach accordingly.

Purpose
Why are you writing the piece? Many times a writer cannot answer that question until at least halfway through a draft. Your purpose may be to inform your audience. You may wish to entertain them. Do you have a point to prove? Are you going to tell a story, make a comparison, give examples, show how to do something, or describe something in detail? Know, before the final draft, what you wish to accomplish. The best finished writing contains forethought.

Voice
Writing often reveals a writer's attitude about his/her subject matter and about his/her audience. These attitudes that come through the text are referred to as the writer's *voice*.

Unity
Any piece of writing you do should be a unified whole. That means you should have a clear thesis, with each paragraph directly relating back to the thesis.

Coherence
This element of writing is often confused with unity. Coherence is about the relationship of the sentences to one another. In order for your ideas to flow, it is important that you use transitional words and phrases. You want to make sure that one thought follows logically and clearly from another. Also, you will want to check that your sentences are organized according to an understandable scheme (most important to least important, least important to most important, chronologically, spatially, etc.).

Voice: Avoiding the Second Person
(Original Version: Chapter 2, Activity 5)

Following is the original paragraph for Activity 5: Voice: Rewriting a Paragraph to Avoid the Second Person. This selection is taken from "Our Changing World," in *America's Hottest Colleges* (2006 Edition), by Lois B DeFleur, President, SUNY Binghamton.

Our world is getting smaller and the pace of change is quickening. Today's college graduate will change jobs as many as ten times over the course of a career, often moving in completely new directions. Most people end up in careers that are fairly unrelated to what they studied in college and find themselves working with colleagues from many different nations and cultures. Successful students think broadly, taking courses that will give them the greatest range of opportunity. The world has become much more interdependent. Health, law, business, and many other fields all operate in a world of permeable borders. Preventing the spread of disease, reducing the flow of illicit drugs, and resolving environmental challenges all require an international outlook. Students who understand other societies and cultures gain a wider base of knowledge and have better communication skills than those who do not.

Finding the Subject of a Sentence

Subjects usually answer, "Who or what is the sentence about?"

> **Example:** Tameka washed her new Mazda.

When you read the sentence, ask yourself who or what is the sentence about? The answer is Tameka.

Subjects often come early in the sentence.

> **Example:** <u>Tameka</u> washed her new Mazda.

A subject is usually a noun or a pronoun.

A *noun* is a word that names persons, places, or things and can function as a subject, an object, or a possessive in the sentence.

> **Example:** The <u>tires</u> were muddy.

A *pronoun* is a word used to take the place of a noun such as *I, you, he, she, it, we,* or *they*.

> **Example:** <u>She</u> filled the bucket with soapy water.

Subjects that are nouns and pronouns can be modified by adjectives.

An *adjective* is a word that modifies (describes or limits) a noun or pronoun.

> **Example:** The new, lipstick-red <u>Mazda</u> gleamed in the bright sun.
> (The adjectives modifying the subject Mazda are *new* and *lipstick-red*.)

The subject can be a compound.

A *compound* is two or more nouns or pronouns joined together by *and, or, either/or,* or *neither/nor*.

> **Example 1:** <u>Tameka</u> and <u>Malcolm</u> took a drive later that afternoon.
> **Example 2:** Neither the <u>heat</u> nor the <u>traffic</u> could spoil their mood.

Finding Hidden Subjects

Since a subject can never be found in a prepositional phrase, the subject of a sentence is easier to detect if the prepositional phrases are deleted.

A *prepositional phrase* is a group of words containing a preposition and an object of the preposition with its modifiers.

> **Example:** After the football game, <u>Tonio</u> took his friend to a diner for a hamburger.

Game, diner, and *hamburger* cannot be subjects because they are objects of prepositional phrases.

Since the subject of a sentence cannot be found in an appositive, deleting appositives can make it easier to find the subject.

An *appositive* is a word or group of words that gives extra information about a noun.

> **Example:** <u>Marketa</u>, a Czech college student, will be coming to live with us.

A Czech college student is an appositive for Marketa because it gives extra information about her.

To find the subject of questions, change the questions to statements.

> **Example:** When did <u>Tonio</u> meet Janessa?
> <u>Tonio</u> met Janessa when they were in high school.

If a sentence that is not a question begins with a verb and gives a command, the subject of the sentence is an understood (although it is not written) *you*.

> **Example:** Take out the garbage right this minute.
> (<u>You</u>) take out the garbage right this minute.

Since *here* and *there* can never be subjects, ask yourself what the sentence is about in order to find the subject.

> **Example:** Here are the magic markers I was looking for.
> (The <u>magic markers</u> I was looking for are here.)

Finding Verbs in Sentences

After you have located the subject of any given sentence, you should have no trouble finding the verb if you pay attention to these three types: action verbs, linking verbs, and helping verbs.

1. Action Verbs

These verbs tell us what the subject is doing and when the action occurs.

> **Example:** <u>Mike</u> <u>drove</u> seventy miles last week to reach a grocery store.
>
> *Mike* is the subject. What did he do? Drive. When? Last week.

2. Linking Verbs

These verbs link the subject to one or more words, which identify and/or describe the subject.

> **Example 1:** <u>Martha Fuller</u> <u>has become</u> a fine surgeon at Mercy Hospital.
> **Example 2:** <u>Rodney</u> <u>is feeling</u> confident about his chances of being hired.
> **Example 3:** <u>I</u> <u>am</u> very hungry.
>
> *Martha Fuller* can be renamed by the phrase *a fine surgeon*.
> *Confident* describes some aspect of the subject *Rodney*.
> *Very hungry* describes the state of being for the subject *I*.

Some common linking verbs are: *feel, grow, look, seem, appear*, and all forms of the verb *to be*.

3. Helping Verbs

These verbs are used to help the main verb express time or special meaning.

> **Example 1:** <u>Eve</u> <u>was reading</u> in the Student Union on her lunch hour.
> **Example 2:** <u>They</u> <u>will be going</u> to Mexico for Spring Break.
> **Example 3:** <u>I</u> <u>have taken</u> the driver's test twice already.
>
> *Was* is a helping verb for the main verb *to read* and helps to describe continuous action in the past.
> *Will* and *be* are helping verbs for the main verb *to go* and they help to describe continuous action in the future.
> *Have* is a helping verb for the main verb *to take* and helps to describe finished action in the past with reference to the present.

Making Subjects And Verbs Agree 1

Subject-verb agreement with pronouns

Pay attention to present tenses, especially when combined with third-person singular pronouns *he, she,* or *it*.

> **Example:** I <u>love</u> watching old movies, but not Eddie. <u>He</u> <u>loves</u> action films.

Subject-verb agreement with *do* and *be*

Use *does, is,* and *was* with third-person singular pronouns *he, she,* and *it* and singular nouns.

> **Example 1:** <u>She</u> <u>does</u> enjoy skiing although she <u>is</u> not very experienced.
> **Example 2:** When he <u>was</u> younger, <u>Ron</u> <u>was</u> a member of the ski club.

Subject-verb agreement with hard-to-find subjects

Subjects are not found in prepositional or appositive phrases. Subjects can be found after the verb in sentences beginning with *here* or *there* and in questions.

> **Example:** There <u>are</u> several <u>things</u> to discuss with Ainsley, president of the literacy council.

Subject-verb agreement with group nouns

A group noun such as *audience, crowd,* or *team* takes a singular verb if the noun acts as a unit; it takes a plural verb if the members of the group act independently.

> **Example 1:** My <u>family</u> <u>is</u> Australian.
> **Example 2:** The <u>association</u> <u>are voting</u> on the important proposal tomorrow.

Making Subjects and Verbs Agree 2

Subject-verb agreement with indefinite pronouns

- Indefinite pronouns ending in *-one, -thing,* or *-body* take a singular verb.

     Example 1: <u>Somebody</u> <u>has taken</u> my favorite pen.
     Example 2: <u>Does</u> <u>anyone</u> <u>know</u> who it was?

- Indefinite pronouns *both, few, many* and *several* take a plural verb.

     Example 1: <u>Few</u> of my childhood friends <u>have</u> children of their own.
     Example 2: <u>Many</u> of us <u>are hoping</u> to get good news.

- Indefinite pronouns *any, all, more, most, none,* and *some* take either a singular or a plural verb depending on the meaning of the sentence.

     Example 1: The <u>apples</u> <u>have</u> some soft spots. <u>Most</u> <u>need</u> to be thrown out.
     Example 2: The <u>salt</u> <u>is</u> damp. <u>Most</u> <u>is</u> unusable.

Subject-verb agreement with compound subjects

- Use a plural verb with compound subjects joined by *and* unless the two subjects compose a single unit.

     Example 1: The <u>celery</u> and <u>green pepper</u> <u>are</u> in the refrigerator.
     Example 2: The <u>mortar and pestle</u> <u>is</u> made of black marble.

- Use either a singular or a plural verb with compound subjects joined by *or, nor, either, either/or, neither, neither/nor, not only/but also*—the verb should agree with the subject closest to it.

     Example 1: Neither the <u>magazines</u> in the living room nor this <u>magazine</u> on the table <u>contains</u> the article I am looking for.
     Example 2: <u>John</u> or the <u>Robinsons</u> <u>are planning</u> to drive us home.

Correcting the Fragment 1

A fragment is a piece of a sentence.

> To be or not to be.
> Rosanna our neighbor across the hall.
> At midnight.
> Swimming, skiing, and hiking scenic trails.
> Is better than nothing.

A fragment can be corrected by adding the missing parts of the sentence.

> "To be or not to be," is the question Hamlet made famous.
> Rosanna, our neighbor across the hall, has invited us to dinner.
> Sandi thought she heard music at midnight.
> Darnell likes swimming, skiing, and hiking scenic trails.
> Something is better than nothing.

A fragment can sometimes be corrected by being added to the complete sentence before it or the complete sentence following it.

> **Incorrect:** Most people today think of laundry as drudgery. Even with the use of automatic washers and dryers. Only a few decades ago. Women were expected to set aside an entire day each week to do the laundry. Now that's drudgery!

> **Correct:** Most people today think of laundry as drudgery, even with the use of automatic washers and dryers. Only a few decades ago, women were expected to set aside an entire day each week to do laundry. Now that's drudgery!

Correcting the Fragment 2

Fragments are often made up of phrases.

A *phrase* is a group of words that belongs together but does not make a complete sentence.

Noun phrase

A noun phrase is a group of words containing a noun and its modifiers.

> **Example:** <u>The gorgeous midsummer sunset</u> lingered for an hour.

Prepositional phrase

A prepositional phrase is a group of words beginning with a preposition and containing an object and possibly modifiers.

> **Example:** <u>After a relaxing and satisfying dinner</u>, the four of us went walking.

Verb phrase

A verb phrase is the main verb along with its helping verbs (auxiliary verbs). It is the complete verb of a sentence.

> **Example:** By next winter, Sam <u>will have been traveling</u> in Asia for nearly eighteen months.

Correcting the Fragment 3

Participial phrase

A participial phrase is a participle plus its nouns and modifiers. A participle is often a present form of a verb ending in -*ing* or a past form of a verb ending in -*ed*. A participial phrase functions as an adjective in a sentence.

> **Example 1:** <u>Eating her breakfast</u>, the child watched for the school bus.
>
> **Example 2:** That woman, <u>reading a poetry magazine</u>, is Ezra's Aunt Linda.
>
> **Example 3:** <u>Utterly exhausted</u>, the soccer team rode home in silence.

Gerund phrase

A gerund phrase is a gerund plus its nouns and modifiers. A gerund is a present form of a verb ending in -*ing*. It can be distinguished from a participial phrase by its function: a gerund phrase functions as a noun in a sentence.

> **Example 1:** <u>Taking the test</u> is necessary. (Subject)
>
> **Example 2:** I will enjoy <u>taking the test</u>. (Direct Object)
>
> **Example 3:** You cannot graduate without <u>taking the test</u>. (Object of Preposition)

Infinitive phrase

An infinitive phrase is an infinitive plus its nouns and modifiers. An infinitive is formed by the word *to* plus the base form of the verb. An infinitive phrase can function as a noun or a modifier. Note: the word *to* can also be a preposition. Look for the base form of a verb following *to* in order to make sure it is an infinitive.

> **Example 1:** Macy loves <u>to sleep late</u>. (Noun/Direct Object)
>
> **Example 2:** <u>To be honest</u>, I love this job. (Modifier)

Combining Sentences Using the Three Options for Coordination

Coordination is the joining of two sentences, known as independent clauses, which are related and contain ideas of equal importance.

A *compound sentence* is a sentence composed of two independent clauses joined by means of coordination.

There are three options for coordination:

1. Use a comma and a coordinating conjunction (*and, but, for, nor, or, yet, so*) between the independent clauses.

> **Example:** Emma wanted to go to the basketball game , but she needed a ride.

2. Use a semicolon, an adverbial conjunction, and a comma between the two independent clauses.

> **Example:** Emma wanted to go to the game ; however, she needed a ride.

3. Use only a semicolon between two independent clauses.

> **Example:** Emma wanted to go to the basketball game; she needed a ride.

Combining Sentences Using Subordination

Subordination is the joining of two clauses containing ideas that are not equally important.

The main point of the sentence is contained in the independent clause, and the less important point is contained in the dependent clause. These clauses are joined by means of subordinating conjunctions (*after, since, because, although, until, unless,*etc.) and relative pronouns (*who, whose, whom, which, that*). Sentences joined through subordination are called complex sentences.

Example sentences to combine (two independent clauses):
Rodney has a great analytical mind. He will be a good engineer.

Combining Sentences Using Subordinating Conjunctions

<u>Because</u> Rodney has a great analytical mind, he will be a good engineer.

Combining Sentences Using Relative Pronouns

Rodney, <u>who</u> has a great analytical mind, will be a good engineer.

Coordination and Subordination
(Original Version: Chapter 7, Test 2)

Below is American humorist James Thurber's original paragraph.

I met Doc Marlowe at old Mrs. Willoughby's rooming house. She had been a nurse in our family, and I used to go and visit her over weekends sometimes, for I was very fond of her. I was about eleven years old then. Doc Marlowe wore scarred leather leggings, a bright-colored bead vest that he said he got from the Indians, and a ten-gallon hat with kitchen matches stuck in the band, all the way around. He was about six feet four inches tall, with big shoulders, and a long, drooping mustache. He let his hair grow long, like General Custer's. He had a wonderful collection of Indian relics and six-shooters, and he used to tell me stories of his adventures in the Far West. His favorite expressions were "Hay, boy!" and "Hay, boy-gie!" which he used the way some people now use "Hot dog!" or "Doggone!" I thought he was the greatest man I had ever seen. It wasn't until he died and his son came out from Hew Jersey for the funeral that I found out he had never been in the Far West in his life. He had been born in Brooklyn.

Correcting the Run-on

A *run-on* is a sentence in which two independent clauses have been combined incorrectly.

There are three common types of run-ons:

1. The fused run-on

The fused run-on is a sentence in which two independent clauses are joined without any punctuation or coordinating conjunctions between them.

> **Example:** Buying a house is a big step it can also be an important investment.

2. The comma splice

The comma splice is a sentence in which two independent clauses have been joined using a comma but without using a coordinating conjunction.

> **Example:** You should tour the house several times, many consumer advocates recommend checking the water pressure and electrical system.

3. The "and" run-on

The "and" run-on is a sentence in which two or more independent clauses have been joined using "and" (or another coordinating conjunction) but without using a comma(s).

> **Example:** Do not sign a contract without getting a building inspection and it is a good idea to apply for pre-approval for your loan and many home buyers are embarrassed to take advantage of a final walk-through before closing the deal.

Choosing Correct Pronouns 1

Pronouns can change form depending on whether they are being used as subjects, objects, possessives, or reflexives.

Subjective Case

Pronouns in the subjective or nominative case are not only the subjects of sentences. They can also be the subjects of dependent clauses.

Singular   I, you, he, she, it, who

Plural   we, you, they, who

> **Example:** <u>I</u> borrowed the car.

Objective Case

A pronoun in the objective case can be the direct object of an independent or dependent clause, or the object of a phrase (prepositional, infinitive, gerund, or participial).

Singular   me, you, him, her, it, whom

Plural   us, you, them, whom

> **Example:** I borrowed <u>it</u>.

Possessive Case

Pronouns in the possessive case show possession and act as adjectives within the sentence.

Singular   my/mine, your/yours, his, her/hers, its, whose

Plural   our/ours, your/yours, their/theirs, whose

> **Example:** I borrowed <u>my</u> father's car.

Reflexive Case

Pronouns in the reflexive case show action returning or being reflected upon its subject.

Singular   myself, yourself, himself, herself, itself

Plural   ourselves, yourselves, themselves

> **Example:** My father usually uses the car <u>himself</u>.

Choosing Correct Pronouns 2

Special cases of pronoun agreement:

Comparisons

When pronouns are used in a comparison, complete the comparison to find out whether the nominative or the objective case is appropriate.

> Nikita is much better at learning new languages than *I/me*.
> Nikita is much better at learning new languages than *I* (am).

Compound constructions

When pronouns are used in a compound construction, take out one of the elements of the compound and use the pronoun that makes sense by itself.

> After *she/her* and *I/me* left for the lecture, our father called.
> After *she* left for the lecture, our father called.
> After *I* left for the lecture, our father called.

Who/whom constructions

When *who* or *whom* is in a clause, cross out everything but the clause containing *who* or *whom* to find out how it functions in the clause. (Ask yourself if the pronoun is the subject or object of a clause or phrase.)

> That poet *who/whom* I told you about just published a new collection.

> *who/whom* I told you about
> I told you about *who/whom*
> (*Whom* is correct because it is the object of the preposition)

> That poet *whom* I told you about just published a new collection.

Choosing Correct Pronouns 3

An *antecedent* is a word or group of words that a pronoun replaces.

> **Example:** The living room <u>furniture</u> we wanted was finally on sale.
> <u>It</u> cost only a third of its original price.

A pronoun must agree in number (singular or plural) with any other word to which it refers.

> **Incorrect:** A <u>lobbyist</u> never tires although <u>they</u> often wonder if their efforts are appreciated.

> **Correct:** The <u>lobbyists</u> never tire although <u>they</u> often wonder if their efforts are appreciated.

A pronoun must agree with its antecedent in person. In other words, don't mix *I*, *you*, *one*, and *they*.

> **Incorrect:** <u>You</u> really ought to travel. <u>One</u> cannot imagine the experiences that are in store for <u>them</u>.

> **Correct:** <u>You</u> really ought to travel. <u>You</u> cannot imagine the experiences in store for <u>you</u>.

The antecedent of a pronoun should not be missing, ambiguous, or repetitious.

> **Incorrect:** <u>They</u> always say, "Better safe than sorry."

> **Correct:** <u>An old adage</u> claims that people are "better safe than sorry."

> **Incorrect:** When <u>Melissa and her mom</u> volunteered for Habitat for Humanity, <u>she</u> said <u>she</u> felt good about the work <u>they</u> were doing.

> **Correct:** When <u>Melissa and her mom</u> volunteered for Habitat for Humanity, <u>Melissa</u> said <u>she</u> felt good about the work <u>Habitat</u> is doing.

Parallel Structure

Parallel structure is the use of similar parts of speech, phrases, or clauses in a series.

> **Example:** I wanted to see the <u>sunset</u>, the <u>constellations</u>, and the <u>moon</u> at the lake.

Phrases in a series should be the same kinds of phrases (infinitive, verb, noun, prepositional, gerund, or participial).

> **Incorrect:** The girls had a great time <u>staying</u> up late, <u>eating</u> pizza, and <u>slept</u> in bunk beds.

> **Correct:** The girls had a great time <u>staying</u> up late, <u>eating</u> pizza, and <u>sleeping</u> in bunk beds.

Clauses in a series should not be mixed with phrases.

> **Incorrect:** I told him <u>about the cabin</u>, <u>about the trip</u>, and <u>what happened</u> when Jacob overturned the canoe.

> **Correct:** I told him <u>about the cabin</u>, <u>about the trip</u>, and <u>about what happened</u> when Jacob overturned the canoe.

Misplaced and Dangling Modifiers

A *modifier* is a word or group of words that functions as an adjective or adverb.

A *misplaced modifier* is a word or group of words that has been placed in a wrong, awkward, or ambiguous position.

> **Incorrect:** She brought the food to the patient <u>that was piping hot</u>.

> **Correct:** She brought the food <u>that was piping hot</u> to the patient.

A *dangling modifier* is a modifier without a word, phrase, or clause that the modifier can describe.

> **Incorrect:** <u>Hanging</u> on her every word, the door burst open and startled the rapt audience.

> **Correct:** <u>Hanging</u> on the lecturer's every word, the audience was startled when the door burst open.

Principal Parts of Verbs

Base Form   (to + verb, also called the infinitive)

                             regular verb: to enjoy
                             irregular verb: to grow

Past Tense   (in regular verbs, just add *-ed*; the past tense of irregular verbs will
                             not be formed by adding *-ed*)

                             enjoyed
                             grew

Past Participle   (in the active voice, it is preceded by *have, has,* or *had*; in regular
                             verbs, the past tense and past participle are the same)

                             enjoyed
                             grown

Present Participle   (base form + *-ing*)

                             enjoying
                             growing

Present Tense Verbs

Present   (present tense form of the verb: add -*s* or -*es* for third person singular)

The present tense is used to show actions happening now and facts/actions that are always true.

> **Example:** His son <u>grows</u> bigger each time I see him.

Present Continuous   (*am/is/are* + present participle)

Use the present continuous to describe most actions occurring in the present moment, especially actions that are constant or ongoing.

> **Example:** Tom <u>is growing</u> fond of cycling.

Present Perfect   (*have/has* + past participle)

Use present perfect to explain a discreet action that began in the past and is ending or continuing in the present. It can describe an event that has just taken place, or an action in which the time is indefinite.

> **Example:** I <u>have grown</u> several types of herbs this summer.

Present Perfect Continuous   (*have/has* + *been* + present participle)

Use present perfect continuous when the continuous or constant action that began in the past is still going on.

> **Example:** Selene <u>has been growing</u> tomatoes in her basement since January.

Past Tense Verbs

Past   (past form of verb)

Use past tense to describe most actions that occurred in the past.

> **Example:** Hillary <u>read</u> *War and Peace* last month.

Past Continuous   (*was/were* + present participle)

Use past continuous to describe a continuous or constant action that occurred in the past. It is often used in conjunction with a past tense verb.

> **Example:** Randall <u>was going</u> into the health food store when he saw his old high school buddy.

Past Perfect   (*had* + past participle)

Use past perfect to describe an action that occurred prior to another past action. It is often used in conjunction with a past tense verb.

> **Example:** Janine <u>had taken</u> the ACT two months before she entered college.

Past Perfect Continuous   (*had* + *been* + present participle)

Use the past perfect continuous tense to describe a continuous or constant action (belief, fact) that occurred in the past but ended due to another action that occurred in the more recent past.

> **Example:** Ricardo <u>had been going</u> to night school for two years when he <u>received</u> a scholarship to Penn State.

Future Tense Verbs

Future   (*will/shall* + base form of the verb)

Use the future to describe most actions that will occur at a later time.

> **Example:** Dominique <u>will travel</u> back to her homeland in June.

Future Continuous   (*will/shall* + *be* + present participle)

Use future continuous to describe an action that will be continuous or constant at a later time.

> **Example:** She <u>will be flying</u> on United Airlines.

Future Perfect   (*will/shall* + *have* + past participle)

Use future perfect to describe an action that will be completed by a given time in the future.

> **Example:** The eighteen-year-old student <u>will have completed</u> two years of advanced language study by the time she returns home.

Future Perfect Continuous   (*will/shall* + *have* + *been* + present participle)

Use the future perfect continuous tense to describe a constant or continuous action that began at a time prior to the point in the future referred to.

> **Example:** At that time, she <u>will have been studying</u> English for a total of eight years.

Using Correct Capitalization

Capitalize the first word of every sentence.

> **Example:** <u>Don't</u> listen to him. <u>He</u> is just jealous. <u>Ignore</u> him.

Capitalize the names of specific things and places.

> **Example:** We went to <u>Devil's Den</u> over the holidays and stayed over night by the <u>Buffalo River</u> at <u>Thunderbird Inn</u>.

Capitalize the days of the week, months, and holidays, but don't capitalize the names of the seasons.

> **Example:** I can't believe that <u>Wednesday</u> is the first day of spring.

Capitalize the names of all languages, nationalities, races, religions, deities, and sacred terms.

> **Example:** I have studied <u>Spanish</u>, <u>Greek</u>, and <u>Hebrew</u> .

Capitalize the first word and every important word in a title. Do not capitalize articles, prepositions, or short connecting words in a title.

> **Example:** I've always wanted to read <u>*A Tale of Two Cities*</u>.

Capitalize the first word of a direct quotation.

> **Example:** My sister shouted, " <u>Hold</u> that thought!"

Capitalize historical events, periods, and documents.

> **Example:** We studied Picasso's <u>Blue Period</u> last semester.

Capitalize the words *north*, *south*, *east*, and *west* when they are used as places rather than as directions.

> **Example:** I was born in the <u>Midwest</u>, but now live on the <u>East Coast</u>.

Using Correct Punctuation

Use a comma to separate items in a series.

> **Example:** The supply list requested large mailing envelopes, packing tape, a stapler, and bubble wrap.

When an address or date occurs in a sentence, each part is treated like an item in a series. A comma is put after each item, including the last.

> **Example:** On May 14, 1998, in Reno, Nevada, my brother was married.

A group of adjectives may not be regarded as a series if some of the words "go together." You can test this by putting and between each item. If you can, use a comma.

> **Example:** The child discovered the fragile, pale blue egg beside the rain gutter.

Use a comma to follow introductory words, expressions, phrases, or clauses.

> **Example:** As you well know, I enjoy talking on the phone.

Use commas surrounding a word, phrase, or clause when the word or group of words interrupts the main idea.

> **Example:** My mother, the perfectionist, uses a razorblade to chop the garlic for spaghetti sauce.

Use commas around nouns in direct address.

> **Example:** Martin, could we plan on a general staff meeting for next Monday?

Use a comma to set off exact words spoken in dialogue.

> **Example:** "It seems crazy," said Greg, "not to invest in flood insurance."

Exercises in Connotation

A. The following groups of words have the same *denotation* or basic definition. Decide which words in each group have a negative sound or *connotation* and which have a positive connotation. Can you identify the reasons for your choices? Do any words in each group have a neutral connotation?

When you have made your choices, find a partner and compare notes. It is possible that you will not agree in every case. Think about why this might be the case. Is it possible that you are both right, depending on the context?

1.   procrastinate/hesitate/stall/play for time/hold off/delay
2.   weak/flabby/feeble/soft/gutless/sluggish/dull/bloodless
3.   energetic/vigorous/forceful/powerful/intense/dynamic/strong/demonic
4.   stench/stink/smell/odor/fetidness/noxiousness/miasma/reek/rankness
5.   quiet/silent/deathlike/tomblike/still/noiseless/hush/tranquil
6.   intelligent/egg-headed/pin-headed/scholarly/brainy/quick
7.   crazy/insane/ill/demented/deranged/looney/nuts
8.   dumb/simple/stupid/idiotic/ignorant/empty-headed/vacuous/unknowing
9.   trusting/unsuspicious/blind/credulous/uncritical/believing/gullible
10. coarse/unrefined/clumsy/crude/natural/refreshing/down-to-earth
11. impulsive/capricious/fun-loving/fanciful/flighty
12. ordinary/average/normal/commonplace/garden-variety/unexceptional

B. For the following words, write several synonyms that have a more positive connotation and several that have a more negative connotation. You may use words or phrases. For more ideas, check your thesaurus.

1. clean	7. intoxicated
2. tired	8. illegal
3. untrustworthy	9. punishment
4. expensive	10. anger
5. impatient	11. acquire
6. marriage	12. workplace

Exercise in Sound-Alikes

Below is a list of 80 pairs of words often confused. These provide an additional challenge for those who have mastered the 48 pairs in Chapter 15. Choose 10 pairs that are not familiar to you, look them up in the dictionary, and then write a sentence for each pair in which the sound-alikes are used and spelled correctly.

Example: In *addition* to receiving the Sunday paper, we are now getting the daily *edition*.

addition/edition	cowered/coward	hour/our
adverse/averse	currant/current	idol/idle
air/err/heir	cymbal/symbol	in/inn
allude/elude	dairy/diary	intense/intents
allusion/illusion	dam/damn	knead/need
aloud/allowed	dear/deer	knew/new
altar/alter	dew/due/do	know/no
amend/emend	descent/dissent	knot/not
amoral/immoral	die/dye	later/latter
aisle/isle	discreet/discrete	lessen/lesson
ant/aunt	doe/dough	liable/libel
assent/ascent	dual/duel	loan/lone
bear/bare	elicit/illicit	made/maid
bazaar/bizarre	emit/omit	mail/male
be/bee	ensure/insure	mall/maul
berry/bury	eye/I	manner/manor
blew/blue	fairy/ferry	meat/meet
bridal/bridle	flour/flower	metal/medal/mettle
boar/bore	gorilla/guerrilla	miner/minor
brake/break	great/grate	morning/mourning
bough/bow	groan/grown	naval/navel
but/butt	hair/hare	pair/parc/pear
carat/carrot/caret	hall/haul	pail/pale
cellar/seller	halve/have	peace/piece
censer/censor/censure	hear/here	pedal/peddle
cents/sense	him/hymn	precede/proceed
chute/shoot	heard/herd	

Standard and Nonstandard Usage

A. These words and phrases should be studied because they are often used incorrectly. Save this list so you can refer to it whenever necessary.

Standard	Nonstandard
all right	alright
a lot	alot
anywhere, everywhere, somewhere	anywheres, everywheres, somewheres
because, since (to introduce a clause)	being that, being as how
different from	different than
in regard to	in regards to
reason is that	reason is because
regardless	irregardless
somewhat, rather	kinda, sorta

B. Study the specific usage rules for the following pairs of words.

amount/number	*amount* is used for uncountable things (the amount of sugar); *number* is used for countable things (the number of guests invited to the dinner)
beside/besides	*beside* means *next to*; *besides* means *in addition to, moreover,* or *also*.
between/among	*between* is used with two persons, places, or things; *among* is used with three or more persons, places, or things
learn/teach	*learn* means to gain knowledge; *teach* means to instruct

Exercise in Supporting Details

Give four examples for each topic sentence to explain, illustrate or clarify the idea.

Topic Sentence: Last winter was the worst winter I have ever experienced.

1.
2.
3.
4.

Topic Sentence: Choosing to remodel the house myself was a huge mistake.

1.
2.
3.
4.

Topic Sentence: Camping can be physically, emotionally, and spiritually exhausting.

1.
2.
3.
4.

Create a thesis statement of your own and list four supporting examples for each.

Topic Sentence: _____.

1.
2.
3.
4.

Exercise in Illustration

Using illustration or example is a good way to clarify and develop your ideas. Below are three ideas for illustration on the topic of credit cards. Brainstorm and write a paragraph for each of the three prompts.

1. Provide a list of major credit card companies.

2. Discuss possible advantages or disadvantages of using credit cards.

3. Provide an anecdote that illustrates a positive or negative experience you or someone you know has had with credit cards.

Exercise in Narration 1

Dialogue

The following exchange between two brothers has been written without fragments, dialect, and interruptions. *First assignment*: Write out the same dialogue the way that you, or someone you know, would speak. *Second assignment*: Rewrite the dialogue in a dialect of your choice. *Third assignment*: Write six sentences of your revised dialogue in direct quotation format, paying attention to the placement of commas, quotes, and other marks of punctuation. For fun, look at Sam Shepard's dialogue choices in the opening scene of *True West*.

Speaker 1:   I heard that Mother decided to go to Alaska. Was that true?

Speaker 2:   Yes, it is true.

Spcaker 1:   Did she leave you in charge of the house?

Speaker 2:   Yes, she did. She knew I was coming down to visit, so she offered to let me stay here.

Speaker 1:   Have you been watering all of the plants?

Speaker 2:   Yes, I have.

Speaker 1:   Have you been keeping the kitchen sink clean? You know that Mother does not like it if there is even a single tea leaf in the sink.

Speaker 2:   Yes, I know.

Speaker 1:   Will she be in Alaska for a long time?

Speaker 2:   I am not sure.

Speaker 1:   It must be nice for you to have the whole house to yourself.

Speaker 2:   Yes, I am enjoying it.

Speaker 1:   There are a lot of crickets around here. There are lots and lots of crickets. Do you have any food? Do you have any coffee?

Speaker 2:   What was that you said?

Speaker 1:   Do you have any coffee?

Speaker 2:   Yes, I do have coffee?

Speaker 1:   That is good. Is it real coffee and not instant coffee?

Speaker 2:   Yes, it is. Would you like some coffee?

Speaker 1:   No, thank you. I brought something of my own to drink.

Speaker 2:   Please help yourself to anything in the refrigerator.

Speaker 1:   Thank you, I will. Please do not worry about me. I can take care of myself.

Exercise in Narration 2

In the following story, events are told out of chronological sequence. Create a chronological outline of the events described. Rewrite the selection according to your outline, supplying details as necessary.

My step-father and step-brother were on vacation in Washington when I decided to leave home. I knew that if I was ever going to leave home, it had to be then. My step-father was a very stern man who had strong views on what an American family should be. However, he wasn't acting like much of a father to me. He was only concerned with maintaining a close relationship with his son. He always sided with Robert, my step-brother, regardless of the situation. Therefore, I typically got in trouble for things I didn't even do. I promptly did my chores every day after school while Josh, my step-brother, sat on his lazy butt and watched television. It shocked my step-father when I left. He never really realized how much I did around the house, nor did he realize how much of a jerk he had been until after I left and it was too late. Just last year he formally apologized for being so cruel all of those years. It must be very difficult for a man with that much pride to apologize to a young man like myself. I admire that very much. I forgave him completely, and since then we have become very close friends.

The stress I endured around the house was unbelievable. This is what eventually drove me to leave. I was only a twelve-year-old boy living a life of "torture." One time, I remember sitting at the table for two hours because I wouldn't eat my entire bowl of soup. My step-father had a strict policy of "take all you want, but eat all you take!" Mom had made some vegetable-beef soup with chunks of meat in it. The meat was very hard; it was too tough for my jaws to handle. If I could have just swallowed the meat, then I could have left the table, but the meat was just too large to swallow and it was just too tough for my tired jaws to shred. I refused to eat it. I sat there for two hours staring at the meat until finally he let me leave. This was one of the few occasions that I won the battle. Constant fighting amongst parents over money, super-strict rules set by my step-father, and constant hatred between my stepbrother and me eventually led to my leaving.

From "My Train Of Life" by Gary Myrick

Exercise in Description

In the following paragraph, add specific details (concrete nouns, adjectives, adverbs, active verbs) to make the writing more vivid.

> When I was young, I lived with my family in a small house in a Western state. At that time, things were not going well. My mother had remarried and her new husband had brought his child to live with us. Home life was a constant challenge and difficult to come to terms with. I decided it was time for a change. The decision I made changed the lives of my family members as well as my own.

In the following example, underline the descriptions that seem the most vivid to you. Write your own descriptive paragraph about a close family member.

> Throughout Anita's interview, her blonde hair stayed tucked behind her ears. Her green, Barbara Streisand eyes were concentrated on her nails as she bit them the same way a mouse nibbles on cheese. Her slender figure sat Indian style on my floor as she blurted out stories of her middle school, high school, and college experiences.

In the following example, change ten words and/or phrases to give the scene a sense of foreboding.

> It was an unusually hot morning. As we pulled into the dusty parking lot that had only about ten or eleven other cars in it, I gazed to my left, then to my right. To my left I saw a trailer and two enormous planes. To my right I saw nothing but an open field and sky. As we filed out of the temperature-controlled van into the blistering sun, I was beginning to wonder what I had gotten myself into.

Exercise in Process Analysis

Write clear and simple steps to the following processes, keeping in mind a particular audience. Use complete sentences and transitional words and phrases.

1.　Write official directions to tell office workers how to use the fax machine properly.

2.　Explain to a driver's education student how to parallel park a car.

3.　Tell a close friend how to dress for an important job interview.

4.　Show a five-year-old how to make a favorite sandwich.

Practice in Comparison or Contrast

Organize the following supporting details into a block outline, and a point-by-point outline.

Laundry 1898

1. My grandmother boiled water for laundry in the same black cauldron where she made lye soap.
2. She shaved a bar of lye soap into chips, which she put in the boiling water.
3. After sorting her family's clothes, she placed several items of clothing into the soapy water and boiled them for a few minutes.
4. She lifted each piece of clothing out of the water with a sturdy hardwood stick.
5. She rubbed any stain with a bar of lye soap.
6. She scrubbed the clothes on a ripply washboard.
7. She rinsed clothes in another tub of cold water.
8. She wrung out the clothes in a wringer.
9. Afterwards, she took the clothes outside and pinned them to the clothesline.
10. Then she ironed everything.
11. She heated the flat irons on her wood cookstove.
12. At last, she would fold each item of clothing or hang it in the oak wardrobe.

Laundry 2007

1. I buy my soap, which comes in powdered or liquid form, at the grocery store.
2. I also buy bleach, stain remover, and fabric softener (either liquid or sheets).
3. I sort my clothes and use stain remover on any spots I find.
4. I set my automatic washing machine to the proper setting and put soap in the machine as it fills.
5. I place the clothes, sorted according to color and fabric, in the machine.
6. The hot water comes from a gas water heater through the pipes into the machine.
7. After the cycle is finished, about twenty minutes later, I take the clothes out of the washing machine.
8. I quickly place them in the automatic dryer, along with a fabric softening sheet.
9. I choose the correct setting by turning a knob.
10. Then I press a button to start the dryer.
11. When the clothes are dry, I take them out and only need to iron a few items with an electric iron.
12. Finally, I fold the clothes and put them in a chest of drawers or hang them in the closet.

Two Methods for Comparison/Contrast Outlines

Block Outline

I. Introduction: Introduce both of your subjects that you will be comparing or contrasting. You may do this by telling a story that mentions both, telling two brief contrasting anecdotes, or giving background information about both (just to name a few possibilities).

II. Body.

    A. Subject 1.

        1. Point 1.

        2. Point 2.

        3. Point 3.

    B. Subject 2.

        1. Point 1.

        2. Point 2.

        3. Point 3.

III. Conclusion: You might explain the meaning of the comparison or contrast of your subjects, or tell your reader why Subject 2 is superior/inferior to Subject 1 based on the information you provide, among other things.

Point-by-Point Outline

I. Introduction: Introduce Subjects 1 and 2 (same as above).

II. Body.

    A. Point 1.

        1. Subject 1.

        2. Subject 2.

    B. Point 2.

        1. Subject 1.

        2. Subject 2.

    C. Point 3.

        1. Subject 1.

        2. Subject 2.

III. Conclusion: (same as above.)

Note: You may have more than three points for comparison or contrast. Typically, a comparison/contrast essay does not have more than two subjects.

Cause and Effect Exercise 1: Surveys and Polls

When composing questions for surveys or polls that will attempt to discover patterns of opinion or behavior in a cross-section of people, it is important to ensure that each question gives rise to a limited number of responses. The questioner must give enough range in the possible responses so that those being surveyed or polled do not feel that they are being "led" to respond in predetermined patterns. Remember: the goal of good surveys and polls is to uncover truths, not to find answers that reinforce at all costs your particular position on an issue.

Directions: Choose one of the following survey topics and compose 10–15 questions that will have limited responses. When you are satisfied with your questionnaire, conduct your survey by finding a good cross-section of people, reading each question in a professional manner, and jotting down their responses to each of your questions:

1. You are researching the negative effects of sugar (particularly candy) on adult behavior. You wish to know more about the average candy consumption of the population.

2. You want to discover the causes of the general boom in interest in recycling. Compose questions that will determine recycling habits and/or opinions on the matter.

3. You are writing a report on the causes of teenage drug addiction. Survey a wide number of people, especially teenagers. Hint: You might want to conduct the survey at a mall.

4. You wish to conduct a poll on the effects of the current political system on people's lives. Make sure you ascertain whether or not informants are aware of the current system. Ask about their political leanings.

Note: Once you have conducted your survey, tabulate your answers and draw tentative conclusions based on your findings.

Cause and Effect Exercise 2: Interviews

The principles of composing interview questions are nearly the opposite of those for surveys and polls. In an interview, you will devote a significant amount of time to listening to one person or a limited number of people. Your questions should therefore be as open-ended as possible in an effort to elicit longer answers from the person being interviewed. The tone and phrasing in which an answer is given will be of interest to you. If your subject does not respond at first, part of your job is to probe into reasons for reticence. Many times interviewers find that using a tape recorder makes an in-depth interview feel more like a conversation.

Directions: Make an appointment to interview someone concerning the effects of education. Set a time limit (e.g., 20–30 minutes). When the interview is finished, choose three interesting answers and write down the direct, *verbatim* quotes following your questions.

Basic Classification Outline

    I. Introduction: Introduce the subject you wish to classify and break it down into its distinct categories.

    II. Body: For each main category or class, use examples that make up the class.
- A. Class 1.
  1. Example 1.
  2. Example 2.
  3. Example 3.
- B. Class 2.
  1. Example 1.
  2. Example 2.
  3. Example 3.
- C. Class 3.
  1. Example 1.
  2. Example 2.
  3. Example 3.

    III. Conclusion: Explain what can be learned from using your particular system of classification.

Exercise in Writing A Definition

Choose one of the following concepts that you are familiar with as a topic of your definition essay or paragraph. Then follow the steps below.

1. An educated person	11. Conservative
2. Afterlife	12. Liberal
3. Role Model	13. Nepotism
4. Fast Food	14. A civilized society
5. Family	15. Plagiarism
6. Creativity	16. Faith
7. Business Sense	17. Wilderness
8. Oppression	18. Narcissism
9. Culture	19. Art
10. Morality	20. Charity

1. Once you have chosen a concept, brainstorm (e.g., freewrite, cluster, list, etc.) for at least one page about everything you know about the concept. The brainstorm will be submitted with the essay.

2. On a separate sheet of paper, create your own three-sentence definition of your concept.

3. Look up the word or words that make up the name of your concept in the dictionary, and write down the definition(s) beneath the definition you created.

4. Beneath the definitions, note comparisons and conflicts between your own definition and the dictionary's.

5. On another sheet of paper, write down four detailed examples of the concept that you have either experienced, heard of, or read about.

Logical Fallacies

Ad hominem (Latin for "to the man"): An attack on the character or person rather than that person's position on some issue.

> **Example:** My opponent is nothing but a lazy slob.

Ad populum (Latin for "to the people"): An appeal to people's fears and prejudices rather than the merits of a position on some issue.

> **Example:** If we continue to allow gun ownership, we'll all be killed in our homes.

Bandwagon appeal: An appeal to take a position because "everybody else" is doing it or thinking it.

> **Example:** You should buy those shoes since all the stars wear them.

Begging the question: Presenting an opinion or a premise as the truth of a matter.

> **Example:** The death penalty is wrong because it is murder.

Either/or approach: Falsely presenting an argument as if there were only two possibilities.

> **Example:** Either we continue the space program or we cancel all future flights.

Non Sequitur (Latin for "it does not follow"): A conclusion that does not follow from the initial premise. The initial premise could also be untrue.

> **Example:** Jose will be a remarkable doctor because he is very smart.

Note: One cannot assume that Jose will be a remarkable doctor on the basis of intelligence alone.

Hasty Generalization: A conclusion drawn from inadequate evidence. Stereotyping is a kind of hasty generalization.

> **Example:** All French people love to drink wine.

Sample Topics for Persuasive Essays and Research Papers

Below you will find a list of hot topics for persuasive essays or research papers. The questions and ideas that follow the topics are intended to get you thinking about the topic, but are certainly not the only areas of debate. When you pick a topic for a persuasive essay, you must find a focus that will be narrow enough to guide your research and help you pick the most appropriate sources, facts, and statistics for your paper. As always, try to find a topic that you have an interest in finding out more about.

Abortion (Should it remain legal? Should there be exceptions?)

Adoption (infants, older children, interracial)

Affirmative Action (positive effects, negative effects)

Alcoholism (Is it a disease? In conjunction with pregnancy)

Animals and Physical Therapy (Do pets aid the physically challenged?)

Caffeine (Is it good or bad for you?)

Child Abuse (discipline vs. abuse? What should be done to reform child abusers?)

Child Witnesses (Should children be allowed to testify in court?)

Cigarette Companies (Should companies be forced to pay damages to smokers?)

Day Care (Is day care or home care best for young children?)

Drinking Age (What is the most appropriate drinking age? How do U.S. views on this topic compare with those of other countries?)

Drug Addiction (What are the best ways to stop teen addiction and/or reform addicts?)

Elder Care (What is the best way to care for elderly family members?)

Endangered Species (Are endangered species laws too strict or too lax?)

Euthanasia (Should it be legalized?)

Farm Subsidies (Should farmers receive federal aid to help them compete with agribusinesses?)

Foreign Language Requirement (Should it be required for all high school students? When should instruction begin? Which languages should be offered?)

Gay Marriage (Is this issue one of civil rights? Is it a federal or state issue?)

Genetic Testing (Are some forms of genetic testing invasive or harmful?)

Global Warming (What can be done about it?)

Gun Control (What types of weapons, if any, should be controlled? Is the waiting period too short or too long?)

Political Ads (Should political ads be monitored, screened for truthfulness, or regulated?)

EVALUATION
HANDOUTS

Student Editing and Proofreading Checklist

Complete the following checklist before turning in final drafts.

1. Have I read my work aloud to listen for problems?

2. Did I check every possible misspelling in a dictionary or with a spell checker?

3. Did I edit for run-on sentences?

4. Did I fix all comma splice run-ons?

5. Did I edit for fragments?

6. Did I check my use of verbs?

7. Did I check my use of pronouns?

8. Have I checked any punctuation I'm unsure of?

9. Have I checked my use of capital letters?

Rough Draft Workshop: Peer Evaluation Worksheet

Student Writer _____   Student Evaluator _____

Thesis:

Where has the author placed the thesis? Underline it.

Is the thesis sufficiently narrow and interesting? If not, make several suggestions for narrowing or expanding the thesis.

Is there a possible thesis lurking elsewhere in the paper that may be what the writer might prefer to write about?

Examples:

Count the number of specific examples that support the thesis. (An example might be a number, a statistic, a brief story, a clear description, a well-explained quote, etc.)

Do you feel there are enough examples and details to support the thesis and hold your interest? If not, help the writer to brainstorm for more examples.

Are the examples clear and effective? Does the author use names, dates, titles, places, colors, shapes, etc.? Mark vague or uninteresting examples with an asterisk (*) in the margin of the paper.

Overall Impression:

What do you especially admire in this draft? Are there any aspects you would like to emulate in your own writing?

What would you like to know more about?

What would you like for the writer to tell you in the conclusion?

Additional Comments:

Revision Workshop: Peer Evaluation Worksheet

Student Writer _____   Student Evaluator _____

1.   What strategy does the author use to grab your interest? Could the introduction be more exciting? If so, make several suggestions for improvement.

2.   Does the essay pull you through from beginning to end? If not, put an arrow at the point or points where you begin to lose interest.

3.   Underline the paper's thesis. Draw a wavy line under the topic sentence of each paragraph. If you cannot detect a topic sentence in a given paragraph, jot down the controlling idea in the margin of the paper.

4.   Number the paragraphs in the paper. According to what principle are they organized?

5.   Are there long paragraphs that are really two or more paragraphs in disguise? If so, write down the numbers of the corresponding paragraphs.

6.   Are there any short paragraphs that really belong with another paragraph? If so, give the numbers of the paragraphs.

7.   How do you feel at the conclusion of the essay? Does the author sufficiently sum things up and leave you feeling satisfied? Are there loose ends that leave you hanging? Make several suggestions for improvement.

8.   Copy one of the paragraphs of the paper into your journal and revise by deleting unnecessary words and phrases, adding specific examples, and reorganizing material for better rhetorical effect as necessary. When you are satisfied with what you have done, share the revision with the author with the understanding that your revision is one of many possible ways to revise and edit.

9.   What do you admire about the author's style, use of language, storytelling ability, clarity, precision of details, musicality, etc.

Rough Draft: Instructor Evaluation Sheet

Student   _____

Focus   20 points   _____points
Does the paper have a narrowed thesis?
Do the paragraphs have topic sentences or controlling ideas that clearly relate to the thesis?

Organization   20 points   _____points
Do the ideas follow a logical progression?
Are there adequate transitional paragraphs, words, and phrases?
Does the writer use a clear pattern of organization in both body and paragraphs?

Development   20 points   _____points
Are there enough details, statistics, facts, and examples to make the writer's position clear and define concepts?
Is there adequate explanation of quotations?
Are examples and quotations appropriate and well integrated?

Introduction and Conclusion   20 points   _____points
Does the introduction grab the reader's attention and show signs of technique and attention to audience?
Does the conclusion sufficiently wrap up loose ends and leave the reader with a provocative thought?

Grammar and Mechanics   20 points   _____points
Is the essay free of spelling errors, run-on sentences, sentence fragments, and incorrect usage?
More than 4 major usage errors, or 2 major usage errors and 4 additional errors, or 8 minor errors will result in a score of 0.

Total points out of 100 =_____

Instructor's Comments and Suggestions for Revision:

Grammar and Mechanics: Instructor Evaluation Checklist

Major Usage Errors
Fused run-ons   _____
"And" run-ons   _____
Comma splices   _____
Fragments   _____

Minor Comma Errors
Excessive comma use   _____
No comma after introductory phrase/s   _____
No comma after introductory clause/s   _____
No commas around nonrestrictive modifiers   _____
No commas around vocatives/sentence adverbs   _____

Spelling, Quotation, and Capitalization
Capitalization errors   _____
Spelling errors   _____
Sound-alike word misspellings   _____
Look-alike word misuse   _____
Quotation punctuation errors   _____

Agreement
Subject-verb agreement errors   _____
Pronoun-antecedent agreement errors   _____
Pronoun case errors   _____
Faulty parallelism   _____

Modifiers
Dangling modifiers   _____
Misplaced modifiers   _____

Verbs
Wrong verb tense/s   _____
Sequence of tenses errors   _____
Unnecessary shifts in verb tense   _____

Style
Inadequate use of subordination   _____
Inadequate use of coordination   _____
Inadequate use of transitions   _____
Overuse of vague/abstract terms   _____

Revised Draft: Instructor Evaluation Sheet

Student   _____

Focus   20 points   _____**points**
Does the paper have a narrowed thesis?
Do the paragraphs have topic sentences or controlling ideas that clearly relate to the thesis?

Organization   10 points   _____**points**
Do the ideas follow a logical progression?
Are there adequate transitional paragraphs, words, and phrases?
Does the writer use a clear pattern of organization in both body and paragraphs?

Development   20 points   _____**points**
Are there enough details, statistics, facts, and examples to make the writer's position clear and define concepts?
Is there adequate explanation of quotations?
Are examples and quotations appropriate and well integrated?

Introduction and Conclusion   20 points   _____**points**
Does the introduction grab the reader's attention and show signs of technique and attention to audience?
Does the conclusion sufficiently wrap up loose ends and leave the reader with a provocative thought?

Grammar and Mechanics   10 points   _____**points**
Is the essay free of spelling errors, run-on sentences, sentence fragments, and incorrect usage?
More than 4 major usage errors, or 2 major usage errors and 4 additional errors, or 8 minor errors will result in a score of 0.

Improvement   20 points   _____**points**
Have significant improvements been made in the revision of the draft?

                                    Total points out of 100 =_____

Instructor's Comments and Suggestions for Revision:

In-Class Essay: Instructor Evaluation Sheet

Student   _____

Student clearly refers to article or essay question.	**10 points**
Thesis contains a clear argument or position.	**10 points**
Paragraphs are coherent and advance thesis idea.	**10 points**
Examples are clear and appropriate.	**10 points**
Student quotes with accuracy and correct punctuation.	**5 points**
Student addresses an academic audience.	**5 points**
Tone is consistent throughout.	**5 points**
Introduction demonstrates writing technique.	**5 points**
Student concludes essay in the final paragraph.	**5 points**
Conclusion is more than a mere summary of the body.	**5 points**
Student's work has been carefully proofread.	**5 points**
Student has employed a complex vocabulary.	**5 points**
Student has a good sense of phrasing; writing flows.	**10 points**
Student's work is virtually free of usage errors.	**10 points**

Subtotal: _____

Name, course number, or section number is missing.	**−1 point**
Title is missing or is overly vague/general.	**−1 point**

Subtotal minus deductions: _____

Total: _____

Group Work: Instructor Evaluation Sheet

Group successfully completed assignment
(as much as was possible within the given time).   Y / N

Group grasped the core idea behind assignment.   Y / N

All members of group participated in assignment.   Y / N

Group made efficient use of classroom time.   Y / N

Comments:

Summary Assignment: Peer Evaluation Checklist

Student Writer _____   Student Evaluator _____

1. Title, author, date, and publication (of material to be summarized) are clearly stated in the opening sentence(s).

2. Student accurately represents author's thesis and position.

3. Summary contains the main points that develop and support the author's thesis.

4. Summary does not focus on minor points from the essay or selection.

5. Summary does not include the summarizer's opinions or evaluations.

6. Summary is written using verbs in the present tense.

7. Student makes correct use of paraphrasing/quotes.

8. Student uses correct grammar.

9. Student uses varied sentence structure.

10. Summary is free of spelling errors.

Suggestions for improvement:

Summary Assignment: Instructor Evaluation Sheet

Student   _____

1. Title, author, date, and publication (of material to be summarized) are clearly stated in the opening sentence(s).

2. Student accurately represents author's thesis and position.

3. Summary contains the main points that develop and support the author's thesis.

4. Summary does not focus on minor points from the essay or selection.

5. Summary does not include the summarizer's opinions or evaluations.

6. Summary is written using verbs in the present tense.

7. Student makes correct use of paraphrasing/quotes.

8. Student uses correct grammar.

9. Student uses varied sentence structure.

10. Summary is free of spelling errors.

Comments and Suggestions:

Paragraph Exam: Comparison/Contrast and Cause/Effect

Directions

Choose two of the following topics and create a well-written, fully supported paragraph for each. You must choose one topic from the Comparison/ Contrast category and one from the Cause/ Effect category. Narrow and define the topics into workable topic sentences (main ideas). Your Comparison/Contrast paragraph must follow either the block or point-by-point structure with at least three points of comparison. Your Cause/Effect should be strictly cause (covering immediate causes, remote causes, and influences) *or* effect (covering immediate effects and long-term effects). Make sure that each of your paragraphs makes sense, is well organized, and has at least three major details, three corresponding minor details, appropriate transitional words and/or phrases, and a concluding statement. Good luck!

Topics for Comparison/Contrast

1. Compare or contrast riding a bicycle to riding a motorcycle.
2. Compare or contrast watching a movie in a theater to watching a DVD at home.
3. Compare or contrast two restaurants.
4. Compare or contrast two places you have lived.
5. Compare or contrast two jobs you have held or wish to hold.

Topics for Cause/Effect

1. The causes or the effects of excessive salaries for professional sports players
2. The causes or the effects of the Internet on American culture
3. The causes or the effects of the rising divorce rate
4. The causes or the effects of watching too much television
5. The causes or the effects of eating a high cholesterol diet

Final Exam Essay Topics

Directions

Choose one of the following topics and write a well-developed essay according to the ideas we have discussed in class. Make sure that your essay has a thesis, an introduction, a conclusion, topic sentences for the body paragraphs, and plenty of details. Spend at least ten minutes on prewriting and defining/narrowing your topic before you begin the initial draft. You may want to make an outline of your paragraphs before you start writing. Proofread your work very carefully. Your final draft should be 200–300 words long (about two-and-a-half handwritten, double-spaced pages or one full page if typed). You must turn in all drafts and notes with your essay. Make sure to label which version is your final one!

1. Describe a person you are close to in terms of appearance and/or personality and/or habits.

2. Describe, using good concrete details, a beautiful or a horrible place you have visited.

3. Tell a story about a funny and/or embarrassing event in your life.

4. Tell a story about a moment that changed you and/or the way you thought about a particular issue.

5. Compare or contrast two restaurants you have been to, then evaluate strengths and weaknesses of each.

6. Compare or contrast two television programs you have watched, then evaluate strengths and weaknesses of each.

7. Explain to an entering freshman the process of registering for classes, becoming a better student, preparing for a test, or surviving a six-week summer course.

8. Explain the process of making a particular food that you like (e.g., nachos, pizza, lemonade, etc.) for someone who does not know how to cook very well.

Sample Student Writings

Student Writing: Illustration

Worst Vacation
By Josie Heyman

I had the worst vacation at the beach. I was there with my family including four children. First, I lost my nephew. It was a crowded weekend with people everywhere. I looked up, and he was gone. I panicked and started asking everyone if he or she had seen him. After about ten minutes, I sent my husband to the lifeguard stand and went to find his mother. I was relieved to find them together. As if that wasn't enough, I was going out for a swim when I felt an awful stinging in my legs. I rushed out of the water to find I had been stung by a Man o' war jellyfish. He had apparently gotten tangled in my legs. I had been stung from the tops of my thighs to my ankles. To top that, I had an allergic reaction a week later. Finally, I went to the hotel room to soothe the stinging to find I had been out in the sun too long. I was sunburned from head to toe. I was never so ready for a vacation to be over.

Student Writing: Narration

Festus
By Malona Zolliecoffer

Our friends were not home the hot summer day I went to pick him out. As I made my way up to the pen where he was, many puppies come out of a make-shift dog house. They all wiggled, jumped, and licked me through the ratty chicken wire, hoping to be the chosen one. He met my eye quickly. He was light tan and white and had wrinkles from head to toe. Little did I know the future he held with me would leave me in wonder and despair. I named him Festus.

His first year with me brought me lots of laughs, joy, and play. But I will never forget that sultry summer afternoon. He lay motionless against a white lawn chair. He drew my attention by bounding to the back side of the house. Terror went over me as I thought of the worst that could happen – Parvo? We spent many dollars, many vet trips and sleepless nights to bring him back to the dog I once had known.

The following summer came soon, and many memories of him became stamped in my mind. Photos, outside play, and rides on the four-wheeler revolved around him.

Saturday afternoon we left the house. Festus and Ivory stood on the hill in front of our country home. They often went there to play and watch the neighbor 's cattle.

On Sunday we spent the day walking and riding four-wheelers, looking for a clue, a trail, or a corpse. He had vanished without a trace as though God had decided it was his time to go. That day still haunts me in my heart, and tears still cloud my eyes at the thought of him. It is a mystery unsolved over a dog named Festus. He will be in my heart forever. I still love him.

Student Writing: Description

Easter
By Daniel Wolbert

It is early afternoon on a beautiful sunny Easter Sunday just warm enough to wear shorts and shortsleeved shirts. The remnants of fall leaves still pepper the ground. The grass is starting to poke green blades up in some spots, but it is still brown in others. The shade from the naked tree limbs cast intriguing shadows on the ground. You can still see the hillside through the limbs. The cedar trees are at their brightest green of the year, before the insects and heat of summer has turned them brown.

A small dog in the distance watches intently as a father and son hunt Easter eggs hidden earlier by the boy's mother, just enough easy ones to keep his interest and some hidden deep in leaves and holes to make it last. The boy follows his father hoping he will spot the more elusive eggs he missed. The boy is filled with excitement about the magic of the day, peering intently at the ground, hoping to spot another brightly colored egg.

The boy carries a yellow basket that is almost as big as he is, holding it with both hands, trying to keep the treasure within from falling out and breaking on the ground.

It was a simple moment in time that will last for a lifetime in the memories of a father and his son.

Student Writing: Comparison/Contrast

Water Pipes: Copper or P.V.C.?
By Daniel Wolbert

Choosing water piping for your new or existing home can be a difficult and even costly decision. Most professionals think copper is the only choice, but I believe there are benefits to both types. Let's begin by exploring the major differences between the two most common types of piping; there are others, but most are either illegal or outdated. Copper pipe comes in ten- and twenty-foot sticks or sections. It is rated by the wall thickness. The most common copper pipes are types L and M, the latter being the thickest and the most durable. Copper is joined together by copper couplings, which are sweated with a cleaning flux, solder and torch, providing an extremely solid and long lasting joint. P.V.C. pipe also comes in ten- and twenty-foot sticks. It is also rated by wall thickness. The only type still rated for use in water systems is Schedule Forty; there are others, but they are primarily used for sewer and drainage applications. P.V.C. comes in two types: P.V.C. for use with cold water and C.P.V.C. for use on hot water. They are not interchangeable. P.V.C. is joined with couplings and a fusion type glue. C.P.V.C. is joined using couplings and a filler glue. The joint on P.V.C. is usually fairly weak and needs support to keep from separating. Now let's look at price. Copper pipe is very expensive to purchase, and labor costs are usually at least three times that of P.V.C., but once installed properly, it will last indefinitely. P.V.C. is inexpensive and easy to install, but it can be easily damaged. In new homes, where cost is usually not a big factor, I highly recommend the use of copper. In existing homes, where cost or length of service is a problem, I recommend P.V.C. There is no doubt that copper pipe is the best; but, if installed properly, P.V.C. is a viable alternative for temporary or low cost use.

Student Essay: Narration

Fourteen Days of Uncertainty
By Heather Bridges

Life as a twelve year old was perfect, or so I thought. I was a carefree sixth grader. Okay, so I did worry a little, but they were all insignificant things like what lunch was going to be, if I was going to be late for school, which kickball team I would be on. Then one day everything changed. Life all of a sudden was not quite as happy anymore. Now it was tense, sad, and worry-filled.

All these uneasy feelings began when one Sunday morning I woke up and realized that my neighbor, Lucy, was at my house instead of my mom and dad. This, however, was not alarming to me because she was more than a neighbor. She was more like a grandmother to me and my brother. She was at the hospital the day I was born. Many days my brother and I resided at her house after school. However, this specific day she was not herself. The first thing she told me when I woke up was that my dad was in the hospital. Although she attempted not to look overly worried, her face told it all. From her puffy, red eyes to her tense, nervous demeanor, it was impossible for her to hide the seriousness of what had happened. She told me that my mom was going to call when she was told more about the situation. Even though it had only been an hour-and- a-half until my mother called, it seemed like an eternity. She talked to Lucy first then me. Her voice was soft and shaky, as if she were crying. She told me that my dad had a heart attack earlier that morning and that everything should be fine. I did not know whether this was the whole truth, but I did know she was trying to assure me that it would all be okay. She knew as soon as she said those words that I would be comforted. For the next fourteen days I did not see my father at all. From what I understood, as soon as his condition was stabilized an ambulance took him to the Air Force Base Hospital. After all of the blood work and tests had been run, the doctors decided which procedure would be best. They decided to perform an angioplasty and give him medication instead of bypass surgery. This decision was based on his age. He was only forty years old. The angioplasty and medicine worked well, but over the next three years he was very uncertain about his health. This caused him to panic every time he had angina, which resulted in many trips to the emergency room and several two to three day stays in the hospital. All of this added extra stress on the whole family. Therefore, my brother and I tried our hardest to help around the house and not bother them too much.

All of this caused me to feel extremely uneasy about the stability of my family. I had never even imagined how it would be without having my dad around. The emotional, not to mention the financial, difficulties on my mother would have been like a huge black cloud hovering over her. So many horrible thoughts came to my mind during those fourteen days in particular. Even after he had the operation and came home, I still was not myself. Life was not the same anymore. Now I was more withdrawn from people and much quieter, which is something that I normally was not. I was very worried for quite a long time. For instance, every time I would hear sirens I would wonder if it was my dad in the ambulance. Guilt was another feeling I had. Every time I would go play with friends or just ride my bicycle around the block, I would think of how my dad was at home sick and could not do any of these things anymore.

It has been seven years since his first heart attack. During this time he had more heart-related problems. The doctors decided after all of these problems that bypass surgery was now a step that had to be taken. He had double-bypass surgery in January of 1995. Since then, his health has improved tremendously. We feel more at ease with his health today than we did five or six years ago. Therefore, my life, and his, are pretty much back to normal.

Student Essay: Narration

Memories from 7th Street
By Treyson Hopkins

I still drive by the house on 7th Street every now and then, despite the fact that I know what I'm getting myself into. I know memories will be stirred up, wrapped in emotions ranging from carefree happiness to lonely sadness, from top-of-the-world confidence to worried uncertainty. Those memories and emotions stay with me, leaving me confused and insecure about my childhood.

I know I will think of my mom and dad; they usually come first. Sure, I will remember how *I* was with them – listening and laughing as my mom eloquently recounted a story about what so-and-so did at work that day, or playing catch for hour after hour with my dad in the alley; I was never more happy and content than during those hours – but mostly, I remember them being together. When we lived in that house, their relationship was perfect. Of course, it was not really perfect; it would only appear that way to a naïve young boy, so in my memories, everyone was happy then.

Yet, I doubt that anyone who drove by our house during the eleven-and-a-half years we lived there could imagine its residents ever thinking fondly of it. Our house was a perpetual work-in-progress. Whether it was a sprawling stack of decaying wood that had been stripped off the house from God knows where and left unkempt in the yard or the yard itself looking like a World War II battle front with trenches dug and mounds of earth piled high in preparation for the laying of the foundation, there was always something about our house that made passersby slow down so they could give it a long, judgmental look. The inside of the house too was usually in shambles. It was common to see piles of dust from sanding and sawing, walls that were stripped down, leaving their innards – the framing and wiring – exposed, or in some cases, walls that were nothing but thick sheets of semi-transparent plastic. That was the environment in which I grew up. And I miss it.

Seeing the house also makes me think of myself and how different I felt when I lived there. Back then, everything was so stable and certain. I never had to worry about things like moving away or divorce. The only problems I had to deal with could be solved with logic, like, where am I going to take a leak now that they're working on the bathroom? or, how am I going to get across that gaping hole in the floor? Therefore, since I had never experienced any real problems, I arrogantly assumed there was no problem I could not solve, no situation I could not control.

Naïveté and innocence were not the only things responsible for my self-concept of invincibility. I was a popular kid; I excelled both academically and athletically, so things came pretty easy for me. In fact, I don't remember ever really having to work for anything when I was younger. There was one area, however, where I did not mind putting in the extra effort: baseball. I loved to play baseball, mostly because I was so good. I was able to leave after each game with my head held high and bubbling over with confidence, knowing I had just controlled that game, and I loved that feeling of total control. It was after one such game that my sky-high ego was brought back down to earth. During the longest car ride of my life, I was told that in the fall, my family would be moving in order to accommodate my dad in his new job.

How could they do this to me? I wondered. Moving didn't fit with my simple, stable life. For days I cried the tears of a selfish 11-year-old incapable of putting his father and family before himself. I felt as if I had absolutely no control over my life. And I was convinced that I was right, and that everyone was going to see what a huge mistake they had made by moving.

However, shortly after the move, to my surprise, cards began falling into place. I was accepted socially in no time. I grew to like the new town just as much, if not more than my former home. And it was pretty sweet living in a brand new house where you could walk around barefoot without fear of stepping on a nail or live wire. In fact, I was probably happier than ever, and it wasn't long until I began feeling invincible again, ignorant of the stirrings of a sinister serpent: separation, which would eventually claim my family.

When my parents told me they were divorcing, I was bombarded with an arsenal of emotions. Obviously, the anguish of having to leave behind one of the two people I loved most in the world was devastating. However, when I could no longer cry tears of dejection, a new source was tapped. I was again in a situation in which I was neither in control nor capable of solving the problem, and the realization that I could not fix every problem I encountered in life and would have to accept some things and learn to cope, scared me.

Obviously, I would never wish these things upon anyone, but the maturation that I was forced to undergo as a result of the helplessness I felt, improved my approach to life. I am thankful now for the move and divorce – as if anyone can truly be thankful for such demoralizing events – out of fear of what I might have become if I had been allowed to go on much longer without a reminder that no one gets to control everything. Sure, my life is better now, materially and emotionally for the most part, but whenever I see the house on 7th Street, I am reminded of how I once had a life so simple amidst so much external chaos. And I miss it.

Student Essay: Process

How to Make Tomato Sauce
By Rossano Cherubini

In Italy, since the times of the ancient Romans, cooking and eating have always been represented as an art rather than just satisfying the basic human need for food. Since then, Italian cuisine has been famous throughout the world as a traditional, simple and healthy one. The traditional Italian dish is pasta, and the indispensable element in pasta cooking is "La Pummarola," the tomato sauce. It is the base of all the so-called "red sauces," and it can be seasoned to suit personal tastes. However, the Italians usually say that the simplest is the best, and, of the many sauce recipes, this is a simple one. You will find that it will not be necessary to drive to the grocery store, because the things that you need are among the most common. In fact, the only ingredients needed to make this sauce are two pounds of tomatoes, an onion, two stalks of celery, and a carrot. Toward the end of the preparation, salt, pepper, and virgin olive oil are added for seasoning. The only equipment necessary is two saucepans, a strainer, a chopping knife, and a spoon. By following these simple steps, anyone can make the perfect Italian tomato sauce.

You should begin your sauce by preparing the vegetables, and for this you will need to use the chopping knife. First, peel one carrot and cut it lengthwise into strips. You will get four to six strips, depending on the size of the carrot. Second, you have to dice the strips into small cubes. Similarly, you dice two stalks of celery, trimming off the leafage. The onion, like the carrot, has to be peeled, but minced thinly rather than diced. Regarding the tomatoes, they should be soft and ripe for this recipe. You begin preparing the tomatoes by first washing them in cool running water. Second, placing the tomatoes with the stem up, you cut them in half from top to bottom and trim out the cores. Third, the tomatoes should be cut into quarters, and then diced. The carrot, onion, and celery are used and recommended not only for their complementary flavors, but also for the fact that they act together as a counter to the acidity of the tomatoes.

Now that all the ingredients are ready, you can start the actual cooking of the sauce. Take one of the two saucepans and put in the tomatoes so that they completely cover the bottom of the pan. Next, you can add the carrot, onion, and celery on top. You need to make sure that this is the exact sequence of vegetables in the pan and for a good reason: while cooking, the tomatoes will give off liquid and it is this liquid that will take the place of butter, which is normally used to sauté vegetables. On the other hand, if you put the carrot, onion or celery first, they would burn and stick to the bottom of the pan. Once all the vegetables are in the pan, you need to cover and cook slowly on a low heat for forty-five minutes until all the ingredients are soft. This may seem like a long time, but it is fundamental to allow the flavors of the tomatoes and those of the other vegetables to blend.

Once the sauce has been cooked for the given length of time and the vegetables are soft enough for mashing, you should be ready for the next step: straining the sauce. What you need now is the second saucepan and the strainer. First, place the strainer over the top of the saucepan. Second, you have to pour the vegetable mixture into the strainer.

Third, you will want to use the spoon to press the mixture through the strainer so that as much as possible drains into the saucepan. You will have some of the mixture remaining in the strainer, but you can scrape the pulp from the outside bottom of the strainer and add it to the sauce. Now, all you have to do is reheat the sauce. While stirring slowly, add salt and pepper to taste, and two tablespoons of virgin olive oil. The sauce at this point has enough character to be served with any type of pasta, or, at your choice and with double or triple quantities, the sauce can be frozen in small portions and stored in your freezer. If this is the case, it will be always ready by only reheating it in a pan with a tablespoon of olive oil.

Finally, your sauce is ready to cover a steaming plate of spaghetti. At this point, in order to have a true Italian sauce, you need an Italian final touch: fresh basil. However, do not make the mistake of chopping it, because Italians believe that it will bring bad luck. You must break the leaves into small pieces with your fingers and put them in the sauce along with the salt, pepper, and olive oil. After you have done this, you need to let the sauce simmer for about five more minutes in order for the basil to lend its flavor. Of course, you can always use ready canned tomato sauces and artificial flavors, but you will miss the pleasure of cooking and a great taste that will really impress your guests. Buon Appetito!

Student Essay: Classification

A Powerful Team
By Michael Hadley

Three different classes of workers make up the restaurant business. These three classes have shaped this business as it is known today. The employees and managers both work inside the stores and are responsible for making the money. The office workers only work in the stores on special occasions and are responsible for managing the money. These three different jobs have a great effect on the way the business is run. In fact, without the employees, managers, and office workers, there would be no business at all.

The employee is considered to be the first class in a business. Most employees are teenagers making just above minimum wage on an hourly schedule. Just because they are the first class does not mean that they're not important. As a matter of fact, the employees are crucial to the business. They are the individuals that cook, clean, and deal directly with every customer. As people in the restaurant business know, dealing with the customer is the hardest task. For example, an employee must greet the customer and take his or her order. Then, the employee must rely on fellow employees to get the order correct and have it ready in time. Once the food is ready to serve, the employee must be friendly and the customer must be satisfied.

The second class in the restaurant business is the manager. The manager also has an important job. Because the manager has more authority and works longer hours, he or she makes more money. It is important to remember, however, that a manager 's job is not any more important than an employee's. Most managers deal less with the customers and more with the employees. The manager must make sure the employees are doing their jobs correctly. The manager's job requirement is to train new employees, deal with the customer on special occasions, and make sure the store is operating the correct way. For example, if the bathrooms are dirty, then it is the manager's job to make sure they get cleaned. Also, if a customer has a problem, the manager must do his best to fix it.

The third and highest class in the restaurant business is the office workers. This includes the accountant, store supervisor, maintenance crew, and owner or operator. Their jobs are to make the paychecks, keep the restaurants in good condition, train the managers, and keep all the paperwork up to date. Office workers usually make the most money and have a higher education and degree. Although their job is very important to the business, these workers tend to deal with customers even less than the manager. However, on occasion an angry or pleased customer might go to the office to voice his or her opinion.

The employee, manager, and office worker are crucial to the restaurant business. They all have very different jobs, but they are of equal importance. The employee must make the customer happy and serve great food, the manager must make sure the employees are doing their jobs, and the office workers must keep the business going. Their jobs form a very powerful team of workers and make the business what it is.

Student Essay: Persuasion

Leibovitz Revealed
By Yarrow Allen-Hickey

I have always been drawn to photography. I love how it captures raw emotions and single moments in time. It documents inner personalities that people are not usually comfortable showing the world, along with showing different sides of people. Photographs linger in people's minds long after the image is taken and captures people and events that the general public are not usually exposed to. One of my favorite photographers is Annie Leibovitz. I think that it is her portrayal of the human form and people's public and private selves that makes her unparalleled in the field of photography.

Annie Leibovitz breaks the boundaries of social norms with her photography subjects. In one famous photograph she has John Lennon completely naked, wrapped around his wife Yoko Ono who is fully dressed. In a society where men are never physically exposed, having a male role model stripped in the same way women usually are, is a shock to the beliefs of social codes. Another photograph shows a very pregnant Demi Moore posing nude. In American society, women who are not of the desirable skinny body type are usually kept out of pictures. To have a pregnant woman appearing on the cover of Vanity Fair magazine demonstrating confidence and love for her body is bold. I think that Annie Leibovitz addresses many of these stereotypes as well as other issues through the human form. She is able to do this by drawing attention to social norms and issues that are not ordinarily addressed in mainstream media.

In her photographs, Annie Leibovitz captures both the subject's inner self as well as the self that the outside world sees. I believe that she emphasizes an aspect of a subject's public persona while at the same time portraying that subject in a personal way. She has a series of photographs that show Vegas Showgirls in their costumes. Next to each picture is another one in which the same woman is not made up and is in her street clothes. The fantasy vs. reality of their two personas is startling and makes each woman seem more human. In her exhibits there are also pictures of domestic abuse victims next to beauty queens and one is faced with the different levels of society. She uses both famous and non-famous people to create art that makes a statement about the world and the people in it. It is this ability to capitalize on different aspects of society that sets Leibovitz apart from other photographers.

Annie Leibovitz is also very well regarded in the photography world and is the first woman to have had her work exhibited at the National Portrait Gallery in New York City. At twenty-two she was the youngest photographer to become chief photographer for the magazine Rolling Stone and concert tour photographer for the Rolling Stones. She is often compared to portrait photographer Arnold Newman and people say that it is her bold and creative use of the human form that pushes her ahead.

Annie Leibovitz's photographs are different from her fellow artists because she is able to take the human form and use it to convey her message. She portrays the woman underneath of Vegas Showgirls, she undresses the man and leaves the woman fully dressed, and she brings the pregnant woman's form out into the open. She expands society's beliefs on social codes by enabling people to see different views. She is recognized throughout the art world and her photographs are displayed at very prestigious locations. I think that for these reasons Annie Leibovitz is set apart from her contemporaries and is a wonderful photographer.

Student Essay: Persuasion

Beyond the Paycheck
By Jessica Richard

In today's music it is becoming very hard to find a musician or group who has not "sold out" yet. It is much too common to see stars in commercials or advertisements endorsing just about any product that you can think of, from soft drinks to make-up. Neil Young is one artist who has kept true to his music and not done this. He is one of the few artists who only creates music for himself and his fans, not for the sole purpose of making money.

Today, many would argue that endorsing products and making television commercials is essential, that without this stars would have no popularity. This has happened as a result of our society. It used to be a rarity to see as many celebrities on television as we do today. Now it has become something so popular that musicians are considered "nothings" if they not have their name on a brand or even their own brand. Neil Young has done neither of these things. As a protest to his peer's actions, he wrote and released the song called "This Note's For You" on the *Lucky Thirteen* album in 1988. In the first verse of the song a listener can grasp his idea right away.

> I ain't singin' for Pepsi
> I ain't singin' for Coke
> I don't sing for nobody
> Makes me look like a joke
> This note's for you.

The rest of the lyrics of this song go on to explain he won't sing for beer, politicians, or endorsement money because he's "got the real thing, baby." His lyrics for this song prove that he does have the real thing, the act of relying solely on the music to popularize himself, and this is how it should be. A musician should not become well known because we have seen his or her face plastered over billboards everywhere. They should become well known and respected because their music evokes an emotion in people and makes them want to listen to it more.

With Neil Young's album, *Trans*, released in 1983, he proved again that he loves his music and not only the money he makes from it. Throughout the whole album he distorted his voice with vocoders, octave dividers, and synthesizers. The music of this album was also very computerized and employed the use of drum machines. Young made this album to relay his attempts to communicate with his son Ben, who has cerebral palsy. At the time, Ben was going through a therapy program to enable him to communicate better and it was a tough and rigorous process. The whole album was an expression of the frustration of a handicap. Even though Young was highly degraded and just about every critic out there basically trashed his album, he took it with a grain of salt. Even though the album did not sell many copies and was not successful in the least, he treasured it because it meant something to him other than a paycheck.

Neil Young is a musician who should be idolized and looked up to by all, but unfortunately will never be because of the abundance of greedy, money-loving hounds in the music industry today. Today musicians are too materialistic, they don't care about their songs evoking emotions, but instead about how big their houses are and how fast their cars go. One could argue that the money that comes from advertising and promotions is part of their income, but if you are a musician shouldn't your income result from performing and selling you music, instead of endorsing a drink or face cream?

Following the Progress of a Student Essay: Rough Draft

Witness
By Christina Owsley

Continuously I search for a solution of how I feel about being stereotyped a Jehovah's Witness growing up. Although currently I am removed from the religion I don't necessarily think bad of it. It has caused much division in my life in the aspect of me trying to be something that I really wasn't. I will take you through my life from past to present.

Through my life I was always the odd child. I didn't do what the other kids did or wear the clothes they wore. This was because my parents were Jehovah's Witnesses. Witnesses don't believe in celebrating any holidays including birthdays. They do celebrate Anniversary's though. Up until about eight years ago they would publicly remove you from the church if you sought out a higher education than high school. Partially because of this my father worked a low paying job as a janitor. My mother was a housewife because this is what the religion favored at the time. Our family didn't have the money for daily essentials, and defiantly not enough for new clothes. My brother and I were constantly ridiculed about our hand me down and garage sale clothes. Aside from the clothing my brother and I weren't allowed to do any of the social activities other children did. This included holidays, after school sports, and school dances.

Holidays are probably the largest difference that set us apart from others. I remember once when I was in third grade, and I had a teacher named Mrs. Miller. When school started my parents had come in to discuss the Witnesses views on things with her. This was supposed to give her knowledge as to what I could and couldn't do in school.

Well Christmas time rolled around and all the third grade classes filtered into our classroom to learn Christmas Carols from a visiting music teacher. Mrs. Miller paid special attention to see if I was singing or not. She noticed I wasn't, so she pulled me to the front of the classroom to watch me sing. Soon she figured out I was lip sinking. I thought by lip sinking God would know I wasn't really singing so it would be all right. Mrs. Miller was dead set on me singing though. This time she turned the music on low and tried to make me sing this Christmas Carol. Only now I was singing alone in front of all the third graders. I started to, but immediately burst into tears of embarrassment, and tried to leave the room. As soon as I reached the door Mrs. Miller stopped me. She sent me to the back of the room until I calmed down. The other children thought me being the object of humiliation was tremendously amusing. This is just one example of many similar situations.

In fifth grade I was starting to develop my own opinions of the religion. This is when the difficulty for my parents really began, because I rebelled against anything they said or did. I decided I truly did not like the religion because it made me so different. Any chance my brother and I had at fitting into a social click was diminished by our involuntary lack of socialization. We were invited to birthday parties and couldn't go. We had to leave the room if a celebration of any sort was going on. I even remember being asked by the coach of the basketball team to join but couldn't because of religious reasons. Kids noticed that we were different, and didn't akin to it.

After eighth grade graduation my parents didn't like the few "worldly friends" I had somehow made. A "Worldly friend" means a friend outside of the church. They decided to home school me for high school. Again they were trying to socially removing me. History had already proven, and would prove again that this would be detrimental.

At age fifteen I had somehow scraped and borrowed enough money to buy a car. Now when I was in trouble, they took the keys away, but I had an extra set ready. They disabled it, and I fixed it. I was always a step ahead of them. They had lost complete control by age sixteen. I worked two jobs at this age also. One day before work my mom and I got in an argument. She told me, "If I couldn't live by her rules, I couldn't live in her house." Those were the words I had been waiting for. I packed my bags and left for work with no plans of returning to her house.

That's right I didn't return, because when I got off work my probation officer was waiting for me. He took me to an attention home where I lived for a month. While I was there I received a lot of counseling. I came to the realization that I was trying to get rid of the "odd Jehovah's Witness girl" stereotype I had been living with.

When I returned home things changed some but I was still pressured to be a Witness. I was still sixteen and much to my parents dismay found a steady boyfriend. At the age of seventeen I became pregnant with our first child. Then at nineteen I walked down the wedding isle to marry that same boyfriend. I was four months pregnant with our second child at this time. I supposed I succeeded in getting rid of the stereotype I wanted gone.

Now that I am older I realize who I really am and what I stand for. I can't believe some of the things I did to the ones I love. I wish I could go back and change time, however that's imposable. All I can do now is move forward, and try to let the ones I love know how much I love them. I have went back and studied the bible with some Jehovah's Witnesses, and found that I didn't agree with some of their major beliefs. So to my parents dismay I will never be a Jehovah's Witness again. This may trouble them, but I know that everything will be all right. I hope to raise my children without any stereotypes.

Following the Progress of a Student Essay: Final Draft

Witness
By Christina Owsley

Through my life I was always the odd child. I didn't do what the other kids did or wear the clothes they wore. This was because my parents were Jehovah's Witnesses. Witnesses don't believe in celebrating any holidays including birthdays. Up until about eight years ago they would publicly remove you from the church if you sought out a higher education than high school. Partially because of this my father worked a low paying job as a janitor. My mother was a housewife because this is what the religion favored at the time. Our family didn't have enough money for daily essentials, and definitely not enough for new clothes. My brother and I were constantly ridiculed about our hand me down and garage sale clothes. Aside from the clothing, my brother and I weren't allowed to do any of the social activities other children did. This included holidays, after school sports, and school dances. I continuously search for a solution of how I feel about being stereotyped a Jehovah's Witness growing up. Although currently I am removed from the religion I don't necessarily think badly of it. But it has caused much division in my life in the aspect of me trying to be something that I really wasn't.

Holidays are probably the biggest difference that sets us apart from others. I remember once when I was in third grade, I had a teacher named Mrs. Miller. When school started my parents came in to discuss the Witness' views on things with her. This was supposed to give her knowledge as to what I could and couldn't do in school.

Well, Christmas time rolled around and all the third grade classes filtered into our classroom to learn Christmas carols from a visiting music teacher. Mrs. Miller paid special attention to see if I was singing or not. She noticed I wasn't, so she pulled me to the front of the classroom to watch me sing. Soon she figured out I was lip-synching. I thought by lip-synching God would know I wasn't really singing so it would be all right. Mrs. Miller was dead set on me singing though. She turned the music on low and tried to make me sing this Christmas carol. Only now I was singing alone in front of all the third graders. I started to sing, but immediately burst into tears of embarrassment, and tried to leave the room. As soon as I reached the door Mrs. Miller stopped me. She sent me to the back of the room until I calmed down. The other children thought me being the object of humiliation was tremendously amusing.

In fifth grade I was starting to develop my own opinions of the religion. This is when the difficulty for my parents really began, because I rebelled against anything they said or did. I decided I truly did not like the religion because it made me so different. Any chance my brother and I had at fitting into a social clique was diminished by our involuntary lack of socialization. We were invited to birthday parties and couldn't go. We had to leave the room if a celebration of any sort was going on. I even remember being asked by the coach of the basketball team to join but couldn't because of religious reasons. Kids noticed that we were different, and didn't relate to it.

After eighth grade graduation my parents didn't like the few "worldly friends" I had somehow made. A "worldly friend" means a friend outside of the church. They decided to home school me for high school. Again they were trying to socially remove me. History had already proven, and would prove again that this would be detrimental.

At age fifteen I had somehow scraped and borrowed enough money to buy a car. Now when I was in trouble, they took the keys away, but I had an extra set ready. They disabled it, and I fixed it. I was always a step ahead of them. They had lost complete control by age sixteen. I worked two jobs at this age also. One day before work my mom and I got in an argument. She told me, "If you can't live by my rules, you can't live in my house." Those were the words I had been waiting for. I packed my bags and left for work with no plans of returning to her house.

That's right, I didn't return, because when I got off work my probation officer was waiting for me. He took me to a detention home where I lived for a month. While I was there I received a lot of counseling. I came to the realization that I was trying to get rid of the "odd Jehovah's Witness girl" stereotype I had been living with.

When I returned home things changed some but I was still pressured to be a Witness. I was still sixteen and much to my parents' dismay found a steady boyfriend. At the age of seventeen I became pregnant with our first child. Then at nineteen I walked down the wedding aisle to marry that same boyfriend. I was four months pregnant with our second child at this time. I supposed I succeeded in getting rid of the stereotype I wanted gone.

This stereotype affected me immensely in life. I was so caught up in destroying the image of a Jehovah's Witness I lost who I really was. I became a person who did appalling things. Now when I think back over my childhood I realize that my parents were raising me in the best way they knew how, according to their beliefs. I was raised in a loving household, even if it did have a twist to it. My dad came out of an extremely abusive household and managed to break the cycle with his own family. In my adulthood, I have told him many times how proud I am of him for this. But I have also told them my opinion of their religion, and the affects of them raising me as a Jehovah's Witness. I think in a family there should always be the option of a different opinion, even from a young age.

Sometimes I still find myself trying to prove to people that I am a decent person. The odd Jehovah's Witness stereotype has certainly left its mark. But now that I have my own children, I realize how little I care what others think. I have decided to accept myself the way I am in order to be a good parent. My goal for my children is for them to know the sky is the limit. I would also like them to always keep an open mind. Speaking from experience I can say, "No one knows what's on the other side of the fence until you have actually experienced it." I will let my children make their own mistakes, and succeed at their own successes. I would like to raise them free of any stereotypes imposed on them, however impossible this may sound.

Exit Exam Question

Directions: Write a focused and developed response to the following prompt. You will have fifty minutes to complete your response.

Consider the biggest challenge you have faced since arriving at The University of Montana. Briefly describe the challenge and your response to it. Then consider and explain what you have learned about yourself from that response.

Student Exit Exam

By Kirk Scramstad

Since my arrival at the University of Montana I have been faced with many challenges that I have never had to deal with before. However, the one challenge that is the biggest for me is finding good quality friends like I have at home.

A good quality friend is one who does anything for you at any time. The friends that I have at home in North Dakota are these types of friends. I could call them up at five in the morning and they would be on my doorstep as soon as they could no matter the distance they had to travel. The friends that I have here in Montana at the University are basically party friends, the kind of friends that you have a great time hanging out with but you can't really count on in your times of need. If I had to sum up my friends in both places in one word I would say my Montana friends are acquaintances and my North Dakota friends are family.

This has had made me feel like a worthless person at times out here. My reaction to this has included feelings of deep sadness and being very upset at times. It has made me feel like I don't know a single soul in this universe. But this has also helped me become even better friends with my ones at home. It has really put them to the test with the late night phone calls, and believe me, they all passed. This has helped me make new friends as well as strengthen the friendships I have at home.

From this I have learned a lot about myself. I have learned what the true definition of a friend is to me. This reaction has taught me that to call someone a friend is a very powerful thing. Friend is a word that I do not throw around, but rather a word that I use to identify the people that mean the most to me. I have learned that I have to value the time I spend with the people I love and the people that love me. I have learned that friends are really people you can depend on in times of need. But most of all I have learned that that my friends in North Dakota truly do shape me as a person and who I am today.

Making new, good quality friends has been my largest challenge in Montana. However, because of this my friendships at home have been strengthened and I have made some new friends here as well. I have learned a lot about what true friends are, from the late night phone calls, and how these friends have shaped me to make the human being that I am today.

Collected Assignments

35 In-Class Activities

IN-CLASS ACTIVITY 1.   Bring in selections from famous writers' diaries and journals (either copy for all of the students or read aloud). After reading the journal entry, read a selection from that writer's creative work. Good examples for this would be Virginia Woolf's diaries and a selection from *To the Lighthouse* or John Cheever's diaries and the ending to his short story, "The Swimmer." Other famous diarists include Anais Nin, Sei Shonagon (*The Pillow Book*), Samuel Pepys, Sylvia Plath, and Benjamin Franklin. A good resource for this activity would be *The Poet's Notebook: Excerpts from the Notebooks of 26 American Poets* edited by Stephen Kuusisto et al. (Norton, 1997). No matter which examples you decide to use, students will surely appreciate being able to study actual examples of the journal in action.

IN-CLASS ACTIVITY 2.   *Exercise in Coherence*: Have students underline every logical connector or transitional word or phrase in the sample paragraph given in the section on coherence in Chapter 2. Ask them what they think is lost by deleting these words. Often, they will easily get the point. **Exercise in Unity**: Draw a large umbrella on the board or on a transparency. Within the umbrella, write a topic sentence such as "Stress can cause many problems in a student's life." Tell students that only people who belong to that topic sentence can stand under the umbrella, and then give them supporting details, one at a time, and ask if these details belong under the umbrella or outside (in the rain). This is just one quick visual device to help them relate "umbrella" to "unity."

IN-CLASS ACTIVITY 3.   Divide the chalkboard in half and list all of the parts of speech on each half. Choose any reading from the textbook, toss a coin to see which team goes first, and then the first team works to find the subject and verb of the first sentence of the chosen reading. If their answer is incorrect, the question goes to the other team. If neither team gets the answer correct, the first team to correctly identify another part of speech within the same sentence receives a point. Then go on to the next sentence until ten sentences or twenty minutes have expired–whichever comes first. The winning team should get a small prize. Candy or a reduction in that night's homework are incentives that often work well!

IN-CLASS ACTIVITY 4.   Bring in a 10-minute videotape or DVD of a sporting event. Have students practice being sports announcers giving a play-by-play account of the action. If the technology is not available for video or DVD, give directions to several students to mime a specific action while a panel of students gives a moment-to-moment account of what they are doing. Keep track of any mistakes that students make in subject-verb agreement and discuss these mistakes when the exercise is over.

IN-CLASS ACTIVITY 5.   Have the class visit a campus commons or community center. It is important that students are able to witness many people doing different activities. Have students write for fifteen minutes about all of the activities they see using the present tense. Upon returning to class, have students exchange papers and look for subject-verb agreement errors.

IN-CLASS ACTIVITY 6.   Magazine advertisements are filled with sentence fragments. There are several reasons for this–fragments can be emphatic, they stand out from sentences because they are unusual or even irritating, and they can create a conversational tone. Find an assortment of ads that contain fragments and give several ads to each group. Have the groups identify all of the fragments in the ads. Then have students change each fragment into a complete sentence. Next, have the groups analyze the difference the complete sentences make on the overall tone of the ad. When the groups have had sufficient time to work, have them present their findings on one or two of the ads to the rest of the class.

IN-CLASS ACTIVITY 7.   Provide class groups with a list of short choppy sentences that relate to the same topic. The groups must create a "paragraph" that sounds good and makes sense by combining the sentences appropriately. You may wish to specify that students use all of the methods of coordination at least once; or you may wish to hone their critical skills by leaving the choice up to them, and then ask them to articulate the reasons for their choices.

IN-CLASS ACTIVITY 8.   As a class, read "Darkness at Noon" by Harold Krents (in Chapter 27). Go through it slowly to identify dependent and independent clauses. When students experience difficulty, help them identify and eliminate all of the prepositional phrases to get to the basic sentence. Give them the answer if they continue to be confused.

IN-CLASS ACTIVITY 9.   Have students bring in their versions of the paragraph given in Test Two. Provide students with the handout of the original found in Part 4 of this manual. As a class, analyze how American writer James Thurber combined ideas. Have students compare Thurber's choices with their own.

IN-CLASS ACTIVITY 10.   Have each student exchange work with another student in class. Have students closely examine each other's work for fragments and run-ons and then have them provide solutions for fixing problem sentences.

IN-CLASS ACTIVITY 11.   Have students write down a story you are about to tell them. They are to transcribe your story word for word. Proceed by telling a rambling story in which most of your sentences are connected with "and." When you have told the story twice (exactly the same way both times), ask students to look over their version and eliminate run-ons by using the three methods of coordination and subordination. When they finish, have several read their finished products aloud.

IN-CLASS ACTIVITY 12.   Create a deliberately confusing paragraph in which it is impossible to tell the antecedents of the pronouns. Write this paragraph on the board. Have students fix the pronouns so that the paragraph makes sense.

IN-CLASS ACTIVITY 13.   Bring in newspaper headlines that have gross (and often funny) dangling modifiers or find examples of dangling modifier bloopers in magazines (*Reader's Digest,* for example). Have students work on fixing the errors.

IN-CLASS ACTIVITY 14.   Ask for a student to volunteer to tell the class about some incident that has occurred recently. The rest of the class should listen and list the verbs used by the student. Are the verb tenses used accurately and consistently?

IN-CLASS ACTIVITY 15.   First, tell students the following short made-up story: A man and woman meet at the local Wal-Mart and fall instantly in love. Unfortunately, the man is there to buy a few items for his flight home to another state or a foreign country. The woman is there because she needs directions to the nearest medical center. After finishing the story, have students get into groups to write their own versions of the story, packed with name brands, geographical locations, and dialogue. Have each group write a clean copy to submit for an activity grade.

IN-CLASS ACTIVITY 16.   Write the following paragraph on the board or show it on the overhead projector:

> The small child turned the bowl of pasta over on the floor and sat down in it. Her mother was not happy about the child's action. After speaking loudly to the child, the father got something from the sink to help pick the pasta off the floor. The child spread the food across the floor and smiled.

Ask students to go through the paragraph sentence by sentence and change neutral words and phrases into words and phrases that give a negative connotation to the child's actions.

IN-CLASS ACTIVITY 17.   Have students look up the word "loose" in the dictionary. Have them make a list of the different kinds of information they find out about this word. Then have students compare with each other how many different items they have found.

IN-CLASS ACTIVITY 18.   Show the class current headlines from newspapers. Then have them convert the headlines into complete sentences. If the sentences do not yet contain a controlling idea, lead them through the steps needed to create one or more controlling ideas. Then have students identify the controlling ideas in headlines from letters to the editor. You may want to copy one letter to be looked at by the entire class, having them identify the topic sentence in each paragraph.

IN-CLASS ACTIVITY 19.   Have students bring to class the assignments in which "vague" or "not specific enough" has been written in the margins. If this is not feasible, the instructor can provide paragraphs containing vague writing. Have students alone or in groups write the paragraph/s over by including lots of supporting details. This gives students an opportunity to incorporate everything they have learned in Chapter 16 with the newer information about supporting detail. A good way to wind up this exercise is to have groups of students read their paragraphs aloud so that everyone can hear all of the possibilities.

IN-CLASS ACTIVITY 20.   Ask the class to choose a writing topic and put the topic on the board. Give students the following illustration paragraph structure and ask them to write eight sentences employing the structure.

- First Sentence: Make a claim about your topic that needs to be proven (Topic Sentence or Main Idea).

- Second Sentence: Give one good reason that claim is true (First Major Detail).

- Third Sentence: Give a specific example that explains or clarifies that reason (Minor Detail supporting Major Detail).

- Fourth Sentence: Give another good reason that your claim is true (Second Major Detail).

- Fifth Sentence: Give a specific example that explains or clarifies the second reason (Minor Detail supporting Major Detail).

- Sixth Sentence: Give your last and best good reason that your claim is true (Third Major Detail).

- Seventh Sentence: Give a specific example that explains or clarifies your last, best reason (Minor Detail supporting Major Detail).

- Eighth Sentence: Write a neat, concluding statement that sums up your position.

*If you have your students use this chart several times, their writing will begin to sound better to them. It is an excellent way to build their confidence before working with more complicated patterns.

Ask a student to volunteer to tell a story to the class. It could be true or fictional. Set a time limit. Use this story to discuss the basic elements of narration. Ask students to decide whether or not they think the story was true or not. On what did students base their decisions?

IN-CLASS ACTIVITY 21.   Have students bring in their favorite paragraphs from novels or short stories of their choice. Read them aloud and discuss the aspect of description in each selection.

IN-CLASS ACTIVITY 22.   Have students write for fifteen minutes at the beginning of class about the present moment–the chairs, people, marks on the board, quality of light, what can be seen from the window, etc. Tell them to write sharp, exacting detail. When they have finished, you may want to go over the details they noticed. Which details seemed the "sharpest"?

IN-CLASS ACTIVITY 23.   Provide groups with a set of overly general directions to a common task and have them revise for unity and clarity, making sure to fill in the steps that were omitted.

IN-CLASS ACTIVITY 24.   Work together as a class to compare buying a house to having a baby. Topics that seem dissimilar at first will emerge as having a lot in common: both having a baby and buying a house take about a year from start to finish; the rosy glow of pregnancy and deciding on a home may turn to fear and pain when delivery and closing costs occur, etc. After this exercise is complete, have the students challenge you by trying to come up with a two-part topic that is so dissimilar they cannot imagine any similarities being drawn between the two. Prove them wrong–this is the perfect opportunity to discuss analogy!

IN-CLASS ACTIVITY 25.   Have students get into groups to analyze the many causes of a particular social issue. The groups should produce between twenty-five and forty causes. Then have the groups rank the causes in order of importance. Finally, have the groups decide which of these causes were immediate, underlying, and remote influences. When they have completed this assignment and the class has had a chance to compare notes, have the group work on the effects of the same issue. Students may wish to use the list to formulate their own cause and effect paragraphs. See the handout on Sample Topics for Persuasive Essays in Part 4 for a list of topics you may want to discuss.

IN-CLASS ACTIVITY 26.   Have students sit with their desks in a circle and present an issue to be discussed. Instruct the students to voice their opinions on the issue. Tell the students to listen very carefully to what the others are saying; if any statement seems vague, students should demand that the speaker define his or her terms. Take the discussion very slowly at first so that nothing is missed. If the conversation gets heated, make notes of vague terms on the board and discuss the terms when the discussion concludes.

IN-CLASS ACTIVITY 27.   Turn to Part 6 of the textbook, Further Readings for the College Writer. Study each of the introductory paragraphs and discuss the variety of approaches. Which ones seem particularly effective?

IN-CLASS ACTIVITY 28.   Photocopy and distribute to students the rough draft and final draft of the student essay "Witness," located in Appendix A of this manual. Have students read both drafts. Then place students into groups in which they can discuss the changes the writer made between the rough and final drafts. Discuss the changes the writer made, paying particular attention to the reworking of the introduction and conclusion.

IN-CLASS ACTIVITY 29.   Send students to the library to gather statistics on a topical issue, such as the statistics on drunk driving in their home state in the past year. Then students work together to create a paragraph built on statistical illustration.

IN-CLASS ACTIVITY 30.   Gather class examples of childhood experiences that left profound impressions. List them on the board and, as a class, discuss the ways in which these experiences lend themselves to the narrative mode.

IN-CLASS ACTIVITY 31.   Open up classroom discussion to the ways in which process plays a role in our daily lives. Have the class divide up into three groups: those who are decisive, those who cannot make up their minds about the simplest things, and those who fall somewhere in the middle. Put two situations on the board and have students discuss the processes they might go through to make a decision. Have the groups compare notes.

IN-CLASS ACTIVITY 32.   Hand out copies of two paragraphs that you deem suitable. Have students read the paragraphs, identify the topic sentence in each, and write three-sentence summaries. Have students get into groups and discuss their opinions and eventually come up with a basic outline for comparing or contrasting the works. Ask students to write a three-paragraph comparison or contrast for homework, or, if time permits, in the remaining class period.

IN-CLASS ACTIVITY 33.   Photocopy the "letters to the editor" section of your local newspaper and distribute copies to the class. Have students get into groups and discuss the methods of persuasion for each letter. Are any of the writers using verbal attacks or threats? How do those methods of argument affect the persuasiveness of the letter? *You may want to photocopy and distribute the handout on Logical Fallacies, located in Part 4 of this manual. After you have gone over each logical fallacy, have students re-read the letters to the editor, looking for logical fallacies.

IN-CLASS ACTIVITY 34.   Put the following topic on the board and allow students a specific amount of time in which to respond: The Internet: How It Has Changed Our Lives. Afterward, discuss with students how they approached the topic, what prewriting techniques they used, and how they organized their material.

IN-CLASS ACTIVITY 35.   Give your class the sample exit exam question located at the end of Appendix A in this manual. After students have developed their own responses to the question, pass out the sample student exit exam also located in Appendix A. Have students go through the sample essay and analyze how the student writer organized his material. Open up discussion about how their essays compared to the sample essay. Did everyone organize his or her essay in a similar way? What kinds of topics seemed to work best?

35 Journal and Writing Assignments

JOURNAL ASSIGNMENT 1.   Create a one-page cluster on the word "summer."

JOURNAL ASSIGNMENT 2.   List all the items you would put in a time capsule to be opened in the year 2100. Explain the significance of each item and why you chose it for the time capsule.

JOURNAL ASSIGNMENT 3.   *Analyze an Advertisement*: Find an advertisement in a current magazine and analyze it in terms of its subject, purpose, audience, voice, unity, and coherence. Pay attention to both the written and the visual text. Write a few sentences for each element, describing to the reader what visual or verbal cues helped you determine the audience, purpose, and other elements. Hand in a copy of the ad with your written assignment.

JOURNAL ASSIGNMENT 4.   *Analyze Television Commercials to Discover Audience*: Set aside one hour every night for three nights to watch television, making sure you are watching at the same hour every night. Make note of each advertisement during the hour–what products are being advertised and what target audience or audiences do you think the ads may be aimed at? At the end of the three days, write a paragraph about your findings. Is there a specific audience or audiences these ads are trying to reach? How did you determine audience from watching and taking note of these advertisements? How did the time of day that you watched the television play a role in your research?

JOURNAL ASSIGNMENT 5.   Write about the role public libraries could play in a person's life. What role have they played in your own life? You could describe the building itself, memories of checking out your first book, or the books that you remember being most important to you. What role do libraries play in your life today?

JOURNAL ASSIGNMENT 6.   Write about a physically strenuous activity that you have experienced. You may want to discuss a sporting event, a difficult hike, or any other demanding activity. Describe the event in detail as if it is happening right now, using present tense verbs.

JOURNAL ASSIGNMENT 7.   Write about the activities you have enjoyed during the summer that aren't a part of your life during the rest of the year.

JOURNAL ASSIGNMENT 8.   Harold Krents describes his difficulty in finding a job in his essay "Darkness at Noon." What are some of the challenges that job seekers face?

JOURNAL ASSIGNMENT 9.   Write about your feelings on the current interest in all types of cosmetic surgery. To what extent should people alter their real or perceived flaws?

JOURNAL ASSIGNMENT 10.   Give your personal reaction to a human interest story that is currently in the news.

JOURNAL ASSIGNMENT 11.   Write down your observations about someone you know who has grown up without one of his or her parents. From your perspective, how has it affected this person's life?

JOURNAL ASSIGNMENT 12.   Go through the list of irregular verbs listed in Appendix C in the textbook. Make your own personal list of the verbs you consider most important for you to learn.

JOURNAL ASSIGNMENT 13.   Write your impressions of the last memorable event you attended. For example, you could write about a movie, lecture, concert, or reading.

JOURNAL ASSIGNMENT 14.   Poet Wallace Stevens wrote a poem entitled "Thirteen Ways of Looking at a Blackbird" in which he attempted to get closer to the idea of a blackbird by writing about it in every sense he could think of–some of the descriptions abstract and spiritual, some of them concrete. Think about an object, animal, person, or concept that is interesting and mysterious to you. Try to write down as many different ways you can think of that your subject could be perceived. Be creative and don't avoid the weird–Stevens didn't! Number your perceptions. *To make this assignment even more effective, bring in the poem and read it together as a class.

JOURNAL ASSIGNMENT 15.   Affix a photo of a person from the newspaper, a magazine, or your personal album to your journal. First, describe the person with words that have a positive connotation, making him or her as appealing and attractive as possible. Next, write a description of the same person using words with a negative connotation.

JOURNAL ASSIGNMENT 16.   Why should a person try to build a bigger vocabulary? What plan might a person make to purposefully increase his or her vocabulary? Find five words that are new to you in the dictionary and add them, along with their meanings, to your journal.

JOURNAL ASSIGNMENT 17.   Choose a favorite holiday. In three paragraphs, persuade the reader that this holiday is the most important one of the year. Make sure each paragraph contains a topic sentence.

JOURNAL ASSIGNMENT 18.   Are you a neat person or a sloppy person? Do you wish you were neater or sloppier? Why or why not?

JOURNAL ASSIGNMENT 19.   Choose a saying or cliché that you find interesting. First explain what the saying means in general and then give at least three examples to illustrate how this saying has applied to your own life. A few examples of sayings or clichés are:
- Never let the sun go down on your anger.
- Don't judge a book by its cover.
- Necessity is the mother of invention.

JOURNAL ASSIGNMENT 20.   Cut out a photo from a magazine or newspaper and affix it to your journal. Create a narrative from the photograph, explaining what you think is going on in the picture, and describing what may have happened just before the picture was taken and what happened just afterward. Write about the details of the picture using sensory descriptions.

JOURNAL ASSIGNMENT 21. Practice description and focused freewriting by sitting in a room of your home and describing everything in the room exactly as it looks to you from your perspective.

JOURNAL ASSIGNMENT 22. People today are especially concerned about security and personal safety. Do you consider yourself a risk taker, a cautious person, or somewhere in the middle? Write about the ways that you consciously protect yourself.

JOURNAL ASSIGNMENT 23. Write about your current or future occupation. Compare and contrast the positive and negative aspects of the job.

JOURNAL ASSIGNMENT 24. In what ways (positive or negative) do you believe your environment has affected the person you have become today?

JOURNAL ASSIGNMENT 25. Take several minutes to think about the types of people with whom you attended high school. Then write down four or five descriptive categories to which these people belonged. Once you have established these categories, go back and develop a definition for each category.

JOURNAL ASSIGNMENT 26. Make a list of topics discussed in class so far this semester that you would be interested in writing about further. Choose one of these topics and brainstorm about how you might develop this idea into a full essay.

JOURNAL ASSIGNMENT 27. Brainstorm in your journal about the ways in which the belief system of your parent or parents or those who raised you has impacted your life.

JOURNAL ASSIGNMENT 28. Look back over your day so far. What examples can you give of enjoyable moments? What examples can you give of unpleasant moments?

JOURNAL ASSIGNMENT 29. Write about a childhood experience that has left a profound impression on your life.

JOURNAL ASSIGNMENT 30. Present the sequence of how you mastered an important skill. Address your writing to someone who does not have this skill and who is trying to learn it. Explain the steps in careful detail. Anticipate any difficulties the person may face, and encourage that person by describing any difficulties you had in learning this skill.

JOURNAL ASSIGNMENT 31. What are some of the products or objects you used to have that are no longer manufactured or are now obsolete? Write a comparison of then and now. Which objects do you prefer?

JOURNAL ASSIGNMENT 32.   Find accounts of the same newsworthy event that appeared in two different newspapers, and investigate the manner in which this event is reported. Analyze the differences between the articles in terms of the use of language, the phrasing and size of the headlines, the choice of accompanying photos, and so forth. Does either of the articles persuade the reader to a certain position by outright statements of opinion, or more subtly by using nonverbal cues? Quote directly from the articles and don't assume that the reader of your paper will be familiar with the articles.

JOURNAL ASSIGNMENT 33.   Choose three or four ads from magazines that are part of a political or marketing campaign. Analyze the persuasive techniques employed in the campaign. Describe the ads in detail, and address both the verbal and visual aspects. Is the campaign persuasive? What methods of persuasion does the campaign use?

JOURNAL ASSIGNMENT 34.   Convince someone you care about to stop smoking, drinking, or doing any other unhealthy habit (watching television? dieting too often?) Persuade him or her by using reasons, facts, and statistics about the effects of the habit.

JOURNAL ASSIGNMENT 35.   Read a letter to the editor in your local newspaper. Decide what research the author of the letter has done in order to make his or her claim. Was enough research done, if any? Research the topic yourself and write down your findings. After doing your own research, did your opinion change on the matter?

32 Responding to Reading Assignments

*All readings found in Further Readings section of textbook unless otherwise noted.

RESPONDING TO READINGS 1.   Read "On Writing" by Stephen King. King tells us in this piece that he has enjoyed a wide variety of books over the years. Reflect in writing about the books or other texts (comics, magazines, etc.) that have been a part of your reading life up until this point.

RESPONDING TO READINGS 2.   Read "Why Don't These Women Just Leave?" by Elaine Weiss. Determine the subject, purpose, audience, voice, unity, and coherence of this essay. Pay particular attention to the issue of audience. To whom is this essay addressed? Why?

RESPONDING TO READINGS 3.   Read "The Paterson Public Library" by Judith Ortiz Cofer. Underline the subjects and circle each verb in paragraphs 1–3.

RESPONDING TO READINGS 4.   Read the first two paragraphs of "Should Women Go Into Combat?" by Catherine L. Aspy. Rewrite the paragraphs in the present tense taking care to avoid mistakes in subject-verb agreement.

RESPONDING TO READINGS 5.   Read "Summer Reading" by Michael Dorris. There are five sentence fragments in Dorris' essay. Find all of them. Then turn each fragment into a complete sentence.

RESPONDING TO READINGS 6.   Read "No Comprendo" by Barbara Mujica and write a short summary of the piece, making sure to focus on all the writer's main points.

RESPONDING TO READINGS 7.   Read "Summer Reading" by Michael Dorris. Find five examples of sentences that use coordination to join more than one idea. Rewrite those five sentences using subordination. Read Dorris' sentences and your own versions. Which do you think sound better and why?

RESPONDING TO READINGS 8.   Provide students with a copy of the freewriting example from Appendix A of this manual. Have students fix the fragments and run-ons.

RESPONDING TO READINGS 9.   Students that have completed the chapter's Working Together will be fascinated to read the article written for *Harper's Bazaar* (October 2000, page 328), which follows the story of Princess Meriam Al Khalifa's first months in America, including her marriage in Las Vegas with the wedding supper at Taco Bell. Now that students have read further on this subject, they will be well prepared for writing a response that considers some of the rich themes suggested by this news story.

RESPONDING TO READINGS 10.   Read "Where Have All the Fathers Gone?" (in Chapter 31) Make an outline of the essay, making sure to use parallel structure.

RESPONDING TO READINGS 11.   Read "Unforgettable Miss Bessie" by Carl T. Rowan. See if you can find the twenty irregular verbs given in the past tense form or past participle form. Write down the base form, past tense, and past participle of each verb.

RESPONDING TO READINGS 12.   Read "The Changing American Family" by Alvin and Heidi Toffler. In paragraphs 1, 9, 10, and 17 explain the reason for each capitalization that occurs other than at the beginning of a sentence.

RESPONDING TO READINGS 13.   Read "Dream Houses" by Tenaya Darlington. Identify the metaphors and similes the writer uses to describe both her new and old houses. Why is her use of these devices effective? How does she enrich the meaning of the essay by using these metaphors and similes?

RESPONDING TO READINGS 14.   Read "A Day at the Theme Park" by W. Bruce Cameron. Find the words or phrases with negative connotations in the descriptions Cameron uses. In each case, change the word or phrase to one of neutral or positive connotation. How do these changes affect the piece as a whole?

RESPONDING TO READINGS 15.   Read your college catalogue's position on plagiarism. Paraphrase the policy, being careful not to plagiarize yourself!

RESPONDING TO READINGS 16.   Read "Neat People vs. Sloppy People" by Suzanne Britt. Underline the transitional words and phrases used by Britt. Do you think she has provided enough? Too many? In paragraphs 6 through 12, put a double line under each topic sentence and jot down the controlling idea in the margin.

RESPONDING TO READINGS 17.   Read "Neat People vs. Sloppy People" by Suzanne Britt. Underline examples of good supporting details in the essay. Does Britt use better details in describing the habits of neat people or sloppy people? Explain the differences. Why do you suppose the author made those choices?

RESPONDING TO READINGS 18.   Read "My Daughter Smokes" by Alice Walker. Walker tells her story in a series of anecdotes. Reread her essay and mark the anecdotes that you find the most effective. Are there any that surprise you? Which ones are most effective? What are some of the sensory images that Walker uses?

RESPONDING TO READINGS 19.   Read "My Daughter Smokes" by Alice Walker. Walker discusses various moments in her life and in the lives of her father and sister, some in sequence but all with large stretches of time between them. On a separate piece of paper, plot out a timeline of the different moments of her story and compare this to the organization of these moments in the essay. Why do you think Walker chose to tell her story in the way that she did?

RESPONDING TO READINGS 20.   Read "Dream Houses" by Tenaya Darlington. Go through the essay and circle words that seem particularly descriptive. Which descriptions seem the "sharpest" and why?

RESPONDING TO READINGS 21.   Read "Advice to Parents: How to Communicate with Your Teen" (in Chapter 1). Write your own process piece, giving advice to a person you know well on how he or she could improve communication skills with someone.

RESPONDING TO READINGS 22.   Read "Dream Houses" by Tenaya Darlington. Outline Darlington's essay in terms of comparison and contrast. Does she employ a block format or a point-by-point format? Decide whether the other format would have been more or less effective for her essay and explain your answer.

RESPONDING TO READINGS 23.   Read "Requiem for a Champ" by June Jordan. Decide whether the reading deals with causes or effects or both. Explain your answer in writing.

RESPONDING TO READINGS 24.   Read "I'm a Banana and Proud of It" by Wayson Choy. Choy defines himself through ethnicity/ethnicities. How do you define yourself?

RESPONDING TO READINGS 25.   Read "The Changing American Family" by Alvin and Heidi Toffler. Go through the essay and determine how the authors achieved coherence by using transitional expressions, repeated words, and appropriate use of pronouns.

RESPONDING TO READINGS 26.   Read the student essay "Leibovitz Revealed" by Yarrow Allen-Hickey, found in Appendix A of this manual. Discuss the essay in terms of its thesis, topic sentences, supporting details, and the development of its ideas.

RESPONDING TO READINGS 27.   Read "Requiem for the Champ" by June Jordan. Mark each occurrence in which the author employs an example, extended example, illustration, or anecdote. When you finish, go back and try to identify which type the author relied upon the most.

RESPONDING TO READINGS 29.   Have students read "Memories from 7th Street" by Treyson Hopkins, found in Appendix A of this manual. What is the main point of this narrative? What makes this narrative compelling?

RESPONDING TO READINGS 30.   Locate an instruction manual for an appliance or piece of equipment you have in your home. Analyze the text. Is it clear and easy to follow? Does the manual cover all the important steps necessary to set up or use the appliance? How could the manual be improved?

RESPONDING TO READINGS 31.   Read "The Ugly Truth About Beauty" by Dave Barry (in Chapter 30). Compare how much time you spend on your appearance to how much time other members of your family spend. Do you or other members of your family fit the stereotype that Barry describes?

RESPONDING TO READINGS 32.   Read "Why Don't These Women Just Leave?" by Elaine Weiss. Regardless of your personal opinion on the matter, see if you can write an essay taking the opposite stance.

RESPONDING TO READINGS 33.   Read "Should Women Go Into Combat?" by Catherine L. Aspy. Discuss the specific research the writer has done to produce this essay. Does the research seem well-balanced?